FAY MASCHLER'S
GUIDE TO EATING OUT IN LONDON

CENTURY

LONDON MELBOURNE AUCKLAND JOHANNESBURG

To all my companions. . . .

but particularly to my sister Beth who shares my love of
restaurants and of food, to Tom Maschler who ate
through the bed-rock of research for this guide and who
was a great support, and to my children, Hannah, Alice
and Ben who will probably contribute to the downfall of
a restaurant critic; *one too many dim sum.*
Without the help, practical and emotional, of Hazel
Short and Helen Redmond, this book would never have
been published; they are allies.

Illustrations by Russell Walker

Copyright © Fay Maschler 1986

All rights reserved

First published in 1986 by Century Hutchinson Ltd,
Brookmount House, 62–65 Chandos Place, Covent Garden,
London WC2N 4NW

Century Hutchinson Publishing Group (Australia) Pty Ltd,
16–22 Church Street, Hawthorn, Melbourne, Victoria 3122

Century Hutchinson Group (NZ) Ltd,
32–34 View Road, PO Box 40–086, Glenfield, Auckland 10

Century Hutchinson Group (SA) Pty Ltd,
PO Box 337, Bergvlei 2012, South Africa

Photoset in Linotron Baskerville by
Rowland Phototypesetting Ltd,
Bury St Edmunds, Suffolk
Printed and bound in Great Britain by
Richard Clay (The Chaucer Press) Ltd, Bungay, Suffolk

British Library Cataloguing in Publication Data
Maschler, Fay
Fay Maschler's guide to eating out in London
1. Restaurants, lunch rooms, etc. – England – London –
Guide-books
2. London (England) – Description – 1981 – Guide-books
I. Title
647'.95421   TX910.G7

ISBN 0 7126 9496 X

Introduction

Listening to the tinkle of ice in glasses with one ear,
the ringing of a cash register with the other, I
sometimes feel like what I am – a one-woman band
where restaurant reviewing is concerned. This has its
advantages and its disadvantages (a noticeable one
being my shape). Contributing a weekly article to *The
London Standard* since 1972, I calculate that I must
have reviewed well over 2,000 restaurants. What you
see here, a compilation of newly written descriptions
and appraisals of over 200 restaurants that currently
should engage your interest in London plus some
comments on the general scene, is of necessity a
subjective view. I see myself not so much as a guide
inspector but as an experienced and dedicated
customer who is able to pass on the news. Like any
customer I am prey to prejudices and preferences and
varying states of mind and health and degrees of
enchantment or lack of it with my dining companion.
However, with few exceptions, those being the very
recently opened places, my judgements are based on
several visits. My aim is to be fair, and evaluating a
restaurant as a customer would strikes me as the most
useful response.

Chefs and restaurateurs readily agree that cooking
is an art form but then are furious if they are criticized
the way a concert or a play might be and find it quite
intolerable that a restaurant critic should visit on the
first night. It is tempting in this job to become
sympathetic to the plight of restaurateurs, subject as
they are to same stresses as you and me, but I think
they should not learn their trade at the (considerable)
expense of what they like to call the punters, a phrase
with overtones of gambling. What this guide will do is
take some of the gamble out of what can be the risky
business of choosing a restaurant, be it for work or
play, for haute cuisine or snacking, for romance or
voyeurism.

On reading through the listings you might find
what strike you as glaring omissions. My criterion for
a restaurant being included has been the mental
exercise of imagining myself recommending to

3

someone a particular establishment. I might have to conjure up a visitor from Philadelphia, a chauvinistic French person, someone on a low fixed income wanting to initiate a love affair, one of my teenage daughters' friends . . . but when I cannot think of a good reason based on the restaurant's food or that ungainly expression 'the meal experience', a factor which includes cost, then I have left it out.

Restaurants are maddeningly volatile which can make writing a guide, with its inevitable time lapse between the last word typed and publication day, frustrating, but at the same time it is the restless nature of the business that is part of its appeal. Aside from rising prices which only act as an inhibiting factor to development and to a customer's enjoyment, or, indeed, presence, standards improve with each year that passes. Look at the index for English food and you will see that at last there is a burgeoning pride in the indigenous cuisine. Serious French food now compares competitively with what is available in Paris. Ethnic food, once synonymous with cheap and usually still a bargain, has become increasingly sophisticated and savvy but you have to watch for an unwelcome trickling down of fancy prices onto undeserving food in some establishments, particularly the ones who think nirvana hovers if you offer a cocktail list. The number of restaurants that feature vegetarian dishes shows that a concern for health is impinging and it means that a vegetarian out with a meat eater is no longer just dealt the cheese omelette and conversely, the companion is not obliged to graze on a green pepper stuffed with rice and sultanas.

One of the signs of advancement of standards is the attention paid to detail, by which I mean items like the bread, butter, the choice of cheese, the selection of mineral waters (though the price is often out-of-sight), the effort in procuring fresh produce, particularly herbs and interesting salad leaves, the nearly palpable move to make set-price deals be what they seem. But let there be no mistake, it is competition and the following of food fashions that has led to this, not goodness of heart. Speaking of that begs the question of: *Tipping*. It is a sore subject because there are no norms. Some restaurants include service charge, others don't. Many who do include it deliberately leave you wondering if you are expected to pay more, the chief weapon in this attack being the totals space on the credit card form left blank. My feeling is that unless the waiter or waitress has performed services way beyond the call of duty – like going home to relieve your babysitter – a tip of 15% is quite sufficient. A tip of 12½% is adequate and if you are charged 10% and you have had a good time, some loose change on the table is an appropriate gesture. Check all bills to see whether service is included and if you want to leave extra, do it in cash since otherwise it is the credit card companies who benefit, not Sandro or Sandra. There is no legal requirement to leave even a fixed tip if you consider either the food or service to be below standard.

Another vexed question is that of *Licensing*. It is to be hoped that the licensing laws in England will soon be relaxed. At the moment of writing, in the average restaurant, that is one without a full-on licence or supper licence, you must eat a meal if you wish to drink alcohol, and drinking hours are regulated, usually ending at 3 pm after lunch and at 11.30 pm or midnight in the evening. A wine bar licence allows drinking without meals, a facility extended to customers in premises that are converted pubs, or where someone has hammered the magistrates relentlessly, e.g. Bob Payton (*q.v.*) at The Chicago Rib Shack.

The following notes enlarge on the details printed beneath each entry and explain the implication of some of the indexes.

Average price This is the approximate cost of a three course meal including half a bottle of house wine, tax and service. I have tried not to under-estimate but prices creep up as time moves on and keep in mind the homily delivered to me by a new restaurateur, 'What is charged is based on what was borrowed'.

Set menus The prices given were correct at time of research. Unless otherwise specified they are for a three course meal (some restaurants include coffee and/or service in the price).

Seats This means inside the restaurant. Where tables outside are provided the number of covers is given (apt to vary). The capacity of any private room or area is given.

Music/Entertainment Music can often make or break your dining experience. With the co-operation of the restaurateurs I have given an indication of what might usually be expected, but a guitarist could contract 'flu or a new manager be into Ozzy Osborne, so check if you are concerned.

Wheelchairs Wheelchair access means access to both the restaurant and the lavatories.

Nationality Restaurants are only listed under the relevant heading if they provide distinctly national cooking.

Eclectic With communications being what they are, food no longer falls into neat categories. A chef who travels, who reads, who spends his spare time in ethnic restaurants (as most of them do), who is not trammelled by a rigorous culinary tradition (as most British chefs are not) is open to many influences and inputs. The word international applied to the sort of cuisine that results has a depressing hotel chain ring to it, so I have used eclectic. It describes some of the most interesting and innovative reasonably priced food in London at the moment.

♥   I felt it would be inappropriate for me to award stars or other symbols for excellence applied solely to cuisine. That does seem the province of a team of inspectors. Where there is a heart, there is a restaurant, frequently long-established, which for me has soul (less easy to symbolize) and which fulfils ably what a restaurant should do – make you a little more content with life.

AJIMURA

51–53 Shelton Street, WC2
01-240 0178

For a long time Ajimura was the only Japanese restaurant where dark suits, gold-rimmed spectacles, briefcases and Chivas Regal in your own marked bottle were not *de rigueur*. Now there are others non-middle-aged in style but the Covent Garden location means that the popularity of Ajimura has not been eclipsed. It remains a fine place in which to get to know Japanese cuisine and the menu descriptions make it easy to miss out on the stern and militantly beneficial dishes like spinach wrapped in seaweed. Rice and raw fish, omelette and vegetables wrapped in seaweed (nori) are another matter. A selection makes a fine lunch. If you are a newcomer to the food, the set-price lunch delivers a few useful introductions and the price ameliorates the culture shock often induced by neat, discreet amounts of food for large amounts of money. Sashimi (raw fish) and sushi (raw fish with rice) are both prepared and all the dishes you will have heard of – tempura, sukiyaki, shabu-shabu – are there too. To my mind, sake is the only accompaniment. The decor is the Japanese version of log cabin. Try to avoid peak times when its popularity may impinge on your enjoyment and also your assumptions about the ceremonious quality of Japanese eating.

CUISINE: Japanese	*Also vegetarian dishes*
OPEN: L: Mon to Fri; D: Mon to Sun	
MEALS: 12 to 3; 6 to 11 (Sun till 10.30)	
AVERAGE PRICE: £16. Set Menus: £5 (lunch); £6.60–£17 (dinner)	
CREDIT CARDS: Access, Amex, Visa, Diners	
SEATS: 50	
PRIVATE ROOM: (16)	
Wheelchair access	

ALASTAIR LITTLE

50 Frith Street, W1
01-734 5183

Alastair Little personifies a particular sort of young British chef. He came to catering through no formal training and after gaining a degree in archaeology and anthropology at Downing College, Cambridge. He has energy, aggression, *brio*, a passionate appetite and good looks. As he admitted in an interview in the first edition of British *Elle* magazine, nowadays chefs like himself get fêted in a patronizing way. My view is that it is because at last the English media can get to grips with the subject of gastronomy by slotting it into the category of a hobby, a profitable hobby all right, but one that proves that we knew all along that the French were making too much fuss. Alastair Little's career has spanned many of London's more fashionable restaurants including Zanzibar, L'Escargot and 192 Kensington Park Road. The first restaurant in which he was a partner was Simpson's in the Lower Richmond Road, which I reviewed enthusiastically in 1979. This eponymous place was opened in partnership with his girlfriend Kirsten Pedersten and with Mercedes Downend late in 1985. His approach to food involves a menu that changes twice a day, makes good use of seasonal produce, is basically French but doesn't shy from other influences, and has some agreeably straightforward notions like pasta, bean and sausage soup and boiled fillet of beef with mustard sauce. The kitchen is significantly highly visible from the restaurant and Little's stated aim is: 'I like the food to come out of the kitchen, be plonked in front of the customers and make them happy.' I found the waitresses (his partners) very good at the plonking bit. I have always liked Alastair Little's style and his enthusiasm provides an extra ingredient to the sauces that sometimes is all to the good, but I find the atmosphere of the restaurant too modishly stark. However, modishly stark customers like it. I would advise lunch rather than dinner or perhaps a summer evening rather than a winter one.

CUISINE: Eclectic	
OPEN: Mon to Fri	
MEALS: 12.30 to 2.30; 7.30 to 11	
AVERAGE PRICE: £20	
CREDIT CARDS: Visa	
SEATS: 35	

ANNA'S PLACE

90 Mildmay Park, N1
01-249 9379

Anna Hegarty made a decision that other restaurateurs might like to emulate. Having run a highly successful small expensive restaurant serving food inspired by her home country of Sweden she has elected to treat more people more of the time by re-styling the place almost as a wine bar, with a wine bar's lack of insistence on the formality of a meal. If you wish you may just snack or eat only one course but it would be foolish to confine yourself to that since the food, cooked by Paul Sykes, is exceptional and also different from almost anything you find elsewhere. Gravad lax (marinated raw salmon) was always a speciality of Anna's Place, and is still obtainable, but of more interest to those of us who have learned the easy-peasy technique for gravad lax and thus made it once too often, is gubrora, a mixture of Swedish anchovies, hard-boiled egg and Scandinavian caviar which is served with a raw egg yolk to mix in. Herrings are home-pickled and notably delectable. Meatballs deserve the description Swedish by virtue of the blue cheese sauce and lingonberry preserve that accompanies them. Plain boiled new potatoes and refreshing cucumber salad are the accompaniments – standard ones, it would seem, for the meat dishes. Anna's was formerly known for its prowess with fish so I would suppose the dishes to be good without having yet tried them. There is a particular atmosphere at Anna's Place, attributable to the lady herself, and how you respond depends rather on whether you are the sort of person who loves things like the Living Theatre where the actors quiz you relentlessly about your private life, or whether you faint with embarrassment when a restaurant manager asks if everything is all right. Anna's strong suit is cosy, if somewhat didactic chat, rather like a school matron, but she has been in the business long enough not to overdo it. The waitresses, too, are trained to interpret volubly the list from the blackboard. There is a deliberate policy of leaving some tables free for non-bookers and parties of two might be asked to share. Despite all this (I wanted to sink through the floor at the Living Theatre), I warmly recommend Anna's Place. The wines are fairly priced and the food makes it worth going one or two better than house wine.

CUISINE: Scandinavian	*Also vegetarian dishes*
OPEN: Tues to Sat	
MEALS: 12 to 3; 6.30 to 10.30	
AVERAGE PRICE: £18	
CREDIT CARDS: None	
SEATS: 36	
TABLES OUTSIDE: (16)	
Wheelchair access	

Enzo Apicella

Enzo Apicella, an Italian designer and illustrator, came to London in the Sixties. Over twenty years later his impact on the Italian restaurant scene is still evident. Enzo was the one who threw out the raffia-wrapped Chianti bottles, posters of Sorrento, plastic grape vines woven through trellises, and stipulated white walls, pastel tablecloths, ladderback rush-seated chairs, tile floors and spotlights; Mediterranean rather than suburban. With it went a change, though not a sweeping enough change, from escalope milanese with tinned spaghetti to Italian provincial cooking. The restaurant where the style was set was the Trattoria Terrazza in Soho, originally owned by Mario and Franco, two waiters who had been at the Mirabelle among many other places. After

the success of the Terrazza they built up a group of
restaurants which was bought by Spillers. Now
Kennedy Brookes owns the Mario & Franco name
and premises. Enzo is involved only with The
Meridiana in the Fulham Road. More abstruse
interiors are now designed for some Italian
restaurants but there remains a generation (mine) for
whom romance will always be associated with the
clatter of waiters' feet on ceramic tiles, hands held in
the pool of light focused on a lemon yellow tablecloth –
and the fact that it is chicken Kiev being the most
astonishing thing about pollo sorpresa.

ARCHDUKE WINE BAR

Arch 153, Concert Hall Approach, SE1
01-928 9370

Elizabeth Philip was just one of many people who
lamented the lack of decent eating places
around (and within) the South Bank complex of
theatres, cinema and galleries, but she did something
about it. She opened a wine bar that is an architectur-
ally praiseworthy conversion of two railway arches.
High tech might now seem the builder's version of
nouvelle cuisine but the achievement is a feeling of
space and movement in what is basically a cavern.
There are various levels on which to eat and various
styles of food, one of which is an assortment of sausages
including English oak-smoked, Toulouse, and a Swiss
veal sausage as well as a British banger made by Justin
de Blank. Typical dishes from the evening menu are
artichoke hearts and mushrooms in Parmesan mayonnaise, fresh nectarine with cottage cheese and watercress dressing as first courses, lamb in green ginger and
dark almond sauce, monkfish baked in butter and fresh
herbs among the main courses; enterprising and adequately successful. There is also an after-theatre supper
menu of two courses drawn from the above, plus coffee.
Live music is played most evenings, jazz or classical.
'Bangers, boogie and Brahms' was a phrase they used
to convey the experience when they opened in 1980 but
if they have dropped it now, it is because the place
has evolved. Wines are interesting. Her niftiness in

discovering venues for restaurants in areas gasping for them has led to Elizabeth Philip opening The Footstool, St John's Smith Square, SW1 (01-222 2779) where enterprising, eclectic food with proper English puddings is served at lunchtimes in the crypt of the church.

CUISINE: Wine Bar	Also vegetarian dishes
OPEN: L: Mon to Fri; D: Mon to Sat	
MEALS: 11 to 3; 5.30 to 11	
AVERAGE PRICE: After-theatre Menu: £5.85 (2 courses)	
CREDIT CARDS: Access, Amex, Visa, Diners	
SEATS: 70	
TABLES OUTSIDE: (30)	
PRIVATE ROOM: (15–50)	
MUSIC: Live jazz from 8.30 pm	

ARIRANG

31–32 Poland Street, W1
01-437 6633

Korean is an ethnic cuisine that has only flourished in London in the last decade, the restaurants multiplying like an extended family as a canny waiter spots his chance, leaves the parent establishment and starts up on his own. Unless you happen to be Korean the food strikes me as suited only to the jaded palate. When your appetite is in that *je m'en fous* state of mind hit it with raw beef mixed with fresh pear and sesame seeds or bracken stalks or raw skate doused in chilli sauce. Not all the dishes are so esoteric – and those mentioned happen to be delicious – and if you like Japanese food and Thai food you will find something of the austerity of the former and an element of the sparkiness of the latter combined. The Arirang, which was one of the first Korean restaurants in London (not actually the first, as they like to claim), is an ideal place to begin your voyage of discovery with Korean food. There are set meals, an explanatory menu and helpful waitresses. At my last visit to Arirang the owner made it quite clear that my liking of the noodle dishes was a peasant sort of response to the possibilities but my pride is not dented that easily. I would still recommend them, especially chap che where an assortment of vegetables are included. In general it is a healthy cuisine, much boiled or casseroled in a rather puritanical way. If you are at the end of your tether, a slug of the drink containing ginseng, the root that, as you probably know, is the secret of eternal youth, is advisable.

CUISINE: Korean	*Also vegetarian dishes*
OPEN: Mon to Sat	
MEALS: 12 to 3; 6 to 11	
CLOSED: Christmas Day, New Year's Day and Easter Monday	
AVERAGE PRICE: £15. Set Menus: £6.50–£11; Businessman's Lunch: £3.50	
CREDIT CARDS: Access, Amex, Visa, Diners	
SEATS: 86	
PRIVATE ROOM: (7)	
MUSIC: Taped	

THE ARK

122 Palace Gardens Terrace, W8
01-229 4024

35 Kensington High Street, W8
01-937 4294

The Ark in Palace Gardens Terrace, a wooden chalet true to its name, has particular resonance for those of us who ate out in London in the Sixties. The legendary attractiveness of the waitresses meant that people often went out two by two, however they had gone in. Twenty years ago the bistro-style dishes seemed racy and daring. Now, most of all, it seems cheap. It is a place to go when eating out is what you are doing because it seems too much bother to eat in. There remains a jolly, raffish neighbourhood air to the place and the staff are kindly.

13

The branch off Kensington High Street is, in culinary terms, a more serious affair and has a better French accent. But as far as I am concerned it is the original Ark that stirs the nostalgia; the other is just a competent restaurant.

Palace Gardens Terrace
CUISINE: Bistro   *Also vegetarian dishes*

OPEN: L: Mon to Sat; D: Mon to Sun	
MEALS: 12 to 3; 6.30 to 11.15	
CLOSED: Christmas week	
AVERAGE PRICE: £8–£10	
CREDIT CARDS: Access, Amex, Visa	
SEATS: 78	
TABLES OUTSIDE: (14)	
PRIVATE ROOM: (20–26)	

Kensington High Street
CUISINE: French

OPEN: L: Mon to Sat; D: Mon to Sun	
MEALS: 12 to 3; 7 to 11.30	
CLOSED: Christmas week and Easter	
AVERAGE PRICE: £10–£15	
CARDS: Access, Visa, Diners	
SEATS: 95	
PRIVATE ROOM: (20)	

L'ARLEQUIN

123 Queenstown Road, SW8
01-622 0555

The former editor of *A La Carte* magazine, the foodies' glossy, told me that when she took a photographer to lunch at L'Arlequin he left remarking that he would now like to go and have something to eat. There is a sense of over-refinement at this restaurant of Christian Delteil, managed by his very charming wife Geneviève and letters I have received from readers of *The London Standard* confirm a sort of 'Emperor's new clothes' about some of the dishes. Reduction (say of fumet) can become *ad absurdum* if you are left with a discreet puddle on the plate and pangs of hunger. But for those who like the doll's house aspect of the new cooking there is no denying that M. Delteil (ex Le Gavroche and Chewton Glen Hotel) is a gifted, if cautious, chef. The shyness in his own character seems almost to be apparent in the food. The whole performance is carried out with the utmost decorum, to the extent that bread is proffered by the waiters with tongs. There seems general agreement among critics that the dishes of the day are the ones to go for and I would add to that that fish is where the chef truly excels. The dining room is small, well handled by the smiling Madame Delteil and if a quiet, studious, correct meal is what you want then L'Arlequin is the place. The relative bargain of the set-price lunch can be undone by wines which are marked up with an understanding that it is hard to make a restaurant seating 32 profitable.

CUISINE: French	
OPEN: Mon to Fri	
MEALS: 12.30 to 2; 7.30 to 10.30	
CLOSED: Bank Holidays and 3 weeks in August	
AVERAGE PRICE: £35. Set Menu: £12.50 (lunch)	
SEATS: 32	
CREDIT CARDS: Access, Visa, Diners	
Wheelchair access	

ASTRIX

329 King's Road, SW3
01-352 3891

Crêperies are the tortoises in the fast food race and have some of the virtues of that stoical creature: a certain longevity and an attitude of resignation where flashier competition is concerned. Essentially, making galettes (the savoury crêpes using buckwheat flour) can be speeded up only to a point and since the cook cannot ascertain in advance which of the combinations of fillings you are going to settle upon, your food is, perforce, made to order. As every hostess knows, the sweet, white flour, wheat flour crêpes can be made in advance and bubbled in butter and liqueurs and dolloped with jam without coming to much harm, but here I shall reveal my perception about crêpes – which is that ham and cheese in a savoury galette works best. It works much better, let me tell you, than tinned asparagus or smoked salmon or ratatouille, which are some of the more arcane options. Astrix scores for me on several points. It is reasonable, the tapes played are classical ones, the staff are sunny, and wittily dressed young people who are diverting to watch hang out there. I first reviewed Astrix in January 1973 – this is no jumped-up, opportunistic, batter-in-the-pan enterprise.

CUISINE: Crêperie	Also vegetarian dishes
OPEN: Mon to Sun	
MEALS: 12 to 12	
AVERAGE PRICE: £5–£6 (2 courses)	
CREDIT CARDS: None. Luncheon Vouchers only	
SEATS: 55	
MUSIC: Piped classical	

L'AUBERGE

44 Forest Hill Road, SE22
01-299 2211

I have only once in my life (so far) eaten in a restaurant on Christmas Day and it was at L'Auberge. The chef, Egyptian Mr Sami Youssef, prepared a masterful roast turkey, roast potatoes, Brussels sprouts, etc. On other days he is less traditional, his cuisine being a mildly exotic version of French. Although to mention it seems to annoy the irascible Nico Ladenis disproportionately, it must be recounted that Sami Youssef was in the kitchen of the original Chez Nico in Lordship Lane, Dulwich. Since then he has had a place of his own (called Pyramid in homage, he says, to Fernand Point), worked for the Kennedy Brookes chain and then opened again independently in Forest Hill. It is a family affair – Mrs Youssef works out front – and relaxed; even the good value set-price meals can be ignored in favour of the 'menu paysan' which offers individually priced dishes such as mouclade (mussel stew) and fish pie. Fish is the strong point though I would urge you to try Mr Youssef's approach to calf's liver where there is a gratifying glimpse of the Egyptian in his soul. The simpler main courses tend to be the more successful ones. Having put the restaurant to the ultimate test of my three children on Christmas Day I can vouch for the welcome to families.

CUISINE: French	*Vegetarian meals on request*
OPEN: L: Sun only; D: Tues to Sat	
MEALS: 12 to 2.30; 7 to 10.30	
CLOSED: Boxing Day and 3 weeks in August	
AVERAGE PRICE: £16. Set Menus: £5.95 (lunch); £11.95 inc. aperitif (dinner)	
CREDIT CARDS: Access, Visa	
SEATS: 40	
TABLES OUTSIDE: (10–12)	
MUSIC: Taped classical	*Wheelchair access*

AUBERGE DE PROVENCE

St James's Court Hotel, Buckingham Gate, SW1
01-834 6655

P aul Bocuse and Roger Vergé lending their names, and presumably some of their expertise, to a restaurant in Disneyworld says it all. The third Michelin star means that French chefs can join the cavalcade that takes them (profitably) round the world, demonstrating here, endorsing there, perhaps even flying on an airline they advise. Now is the age of designer-label food. In London you can eat an 'Outhier' at Ninety Park Lane and a 'Charial' at the Auberge de Provence, the first restaurant to open at the Taj Hotel group's new venture, the very grand St James's Court Hotel. At least those last two chefs with restaurants in the south of France have the rationale of their establishments being closed for the winter but then, of course, in Outhier's case he also has to fit in Japan and Thailand. Jean-André Charial, the grandson of Raymond Thuilier the octogenarian owner of L'Oustaù de Baumanière has, at the time of writing, been over twice to the London restaurant, once for the opening and then again months later. He has left a brigade in the kitchen. The menu does reflect the sunshine food of Provence and offers dishes reminiscent of those you might find at the beautiful Baumanière, the possessor of three Michelin stars for over 30 years now. Tomatoes, aubergines, olives, garlic and olive oil predominate in the flavourings and the most successful creation of those I tried was red mullet simply grilled and sauced with a stunningly good olive oil. The petits farcis niçois, stuffed baby vegetables, lacked something, perhaps the warmth of the sun, a rare commodity in Victoria in winter. Pasta with a pistou sauce I have had better in Italian restaurants but I did taste a remarkably good vegetarian dish on the second visit when Charial was on hand. I had met Charial on a trip to India designed to show French chefs the point of the cuisine and he had been much impressed by the use made of vegetables there and, unlike some of the others on that jaunt, he has put the revelations to good use. I have heard good reports of the Auberge since my last visit. It is definitely an interesting addition to the London scene. The admirable simplicity of the menu is too firmly echoed in the surroundings which seem more suited to a coffee shop or pizza parlour but apparently they are going to be changed. Provence wines are excellent and good value.

CUISINE: French Provençal	Also vegetarian dishes
OPEN: Mon to Sun	
MEALS: 12 to 2.30; 7.30 to 11	
AVERAGE PRICE: £30. Set Menu: £15 (lunch)	
CREDIT CARDS: Access, Amex, Visa, Diners	
SEATS: 80	

BAGATELLE

5 Langton Street, SW10
01-351 4185

This is one of the stayers in Langton Street, a street where in the past restaurants seemed to change hands almost monthly. One of the Japanese chefs of the Bagatelle who made its name for restrained and artistic food has left for the restaurant Pier 31 and, who knows, perhaps jumped on from there, but the French food is still reliable if less ascetic. There is always a vegetable soup and a fish soup and there is a palpable nod towards health in dishes like raw fillet of beef marinated in red wine and served with a vinaigrette, the slightly old hat terrine de légumes, the yoghurt sauces on the roulade of fishes (hake, turbot, salmon) and main courses like poached steak (they got there before Anton Mosimann of The Dorchester) served rare with a white wine and shallot sauce. There is that old chestnut, breast of duck served with green peppercorn sauce, but also the more gutsy confit of the same bird. Fish dishes vary according to the marketing and they are usually well handled. Separate prices for vegetables, potatoes, salads, and a cover charge are all building bricks towards a considerable bill. The surroundings are cool and stylish; upstairs, to my mind, preferable to down and the garden best of all if the weather colludes. If this slightly unmotivating description is causing you to wonder how mere is this bagatelle, try it out at lunchtime when a set-price menu keeps the cost in check.

CUISINE: French	
OPEN: Mon to Sat	
MEALS: 12 to 2; 7 to 11	
CLOSED: Bank Holidays	
AVERAGE PRICE: £20. Set Menu: £11 (lunch)	
CREDIT CARDS: Access, Amex, Visa, Diners	
SEATS: 50	
TABLES OUTSIDE: (30–35)	

BANGKOK

9 Bute Street, SW7
01-584 8529

This Thai restaurant was diverting residents of South Ken with satay, barbecued chicken and rice-noodle assemblies long before Thai restaurants became 'a thing'. Although nine years ago they moved across the road to slightly larger premises they have sensibly stayed with their simple menu and unfussy surroundings. It may be the equivalent of chop suey as against authentic Cantonese but it has its place, and the place has its devoted regulars.

CUISINE: Thai	
OPEN: Mon to Sat	
MEALS: 12.15 to 2.15; 6.30 to 10.45	
AVERAGE PRICE: £14	
CREDIT CARDS: None	
SEATS: 60	

LA BARCA

80–81 Lower Marsh, SE1
01-261 9221

Luciano (the manager) and Pasquale (the chef) are the owners of La Barca and they run a happy, noisy, crowded ship dependent for an appreciative crew on the casts and the audiences from the nearby South Bank arts complex and the Old Vic. The food is gutsy Italian with more kick and intensity than at the average trattoria. First courses of spare ribs and the prawns in a spicy-hot sauce bear out this contention. I also like the uovo purgatorio, baked egg with a fresh tomato sauce. The problem with that dish is that it might supplant pasta which would be a shame, particularly in the case of spaghetti La Barca with its seafood sauce and the dish named after a friend of mine, pappadelle alla Vera, where home-made pasta is sauced with kidneys, onions and white wine. The fusilli with broccoli is the right choice if you want a more pared-down pasta dish. Of the fish dishes I recommend the sea bass with fennel and pernod and, because I like rustic food, I would choose the cotechino con fagioli, rough sausage with white beans and herbs, from the meat dishes. There are, of course, less calorific items and they make an expensive, but confidence-inspiring steak tartare. The aforementioned Vera says that when she needs consoling, which is quite often, she orders the crêpe La Barca, which is a pancake filled with cream, nuts and brandy. With (the ebullient) service at 15%, La Barca can outdo the price of the best theatre seats, but it makes a rollicking end to an evening out.

CUISINE: Italian	*Also vegetarian dishes*
OPEN: L: Mon to Fri; D: Mon to Sat	
MEALS: 12 to 2.30; 7 to 11.30	
CLOSED: Bank Holidays and Christmas	
AVERAGE PRICE: £20	
CREDIT CARDS: Access, Amex, Visa, Diners	
SEATS: 80	

LA BASTIDE

50 Greek Street, W1
01-734 3300

If Brillat-Savarin can write a book entitled *La Physiologie du Goût*, perhaps a psychologist is well placed to open a restaurant. Nicholas Blacklock, disenchanted with being a psychologist and not enamoured of the restaurants to be found in London, opened his own, D'Artagnan in Blandford Street. It was a success. A popular feature was the regional menu, which took a département of France and presented the specialities at a set price for three or four courses. In the winter of 1985 Blacklock, in partnership with Susan Warwick, moved to these Greek Street premises, formerly Romano Santi, a restaurant in true old-Soho style. The ravages of a fire mean that the building has been gutted and redesigned but mercifully it has been furnished in a comforting, comfortable, manner with muted shades and velvet curtains the colour of oyster mushrooms. The regional menus remain and as well as an à la carte there is a Soho menu which is an invitation to light eating, preferably early or late evening. The management have an easy-going approach. There is no cover, no minimum charge and you are at liberty to switch around among the menus. My, arguably jaded, palate is attracted to the Soho menu with its dishes like boudin blanc with a truffle sauce or grilled andouillettes but those craving cooking with finesse should look to the à la carte with its offerings (typically) of a gratinée of salsify and pistachio nuts, terrine of cooked duck in layers of ox tongue, fillets of roebuck sautéed and flamed in cognac and liqueur, breast of pheasant roasted with a chestnut stuffing. Mr Blacklock strikes me as an intelligent, slightly irascible man and it is a good combination, or anyway an historic one, where cooking is concerned. His own volatility is sometimes reflected in the dishes but on the whole the results are very good. There is little point in giving details of particular dishes from the Menu de la Loire, the one I recently tried, but a creamy chestnut soup, a mousse of fresh eels and pot roasted veal with sorrel and morels will give you some idea of the scope. The wine list is strong and has some interesting French regional bottles. My last memory of La Bastide was a sip of an extraordinary aged bourbon called Old Weller produced by Nicholas Blacklock as a souvenir of his Christmas jaunt to the southern states of the USA. He admired its potency.

CUISINE: French	*Also vegetarian dishes*

OPEN: L: Mon to Fri; D: Mon to Sat

MEALS: 12.30 to 2.30; 6 to 11.30

AVERAGE PRICE: £22. Set Menus: £12.50 (3 courses) and £14.50 (4 courses)

CREDIT CARDS: Access, Amex, Visa, Diners

SEATS: 45

PRIVATE ROOM: (60)

BEAU RIVAGE

248 Belsize Road, NW6
01-328 9992

When I first went to this fish restaurant, so goadingly inappropriately named on a dreary curve approaching the Kilburn High Road, they were unlicensed, a fact that made the whole event – an astonishing range of fresh fish, cooking that had a Mauritian accent, an almost complete absence of customers – cheap and therefore even more delightfully surprising. They have gained their licence and expanded their seating into the basement and reduced the display of fresh fish and shellfish in the window, but the cooking is still good and almonds, paprika, saffron, horseradish inveigle their way into recipes, often with good results. The first course salads are lively and fresh, the fish soups well made and the mussels portugaise popular enough to run out. Sauces on the main course fish dishes tend to be creamy and rich, though often lifted with a julienne of vegetables. What is gratifying is the range of fish. Beau Rivage is now firmly established in the neighbourhood and Saturday night is a big night out. Service would seem to be in part from the family of chef Georges Ng Yu Tin. It is not undeviatingly gracious but can cope under stress. Sorbets, which strike me as the appropriate dessert, are inventive, e.g. pistachio. There is an unremarkable but fairly comprehensive wine list.

CUISINE: French/Fish	*Also vegetarian dishes*
OPEN: L: Mon to Fri; D: Tues to Sat	
MEALS: 12 to 2.30; 6.30 to 11.15	
AVERAGE PRICE: £19. Set Menu: £6.25	
CREDIT CARDS: Visa	
SEATS: 60	

Mark Birley

Unfortunately the urbane Mark Birley only opens clubs which means that some of the nicer food in London, including the best chocolate ice cream ever, is denied to non-members. However, if you know a member or you have some reciprocal agreement from a club abroad, find out how good food in a nightclub can be at *Annabel's, 44 Berkeley Square, W1 (01-629 3558)*, what English country house food and service ought to be like at *Mark's, 46 Charles Street, W1 (01-499 1360)* and, it has to be said, the best Italian food in London at *Harry's Bar, 26 South Audley Street, W1 (01-408 0844)*.

BELVEDERE RESTAURANT

Holland House, Holland Park, W8
01-602 1238

Any time of year – winter has a particular Chekovian charm – the Belvedere is one of the most romantic places in London to eat, and the only good gastronomic use made of the many lovely parks. The restaurant is in a 17th-century building flanked by a courtyard and cloisters with high arched windows on the ground and first floors. Now the news that is not so much bad as unpoetic. It is run by J. Lyons and the prices for the dishes are not for love on the dole, nor even love on a fairly average salary, though the setting is worth saving up for. Prices are in keeping with the services of a Michelin two-star chef, the dishes are not. However, the cooking is by no means incompetent, indeed mostly good, and mercifully the combinations have become a little more simplified recently and have dropped what was a mysterious Scottish theme in the naming. There is a nod, sometimes a bow and a scrape, towards nouvelle cuisine. A few dishes from the menu in front of me are pâté of guinea fowl flavoured with yellow chartreuse and mango, salad of pink grapefruit, orange, lemon and non-fat cheese with truffle and saffron, a fillet of brill oven-baked with halibut soufflé and served on a watercress and cream sauce, fillet of veal sautéed with Grand Marnier, honey, lime and accompanied with a subric of apple and Jerusalem artichoke (I promise you they were more convoluted before) – and there are simpler options. The wine list, which holds no bargains, is backed up with a selection of 92 malt whiskies. On a sunny day, or snowy evening, The Belvedere is somewhere to woo. Peacocks in the park do it . . .

CUISINE: French   *Also vegetarian dishes*

OPEN: L: Mon to Fri; D: Mon to Sat

MEALS: 12 to 2.30; 6.30 to 10.30 (Sat till 11)

AVERAGE PRICE: £35

CREDIT CARDS: Access, Amex, Visa, Diners

SEATS: 65

PRIVATE ROOM: (100)

MUSIC: Piped baroque-style

BEOTY'S

79 St Martin's Lane, WC2
01-836 8768

I doubt if this restaurant has appeared in other serious food guides for many years but I love it for its style, one that is fast disappearing in London. It is Greek/Cypriot food as served in the days before everyone dashed off on package holidays to Corfu (the restaurant has been going for about 25 years), which means it brushes only lightly with authenticity (a fact substantiated by the alternative 'international menu'), is handled with grave charm, in surroundings that are as plush and velvety as the theatres it resides among. What must be a good deal on the rent is reflected in the modesty of the pricing. Downstairs is the nicer room. Only for aficionados of propriety in restaurants. If you like the White Tower, L'Etoile, The Gay Hussar, you will appreciate Beoty's. The Greek dishes – for example the souvlakia – tend to be the more successful.

CUISINE: Greek/Cypriot

OPEN: Mon to Sat

MEALS: 12 to 2.30; 5.30 to 11.30

AVERAGE PRICE: £16. Set Menus: £9.90 (lunch); £10.90 (dinner)

CREDIT CARDS: Access, Amex, Visa, Diners

SEATS: 90

PRIVATE ROOM: (50)

Wheelchair access

LE BISTROQUET

275 Camden High Street, NW1
01-485 9607

Russel Joffe, who has worked in fashionable restaurants including Langan's Brasserie and Odette's, runs this surprisingly nice place. Surprisingly nice because so often the café/brasserie type of venture starts off with laudable intentions, and crumbles. Indeed, this could be levelled at Le Bistroquet which no longer does breakfasts and has abandoned set menus – but does do teas – except for the fact that it has settled into being a lively unpretentious restaurant with a menu that covers most eventualities from dieting to snacking to indulging, the food all cooked with care. In a dieting mood I have enjoyed steamed brill with tomato concassé (hold the creamy sauce) that was perfectly prepared, together with a green salad, a commodity almost impossible to find well made in restaurants, but it was here. My friend Anne speaks longingly of the steak sandwich, a grilled sirloin clamped between two halves of a baguette. There is a pretty courtyard garden at the back. As well as having a creditable wine list themselves they are hand in glove with that enterprising wine firm Bibendum of Regent's Park Road and arrange evenings of tastings. They have a wine bar licence which means you may drink without eating and the Camden Town poseurs often pose at the bar.

CUISINE: French	*Also vegetarian dishes*
OPEN: Mon to Sun	
MEALS: 12 to 2.45 (Sun till 3); 7 to 11.30 (Sun till 11)	
AVERAGE PRICE: £16	
CREDIT CARDS: Access, Amex, Visa	
SEATS: 130	
TABLES OUTSIDE (28)	
PRIVATE ROOM: (30–40)	
MUSIC: Piped jazz, French, classical	

BLADES BARBECUE

94 Lower Richmond Road, SW15
01-789 0869

This restaurant describes itself as Australian Bar B Q which would seem to mean that you get up off your butt and cook your main course yourself. The idea of grilling steak, kebabs, chops, etc. yourself on a gas-fired 'charcoal' grill may or may not appeal, but let me tell you it goes down well with children (as do the hamburgers) as it gives them leave to roam about which is what children, in my experience, like to do in restaurants. To start there are items like taramasalata, mackerel pâté and home-made soup. The main course prices include a baked potato and a salad bar that is quite imaginatively thrown together. To finish there are desserts like chocolate fudge cake with vanilla ice cream. There are Australian wines and beers and hail-fellow service. It is in this guide chiefly because of its appeal to children coupled with reasonable prices. Hazards are loud-mouthed parties, a log jam at the grill or someone pinching 'your' steak.

CUISINE: Australian barbecue	Also vegetarian dishes
OPEN: L: Mon to Fri; D: Mon to Sat	
MEALS: 12 to 2.30; 7 to 11	
AVERAGE PRICE: £12	
CREDIT CARDS: Access, Visa	
SEATS: 70	
TABLES OUTSIDE: (10)	
PRIVATE ROOM: (30)	

BLAKES HOTEL RESTAURANT

33 Roland Gardens, SW7
01-370 6701

This basement hotel dining room designed by raving beauty Anouska Hempel Weinberg has been awarded titles like 'most seductive'. It is a James Bond idea of seductive: shiny black surfaces, strategic mirrors, black cloths and white napkins, the splashes of colour being delivered by the clients and the bowls of tulips or orchids on each table. Food arrives on black plates. I find it more silly than sensual but it certainly overcomes whatever reservations you may have about the idea of eating in hotel dining rooms. I suppose you could say that dining here is a theatrical experience, a thought bolstered by the manager who will anticipate needs you never even knew you had and the menu which is modish and not shy of borrowing bits of finery from other cuisines: viz. the Szechuan duck, sashimi, chicken tikka and teriyaki to trim the Italian, English and French cuisine. The underlying fantasy, I imagine, is a couple holed up in the hotel for a week so in love they don't want to leave the room, managing nevertheless to travel via the food in the restaurant. The lunch menu has 'smaller' dishes – salads and sandwiches – and there is a notable breakfast menu served from 7.30 am which in the Continental version includes cheese or salamis as well as juices, croissant, etc., and in English style gives options like figs, porridge, waffles, kippers, live yoghurt with wheatgerm; in other words considerable thoughtfulness has been applied. I have heard varying reports recently on chef James Robins' finesse but on the whole I think it is a glitzy risk worth risking. There are no bargains on the wine list. Start at house wine at £8.50 and think upwards.

CUISINE: International

OPEN: Mon to Sun

MEALS: 12.30 to 2.30; 7.30 to 11.30

AVERAGE PRICE: £40

CREDIT CARDS: *Access, Amex, Visa, Diners*

SEATS: 40

THE BOMBAY BRASSERIE

♥ *Courtfield Close, SW7*
01-370 4040

The Bombay Brasserie when it opened in December of 1982 (the house astrologer had specified 24 December but marketing sense prevailed and it opened a couple of weeks earlier) changed the face of Indian restaurants in London. There had been smart Indians before (viz. Shezan in Knightsbridge and Kundan in Victoria) but nothing quite as elegant as this and nowhere with the apparent understanding of the special relationship of the English to India. Also the grip of the conventional menu was shattered and instead of the predictable list of mainly Northern Indian dishes there were dishes from Goa and the Punjab, traditional Parsi food and Bombay street snacks, an unheard of thing for a grand restaurant to do but, to my mind, one of the most delicious elements. Bombay is a cosmopolitan city and the menu is designed to reflect this. Eating your way through it will give you some idea of the incredible variety to Indian cuisine, a fact that has tended to be swamped by the popular notion of a curry. The menu is helpful with its descriptions but I would urge you not to miss the sev batata puri in the first course, a beguiling mixture of crisp puris, potato, onion, chillis, gram-flour straws and coriander served with a sweetish chutney. In the same vein, dahi pakodi, soft lentil dumplings marinated in spiced yoghurt and served with various chutneys, is a reminder of the wonderful snacks you get in India, on the whole the second best way of eating to being invited to someone's home. The Parsi speciality of pomfret (a fish) coated with mint chutney and steamed in a banana leaf is another first course worth trying. The main courses are served with a vegetable dish, a potato assembly and lentils which I have known to vary from excellent to only all right. I particularly like the mutton with

apricots (another Parsi dish), the Goa fish curry and achar gosht, a Hyderabad speciality of marinated lamb. Vegetarians fare well with the Bombay and Punjabi thali (a tray on which several dishes are presented at once) and with the à la carte vegetable dishes. Recently two truly hot dishes have been added to the menu, one from the red chilli region of Kashmir and the other from the black pepper region of Kerala. Homemade sorbets make the ideal cooling dessert. Part of the success of the Bombay Brasserie is undoubtedly due to the look of the place which takes the colonial style as its theme. Wicker chairs, revolving ceiling fans, brass-bound chests, potted banana palms, sepia-tinted photographs have become something of a cliché, particularly in the awful 'theme' pubs, but here due to a grand sweep of space and apparently a huge investment, it comes off convincingly and romantically. There is also a conservatory. The set-price buffet lunch (£8.50 at the time of writing) is a bargain and a way to get to know the scope of the dishes. The service is infinitely pleasanter to those they know and the high mark-ups on wine and beer are the other criticism. But it is a place not to be missed.

CUISINE: Indian	*Also vegetarian dishes*
OPEN: Mon to Sun	
MEALS: 12.30 to 2.30; 7 to 11.45	
AVERAGE PRICE: £27. Set Menu: £8.50 (lunch)	
CREDIT CARDS: Access, Amex, Visa, Diners, Luncheon Vouchers	
SEATS: 195	
Wheelchair access	

BRASSERIE DU COIN

54 Lamb's Conduit Street, WC1
01-405 1717

It is as much to promote this area of London – it is one of the more secret 'villages', pedestrianized but not over-gentrified (shoe menders as well as art galleries) – that I include Brasserie du Coin which, like most other self-styled brasseries, adheres firmly to restaurant hours and restaurant mores. The food is competent, interpreting French cooking in a filling, old-fashioned way. Regulars must be conservative souls for the dishes – moules marinière, steak au poivre, etc. – remain steady, even specials go on being specials for a long time, but predictability has its own rewards. The assumptions in the cooking about what constitutes Frenchness are borne out in the decor: gingham table-cloths, that sort of thing. Note the relatively early last orders and weekend closing.

CUISINE: French	
OPEN: Mon to Fri	
MEALS: 12 to 3; 6 to 10	
AVERAGE PRICE: £20	
CREDIT CARDS: Access, Amex, Visa, Diners, Luncheon Vouchers	
SEATS: 100	
TABLES OUTSIDE: (16)	

BRETT'S

16a Coldharbour Lane, SE5
01-733 2041

Brian and Elizabeth Brett who own the restaurant stated their aim as being 'to lift vegetarian food on to a more imaginative level and serve it in surroundings to match'. In a rather unpromising street close to Brixton, they have succeeded in their aim. The restaurant itself is wittily designed –

William Morris goes to Japan was my original summing up and the food, which includes fish dishes, sensibly takes its inspiration from countries where vegetarianism is a hallowed way. Thus there is tempura which includes deep-fried cubes of beancurd served with side dishes of soya, seaweed and Japanese radish. India has lent a chickpea and vegetable curry, Eastern Europe suggested buckwheat crêpes which are stuffed with broccoli in a cheese sauce, and Japan again is the influence behind the land and sea vegetable salad made with rice and millet (millet, as you know, is well balanced in essential amino acids, rich in iron and gluten-free) dressed with a sauce based on soya and given crispiness with triangular pieces of toasted nori (seaweed). Italy, not a country particularly associated with vegetarians, nevertheless can provide a haven for non-meat eaters with pasta dishes, such as shells (made from organically grown wholewheat flour) mixed with various vegetables and dressed with a sauce of sun-dried tomatoes and basil. Brett's also serve a kind of fried polenta and a pâté based on the Genoese sauce pesto. The fish main courses when I visited included snappers cooked with tomatoes and fennel, moules à la poulette and a kebab of marinated fish served with a spicy yoghurt sauce. All of the dishes we tried, with the exception of the curry which just seemed an F-Plan mush, were good and even the side dish of stir-fried vegetables did something revolutionary to cabbage. The puddings, they claim, are sugar-free, but for the natural fruit sugars. Cheeses are British. The choice of coffees includes one made from grains. Some of the information under the section 'We care about your food' seems a bit over-the-top health nutty – I recoil from phrases like 'man's staple food throughout the centuries' – but the experience of an evening at Brett's is an enjoyable one as well as a salutary one. The wine list helps, as do Madeira as an aperitif and malmsey, mead, kirsch and mirabelle as a digestif.

CUISINE: Vegetarian/Fish

OPEN: D only: Mon to Sat

MEALS: 7 to 11

AVERAGE PRICE: £12

CREDIT CARDS: Access, Amex, Visa

SEATS: 38

MUSIC: Piped/Jazz

Kennedy Brookes plc

An organization that describes itself as 'a property
company in the restaurant sector' has changed the
London restaurant scene in the past six years, not
perhaps so much from the point of view of a customer
as from that of an individual restaurateur. With
considerable resources behind them including the
ingenious financial acumen of director Michael
Golder, few aspiring caterers could hope to win out
acquiring premises up against the company that
bought the Mario & Franco group, Joseph
Berkmann's restaurants, the Wheeler's chain and the
various Café des Amis, among other purchases.
Centralized buying and other pooled resources result
in only mild benefits accruing to the customer's bill
and the company's skills do not include imaginative
catering. The only restaurant of theirs to achieve
significant critical acclaim is Hilaire (q.v.). The
ventures that were not takeovers, such as Maxim's de
Paris and the Trocadero are qualified successes. At
the moment of writing there are rumours of upheavals
at Kennedy Brookes and it seems likely that the only
restaurateur on board, Roy Ackerman, who has just
written and produced his first TV series, The Chef's
Apprentice, will move on to be more involved with
activities that gratify him, clues to which might be
found in the aforementioned film, his establishment of
the Henley Arts Festival and his reviving of The
Chelsea Arts Ball. It is said he will bring out a
restaurant guide . . .

BRITISH HARVEST

Hilton Hotel, Park Lane, W1
01-493 8000

B ased on the idea of American Harvest, the let's-be-proud-of-our-heritage restaurant in the Vista International Hotel in the World Trade Center in New York, British Harvest aims to make the most of British produce from eels to elderflower wine. It is a laudable notion particularly if they do support the smallholder or market gardener who can manage to supply an hotel but not a wholesaler, which was one of the original intentions. It is a familiar bleat now, but it remains true that much of the best British produce is exported since the demand at home is not competitive. Perversely, ambitious restaurants wishing to obtain the tiniest vegetables, the rosiest fruit, the briniest shellfish and the most bewitching offal (often exported from Britain) frequently obtain their supplies from Rungis, the market outside Paris. At British Harvest, to underline seasonality there is a monthly menu of specialities as well as what they cannot resist calling a bill of fare for spring, summer, autumn and winter. To give you a taste of last summer, you might have started with a plate of smoked fish – sea bass, scallops, sewin from Wales, and eels from Lough Neagh with cockle salad and followed it by a roasted rack of lamb from the Mendip and Quantock hills served with loganberry sauce and a slice of herb pie. If you think the food and beverage manager doth protest too much, you are right, for the actuality is less poetic than the promise, not helped by tentative service and anodyne surroundings that make you feel not in a corner that is forever England but in the lobby of an hotel that is part of an international chain. However, they are trying hard. As with almost all hotels, prices are idiotically high and even an adherence to the set menu can be scuppered by the cost of the wine. I include British Harvest because I think the idea of the place is laudable and if money is no object it is one more to add to the short list of places specializing in English food, something that silly old tourists seem to want when they come to England.

CUISINE: *English*	*Also vegetarian dishes*

OPEN: *Mon to Sun*

MEALS: *12 to 2.45; 6 to 10.30*

AVERAGE PRICE: *£22. Set Menus: £14.50*

CREDIT CARDS: *Access, Amex, Diners, Visa, Carte Blanche*

SEATS: *85*

PRIVATE ROOM: *(20)*

MUSIC: *Taped classical*

Wheelchair access

♥ # BUBBS

329 Central Market, EC1
01-236 2435

Once the meat market moves, the area around Smithfield is sure to become smarty-arty the way Covent Garden did but, it must be hoped, not quite so. Already restaurants are opening where only caffs were before but Bubbs has been on the scene for years. So they deserve credit for their perspicacity. They also deserve credit for continuing with French bourgeois food when all around were trickling raspberry vinegar on to slivers of duck and serving haricots verts you could count on the fingers of one hand. The last time I ate at Bubbs it was game season and on offer were a first course of a salad garnished with venison and main courses of partridge, teal and civet of hare. What I chose was poached turbot served in a sauce stitched with threads of vegetables. Portions seem to be according to the theory that men have healthy appetites – Bubbs is neatly positioned between Fleet Street and the city – and reflects the importance that the French attach to the business of lunching. Since its opening, the disposition of the space on the two floors has changed. I still prefer the upstairs dining room that has a plainness suited to serious eating. The walls are ox-blood red, the clothes snowy white. There is talk at the time of writing that the owners of Bubbs may be starting a fish and game restaurant on the river, so check that all is in order before booking your table, for lunch, I think, rather than dinner.

CUISINE: French	
OPEN: Mon to Fri	
MEALS: 12.15 to 2.30; 7 to 9.30	
AVERAGE PRICE: £22	
CREDIT CARDS: None	
SEATS: 108	
PRIVATE ROOMS: (30 and 45)	

LE CAFE DES AMIS DU VIN

11–14 Hanover Place, WC2
01-379 3444

Les Amis du Vin is a company, originally a wine company, that has merged with Kennedy Brookes (*q.v.*) with some slightly indigestible nomenclature resulting like the Café Fish des Amis du Vin in Panton Street, SW1, which is the fast turnover theory applied to fish, about which I have my reservations (tellingly not usually necessary). This Covent Garden restaurant (with wine bar in the basement and quieter Salon upstairs) has been popular since it opened in the summer of 1980, perhaps in part because they have stuck quite faithfully to the original concept of good, simple French ingredients, proper French bread, cheeses in their prime, imaginative charcuterie, andouillettes and other less *recherché* sausages. There are well made omelettes and composed salads as well as more structured dishes. Rightly, given its name, there is no pressure exerted to make you feel you should order a three course meal. The wine list is sensibly composed and not over-priced, and special offers are usually available in the basement bar. My reason for not going to Café des Amis du Vin is its noisiness – feet clattering, chairs scraping and remarks bouncing on bare boards. At peak times conversation is precluded – something and somewhere to keep in mind, I suppose, if you are regretting like mad having fixed to meet somebody for lunch.

CUISINE: French	
OPEN: Mon to Sat	
MEALS: 12 to 3; 6 to 11.15	
AVERAGE PRICE: £13	
CREDIT CARDS: Access, Amex, Visa, Diners	
SEATS: 100+	
TABLES OUTSIDE: (40)	
MUSIC: Live classical	

CAFE PACIFICO

5 Langley Street, WC2
01-379 7728

If tacos, nachos, burritos and enchiladas are all a blur to you, it is probably because you have ordered the mixed plate when trying Tex-Mex food. Spicy mince and re-fried beans and mashed avocado and floppy maize pancakes, grated cheese, and chilli-spiked tomato sauce must be carefully marshalled on your plate if you are to get the best out of this species of food, which for me has more allure than either hamburgers or pizzas. Fundamentally you have the *tortilla*, a pancake made from masa harina, ground corn treated with slaked lime. Crisply fried and filled with spicy minced meat, topped with various accompaniments, it is a *taco*. One of these accompaniments is puréed avocado which is *guacamole*. Served with pieces of deep-fried tortilla this makes a good first course. *Nachos* are tortillas fried flat and covered with re-fried pinto beans and melted cheese. *Tostadas* are similar but usually feature meat and shredded lettuce in the garnish. With *enchiladas*, the tortilla is softer, rolled around the filling and usually doused in a sauce. The Tex-Mex

38

food at Café Pacifico does not rise anywhere near the heights of subtlety you might expect if you had read the essential work on the subject, Diana Kennedy's *Tortilla Book*, but consumed judiciously, i.e. separately, the items make fine accompaniment to mugs of Margarita – a tequila-based cocktail served in a glass rimmed with salt. I like the raffish atmosphere here and the anti-decor look but it can be over-crowded and noisy. No evening bookings taken.

CUISINE: Tex-Mex	*Also vegetarian dishes*

OPEN: Mon to Sun

MEALS: 11.30 to 2.45 (Sun brunch from 12); 5.30 to 11.45 (Sun 7 to 10.45)

AVERAGE PRICE: £11

CREDIT CARDS: Access, Visa

SEATS: 115

♥ # CAFE PELICAN

45 St Martin's Lane, WC2
01-379 0309

Would that the brasseries that spring up all over London, using the term because they think it is more chic than restaurant, were like the Café Pélican which is open all day from 11 am with a fluid menu that meets most needs, from a café complet to a crêpinette de pigeonneau truffée aux graines sur feuilles de choux croquant and those idling times in between when tea with pâtisserie or an assiette of cold cuts is what is required. The premises are disarmingly big, winding on and on from the curvy bar near the door practically the length of the block. In the front part it is possible to have just a snack. More formal tables make up the majority of the room. So many can be accommodated – 250 – that booking is usually not necessary. When I was judging the Laurence Olivier Theatre Awards, I constantly had recourse to the Café Pélican which, almost next door to the Coliseum and opposite the Duke of York's, is perfectly placed for after the theatre or indeed the West

End cinema. Most nights recognizable faces are dotted around. The cooking style is modern which some people feel can be translated as small portions. The plats du jour are more gutsy and dishes like the grilled Toulouse sausages or the bavette – that rather tough cut of steak the French favour – with pommes frites and a confit of shallots seem better to suit the French Thirties style of the place than the salmon wrapped in seaweed served with a peppered beurre blanc. The admirability of the concept seems to me to outweigh any hiccups in the cooking, and the service, on the whole, is amiable. There is a set price menu and also a list for children. In other words they would seem to be putting the customer first, a curiously rare restaurant pose.

CUISINE: French	Also vegetarian dishes

OPEN: Mon to Sun
MEALS: 11 am to 12.30 am
AVERAGE PRICE: £22. Set Menu: £10.95
CREDIT CARDS: Access, Amex, Visa, Dinners
SEATS: 250
TABLES OUTSIDE: 15
MUSIC: Pianist
Wheelchair access

CAFE ROUGE

2c Cherry Tree Walk, Whitecross Street, EC1
01-588 0710

Restaurants that open near the Barbican arts centre are to be applauded for offering an alternative to the abysmal catering there. In my first review of Café Rouge I helpfully suggested that were they to simplify the then rather baroque menu – e.g. breast of duck served pink with soya, honey and spring onion sauce, breast of grouse in cherry and port wine – they might become more of a lure for actors, musicians, stagehands, etc.; become a hang-out, the café of the name. I hesitate to take the credit but the menu is now simpler and also slightly cheaper, but still restaurant prices rather than café prices. However, these can be justified by their policy of obtaining fine fish and meat from Billingsgate and Smithfield markets and treating it with some flair: wild Scottish salmon with tomato and basil sauce, noisettes of venison with a gin and juniper sauce, roast barbary duckling with cider and apples. The vegetables are well cooked and are included in the main course prices. Desserts are generally imaginative and they make their own sorbets, some of them flavoured with exotic fruits. There is a well-balanced set-price menu which is the best way of extracting value from the Café Rouge which is a jumble of concepts: name, location (part of a shopping precinct), formally dressed service, eclectic dishes.

CUISINE: French	
OPEN: L: Mon to Fri; D: Mon to Sat	
MEALS: 12 to 2.30; 6 to 11	
CLOSED: Christmas week, first 2 weeks in August	
AVERAGE PRICE: £24. Set Menu: £10.95	
CREDIT CARDS: Access, Amex, Diners	
SEATS: 34	
TABLES OUTSIDE: (20)	
PRIVATE ROOM: (20)	

CALABASH

Africa Centre, 38 King Street, WC2
01-836 1976

It has occurred to me that, as long as you weren't having an illicit affair with a Nigerian, the Calabash would be an ideal clandestine meeting place. In the basement of the Africa Centre the restaurant is redeemed from being too much like a canteen by the fabrics, batik cloths, and the African paintings and carvings. The affair should not be too absorbing since the food – which features dishes from various countries such as Ghana, Senegal, Sierra Leone, Nigeria and also Morocco – is not without its own allure. Avocado, coconut and black-eyed beans served together, but not mushed up, is a good first course. Aloco, cubes of fried plantain served with a jammy sauce, takes more getting used to. Main courses tend to be spicy, but not overwhelmingly so, and some are quite gentle like the poached chicken bathed in coconut cream. Service is laconic, giving you a long time to mull over your problems. Although it does little to promote itself, Calabash is not unwelcoming to outsiders and is welcome respite from relentless trendiness (and overpricing) of many of Covent Garden's other restaurants. House wine is an adequate accompaniment.

CUISINE: African	Also vegetarian dishes
OPEN: L: Mon to Fri; D: Mon to Sat	
MEALS: 12 to 2.30; 6 to 10.30	
CLOSED: Bank Holidays	
AVERAGE PRICE: £12	
CREDIT CARDS: Access, Amex, Visa, Diners	
SEATS: 80	

CAMDEN BRASSERIE

216 Camden High Street, NW1
01-482 2114

When I first reviewed Camden Brasserie I offered the unstartling *aperçu* that if you provide good, well-cooked food, price it sensibly and serve it with enthusiasm, your restaurant will work. I mentioned it in the context of visiting other restaurants whose owners seemed to feel it was probably all right to miss out on one or more of these steps. The Camden Brasserie has been a success from the start: in part because it hit the area at just the right time when the street market was becoming wiser, the boutiques less ethnic and TV AM studios opened, but mostly because what they do they do well and there is a relaxed, easy-going atmosphere. The room is large, the tablecloths are paper over oilcloth covers. On the walls, bare brick or painted white, there are photographs of local lovelies, lovely in the Eighties mode. Good produce is procured and the most satisfactory meal, to my mind, is either fish or meat, charcoal grilled, accompanied by a large wooden bowl of their unputdownable pommes frites. The soup of the day is usually sound. The spicy chicken wings are a nice idea but they can be swamped by the soya saucy marinade. They also serve salads, pastas, a dish of the day. Their link with Camden Wine and Cheese shop ensures that these commodities are well chosen. Recently a pasta restaurant has been opened in the basement. In winter there is a fire, in summer the doors to the street fold back. In other words, it is the sort of place you would be glad to have in your neighbourhood.

CUISINE: International	*Also vegetarian dishes*
OPEN: L: Mon to Sun; D: Mon to Sat	
MEALS: 12 to 3; 6.30 to 11.30	
CLOSED: Christmas and Bank Holidays	
AVERAGE PRICE: L: £12; D: £16	
CREDIT CARDS: None	
SEATS: 75	
TABLES OUTSIDE: (8)	
MUSIC: Piped – mainly jazz and South American	

LA CAPANNINA

24 Romilly Street, W1
01-437 2473

There are various factors that influence one's attitude to food. For me, one was a boyfriend called John Crome. I met him when I was about 17 and because he was in his twenties and working in the film industry, I thought him impossibly mature but consequently rather thrilling. He used to cook for me and use ingredients like green peppers that did not appear in my mother's kitchen. He was intolerant of my refusal to eat a piece of squid in a Chinese restaurant (I ate it) and he said that La Capannina was the most authentic Italian restaurant in Soho. Twenty-four years later you would expect that to be far from the truth, but Italian restaurants in London have developed less than those of other cuisines, and it is not so very far at all. It is still owned by Linda and Gianni Frattini and the dishes of the day feature some homely assemblies such as lentils with cotechino sausage, home-made pappardelle with a sauce of porcini, potato gnocchi, sweetbreads in breadcrumbs and one of the nicest ways, I think, to eat spaghetti: with oil, garlic and chilli. Sadly, they no longer open for Sunday lunch when they used to serve bollito misto. The decor does look dated compared to the style of Apicella and the noise and bustle might not suit everyone but I am attached to the place, in part because it has remained steady for so long. The dishes on the printed, as opposed to typewritten, menu are banal – the first in the list of specialities is deep-fried breast of chicken rolled round garlic butter. For more stories of John Crome, see the entry for The Chanterelle.

CUISINE: Italian	*Also vegetarian dishes*
OPEN: L: Mon to Fri; D: Mon to Sat	
MEALS: 12 to 3; 6 to 11.30	
CLOSED: Bank Holidays	
AVERAGE PRICE: £16	
CREDIT CARDS: Access, Amex, Visa, Diners	
SEATS: 70	
PRIVATE ROOM: (30)	
MUSIC: Taped, varied	

THE CAPITAL HOTEL RESTAURANT

Basil Street, SW3
01-589 5171

The Capital Hotel occupies a place in London restaurant history as signalling the return of interest in hotel restaurants. When David Levin, the owner, conceived this small personalized hotel he was determined that the restaurant should exist in its own right and be the antithesis of those gloomy echoing rooms often associated with hotel dining. To this end he found himself an excellent English chef (Richard Shepherd, now at Langan's Brasserie) and an interior designer whose futuristic style was so dreadful as to be lovable. Now that current interiors fashion is back-to-the-past and the dining room and bar have been duly chintzed, rosied and ruched by Nina Campbell, I rather miss the silvery cladding in the bar and bleak 'good taste' of the brown and beige in the dining room. Thankfully the kitchen remains on view, enough of it anyway to be reassuring rather than distracting. The chef at time of writing, Brian Turner, has been fourteen years at the Capital, five of them as Shepherd's sous-chef, and he has calmly carried on the high standards of cooking, sensibly not imposing himself simply for the sake of sensation or tricksiness; some of the original favoured specialities such as the mousseline of scallops with cream of sea urchins, the hearts of artichoke stuffed à la Nissarda, the potatoes mashed and fashioned to resemble little apples and pears, remain. There is also a set-price menu every day to prevent any lapse into complacence. About this menu Turner has been quoted as saying: 'The food has come from the market that day – and from the heart. I want people to eat it. The à la carte is by no means boring, but the dishes of the day really excite us. I hope my enthusiasm is infectious.' I must admit to not having caught the bug on my last visit, for I chose from La Grande Carte and was so moved by the deliciousness of the brandade of sole (an interesting variation of that emulsion usually made with salt cod) and the coquelet farci au confit d'ail that I finished every scrap, something in the interest of my shape I try not to do. For the regular visitor – and there are many outside the hotel guests – there is a list of fish and meat that can be simply charcoal grilled.

For the Mouton Cadet London Standard Gourmet Competition 1986, with the theme of the rise and rise of British chefs, we chose the Capital Hotel and Brian Turner. The wine list is sound but pricey. They do, however, have the grace to print on the menu a short list of wines 'qui ne sont pas sans mérite'. The Capital is a champion place to suggest to a rich visitor; Harrods is down the road and the wine bar next door, Le Metro (*q.v.*) owned by the hotel is excellent for flurries of economizing.

CUISINE: *French*	
OPEN: *Mon to Sun*	
MEALS: *12.30 to 2.30 (Sun till 2); 6.30 to 10.15 (Sun 7 to 10)*	
AVERAGE PRICE: *£35. Set Menus: £16.50 (lunch); £18.50 (dinner)*	
CREDIT CARDS: *Access, Amex, Visa, Diners*	
SEATS: *40*	
PRIVATE ROOM: *(20)*	
Wheelchair access	

LE CAPRICE

Arlington House, Arlington Street, SW1
01-629 2239

This site has had a chequered career since the days of the original plushy theatrical Caprice. Faces are still to be found here, though, and whilst they may be those of dress designers rather than dramatists the place has a glitz and glamour *de nos jours*: hard-edged rather than sentimental. Shiny black surfaces, stark black and white photographs (by David Bailey), waiters formally dressed, the interior design by Eva Jirinca, also responsible for some of the Joseph clothes shops, owners who are former Langan's Brasserie and Joe Allen managers; it is a cocktail that has proved remarkably successful. Why? My agent who eats there a great deal says it is because they have devised the ideal menu. It is possible to have a cheap meal or an expensive meal, a diet day or a let-it-all-hang-out day. He has a point. The menu is craftily composed to appeal to people who eat out a great deal and value simplicity or harbour back-to-the-nursery longings. There are dishes of the day written on the side of the menu to prevent regulars from becoming bored. Eyeing up the thin customers I might start with crudités and move on to steak tartare spurning the shoestring potatoes alongside and finish with an espresso coffee, drinking Perrier all the while it goes without saying. Other times I have been attracted by the trendy goat's cheese and frisé salad and the sausages served with an onion marmalade. The point is that however you go about it, spending £9 for two as my agent's super-thin wife did, or four times that, the service maintains the same courtesy. Eating at the bar attracts no cover charge and they will do their best to accommodate you there if the restaurant is full. Sunday brunch is a nice event at Le Caprice, with proper country house offerings like fish cakes or smoked haddock. It is perhaps an even better venue than Langan's if the aim of your outing is to look on either the well-known or well-worn phizogs.

CUISINE: Eclectic	*Also vegetarian dishes*
OPEN: L: Mon to Fri, Sun; D: Mon to Sun	
MEALS: 12 to 2.30 (Sun brunch till 3); D: 7 to 12	
AVERAGE PRICE: £22	
CREDIT CARDS: Access, Amex, Visa, Diners	
SEATS: 120	
MUSIC: Pianist each evening, 8 to 12	

CARAVAN SERAI

50 Paddington Street, W1
01-935 1208

This is Afghan food which bears considerable comparison with Northern Indian including an astute use of the tandoori oven, but there are interesting differences. Among the first courses there are dishes reminiscent of ravioli called ashak and mantoo. The vegetarian versions are preferable to my mind, the first being filled with leeks and served in a sauce of yoghurt and cream, the second filled with green peppers and onions and served in a sauce of yoghurt and cream. This sauce also takes the form of soup called shoorba. I also would recommend dalda, barbecued kebabs of minced lamb served with lentils. The lentils are delicious as are the rice dishes. Quite the best dish of rice I have ever had is their kabuli chalaw; basmati rice, faintly shiny with oil, garnished with threads of fried orange peel and almonds. What they refer to as complete dishes have a base of the Afghan version of a naan (wheat flour bread cooked in the tandoori oven) or are accompanied by rice cooked with lentils. At least one of these is worth ordering in the main course. There is a dish called kohi, marinated roasted lamb, rather similar in style to the way Greeks go about cooking lamb (very thoroughly). The room is pretty in an ethnic way and a large china Afghan hound sits beside the door. The service is charming and amazingly sophisticated. If you are keen on exploring the alternative foods that London so generously provides you should not omit a spell in the Caravan Serai. The sister restaurant, Buzkash at 4 Chelverton Road, SW15 (01-788 0599) has an identical menu if the circumstances of your life mean that it is easier to eat in Putney than in Marylebone.

CUISINE: Afghan	Also vegetarian dishes

OPEN: L: Mon to Sat; D; Mon to Sun

MEALS: 12 to 2.45; 6 to 11 (Fri and Sat till 11.30, Sun till 10.30)

AVERAGE PRICE: £18. Set Menu: £5.75

CREDIT CARDS: Access, Amex, Visa, Diners

SEATS: 40

THE CARIBBEAN SUNKISSED RESTAURANT

49 Chippenham Road, W9
01-286 3741

Unlike other ethnic groups, West Indians have been fairly lackadaisical where opening restaurants is concerned, which is a shame since the cuisine has many appealing qualities, not least of them being the root vegetables and the intimations of sunshine. The name of the restaurant is borne out valiantly – an orange sunburst across the window of a dull building in an unprepossessing street. Inside there is a kind of front-parlour-tasteless carpet of many colours but it is not altogether irrelevant to the food, historically a mish-mash of influences. Some of the main dishes resemble curries though with atypical ingredients such as yams and rum (in general there is a happy hand with alcohol as an ingredient). The fish dishes are more particular and it is worth trying the shark if it is available, and also the tuna. Calalou is the traditional soup of the West Indies. The base should be young tender leaves of aroids such as taro or malanga, spinach-like in flavour and spinach can be substituted. Other important ingredients are salt pork, crab and okra which gives a silky texture. The calalou (there are as many ways of spelling it as making it) I tried here was not ace but it gives you the idea. Pepperpot – a soup with a base of fish stock – was suitably spicy. Try a selection of vegetables including dasheen and fried plantain (green banana). With these and the fiery sauces provided it is possible to put together some diverting forkfuls. Rum punch rather than the over-priced wines is more likely to get you in the right holiday mood, a state of mind with which the staff are in sympathy.

CUISINE: Caribbean	
OPEN: Mon to Sat	
MEALS: 12 to 3; 6.30 to 12	
AVERAGE PRICE: £18	
CREDIT CARDS: Access, Visa	
SEATS: 65	
PRIVATE ROOM: (30)	

♥ THE CHANTERELLE

119 Old Brompton Road, SW7
01-373 7390

I t was to The Chanterelle in the 1960s I was first taken out to dinner by a man. I remember I was horrified because the bill came to about £5 and I wondered what on earth might be expected of me later to justify this staggering sum. Also half a bottle of wine had made me giddy enough to acquiesce to anything. The Chanterelle was one of the prototype bistros of that era, designed by Terence Conran, food, then by Walter Baxter not a little influenced (who wasn't?) by Elizabeth David. The stripped pine tongue and groove decor remained a long time and one of my favourite overheard remarks was one man wearily saying to another, 'If they ever redecorate this place they will have to scrape all those old conversations off the walls.' It *is* redecorated – lighter and spacier – and the food is now masterminded by Walter Baxter's partner Fergus Provans. It is an eclectic mixture; on the whole successful gastronomic Franglais. The supper menu is a thoughtful idea and late evening is a pleasant time to spend at The Chanterelle. Incidentally, he kissed me goodnight on the doorstep.

CUISINE: French

OPEN: Mon to Sun

MEALS: 12 to 2.30; 7 to 11.30

CLOSED: 4 days at Christmas

AVERAGE PRICE: L: £11; D: £15. Set Menus: £6.50 (lunch); £10.50 (dinner); Supper Menu (after 10 pm): £8

CREDIT CARDS: Access, Amex, Visa, Diners

SEATS: 42

TABLES OUTSIDE: (10)

LE CHEF

41 Connaught Street, W2
01-402 7761/262 5945

I used to like this restaurant rather better than I do now – something to do with the evolving nature of the restaurant business and the static assumptions here of what constitutes French food and French atmosphere. However, Alan King's cooking has a following and the more rustic dishes can be successfully authentic. The various set-price meals help keep the bill in check. It can come as something of a shock otherwise, particularly if you have had a meal along the lines of the last one I tried which started with egg mayonnaise, an assembly requiring few skills and in that case seemingly the one of unscrewing a lid off a jar. The decor is what is popularly believed to be bistro style. The cheeseboard is of note and I would certainly advise scheduling that course into a meal at Le Chef.

CUISINE: French	*Also vegetarian dishes*

OPEN: L: Tues to Fri; D: Tues to Sat

MEALS: 12.30 to 2.30; 7 to 11.30 (Sat till 11)

CLOSED: August

AVERAGE PRICE: L: £19; D: £24. Set Menus: £13.75 (lunch); £17.50 inc. ¼ bottle wine (Sat dinner)

CREDIT CARDS: Access, Amex, Visa

SEATS: 48

TABLES OUTSIDE: (10)

PRIVATE ROOM: (20)

MUSIC: Piped French

THE CHELSEA ROOM

Hyatt Carlton Tower Hotel
Cadogan Place, SW1
01-235 5411

I include this hotel restaurant overlooking the gardens of Cadogan Place because I respect the skills of the chef Bernard Gaume and indeed those of the restaurant manager Jean Quero. But the combination of the prices and the rather static quality of the haute cuisine, much of it over-rich for present day appetites, makes me hesitate to push it except if you happen to be in the area and on an expense account. Perhaps the way to approach The Chelsea Room is via the set-price lunch which includes half a bottle of wine, but don't anticipate complicated cooking: an avocado with herb dressing and a fillet of turbot bonne femme are two of the choices of the set menu in front of me. Some chefs say they prefer to work in hotels as the responsibility is less, the free time and holidays can be relied upon, luxury ingredients are easily procurable. It is not the recipe for zing.

CUISINE: French	
OPEN: Mon to Sun	
MEALS: 12.30 to 2.45; 7 to 11.15 (Sun till 10.15)	
AVERAGE PRICE: £38. Set Menu: £16.50 inc. ½ bottle wine (lunch)	
CREDIT CARDS: Access, Amex, Visa, Diners	
SEATS: 80	
MUSIC: Pianist in the evening	

CHEZ GERARD

8 Charlotte Street, W1
01-636 4975

A simple formula well executed seems a surprisingly difficult achievement for restaurants but, along the lines of L'Entrecôte and its clones in Paris, Chez Gérard does steak and chips and does it well. They used to be the other side of Charlotte Street but crossing the road has not robbed the frites of their moreishness nor the cheeseboard of its worthiness of another bottle of the house claret. The waitresses can be terse or tasty. I suspect women customers might find the former, men the latter. If you are in a party and one baulks at the idea of charcoal grilled meat and french-fried potatoes, there are alternatives on the menu and the first courses, which might include moules marinière in season and onion soup just to prove to you this is a French restaurant, are not sketchily made. It's a nice place for an alternative Sunday lunch.

CUISINE: French	
OPEN: L: Mon to Fri, Sun; D: Mon to Sun	
MEALS: 12.30 to 2.30; 6.30 to 11	
AVERAGE PRICE: £19	
CREDIT CARDS: Access, Visa	
SEATS: 95	
TABLES OUTSIDE: (16)	

CHEZ NICO

129 Queenstown Road, SW8
01-720 6960

Nico of the title is Nico Ladenis who in 1985 moved to Shinfield near Reading (see Worth a Drive) to grander premises, also called Chez Nico, that should, in time, bring him his third (deserved) Michelin star. Phillip Britten who has worked with Nico for the past four years is now head chef in Battersea and also has a stake in the business. Cooking goes on much as usual but Britten, I think, will slowly develop his own style, though it would only be a pity if he moved away from the hallmarks of Nico's approach: vehement saucing, meticulous attention to detail, particularly apparent in the vegetables, an obvious greater fondness for meat than fish (refreshingly unfashionable), the best and most luxurious of ingredients. It *is* a pity that reports would seem to indicate that Britten has also assumed the mantle of high-handed behaviour towards customers, insisting that only customers who book can be let in, insisting they turn up on the dot, expecting them to consider the kitchen rather than having the kitchen consider them – so what if everyone wants the same main course? Eating out should be fun. However, he works with a small staff and patently wants everything to be of the highest order, so understanding must be expected from both sides. Also once you tuck into your mousseline de canard au beurre de cèpes or a boudin of foie gras avec sa macédoine de légumes à l'huile de noisettes, followed, perhaps, by les deux cailles au chou rouge, sauce porto or filet de boeuf persillé aux truffes, it is fun and there is gratification. The decoration of the room has been changed, unarguably for the better. There is a greater feeling of spaciousness and an impersonality that suits restaurants – I have never liked the 'my drawing room' approach. At dinner the price of the main course, which at the moment of writing starts at £21, includes a choice of first course. Cheese, desserts and coffee are extra but prices include tax and service. Phillip's fiancée charmingly manages the serving. You will notice the set-price lunch among the index of lunchtime haute cuisine bargains and Queenstown Road is nearer than you think, with parking no problem.

CUISINE: French	
OPEN: L: Tues to Fri; D: Mon to Sat	
MEALS: 12.30 to 2; 7.30 to 10.45	
CLOSED: 4 days at Easter, 3 weeks in summer, 10 days at Christmas	
AVERAGE PRICE: £38. Set Menu: £14.50 (lunch)	
CREDIT CARDS: Access, Amex, Visa, Diners	
SEATS: 31	
Wheelchair access	

CHIANG MAI

48 Frith Street, W1
01-437 7444

On Thursdays the plane from Bangkok arrives with the ingredients necessary to authentic Thai food, a commodity on offer here in an environment that is designed to represent a Thai wooden stilt house. The owners also have a shop in Craven Terrace, W2. Because it is still relevant and, though I say it myself, informative, I am quoting some of my original review in *The London Standard*.

'The menu runs to 110 items, many tempting you away from the set-price lists which I know are there to help but always strike me as the sap's way out.

'The section entitled appetizers includes items like satay and tempura that are more familiar to the Western palate and various dumplings and spring rolls that on past experience I would recommend. The soups are also probably good but the other 60 dishes beckoned and we moved on to pad ped which is a dry chicken curry with a coconut flavoured sauce and an ingredient which they call basil leaves but which is sharper and more fibrous than basil as we know it.

'We also had pahd woonsen which was a delicious assembly of fried pork with Chinese mushrooms and transparent noodles. The flavours were subtle and did not pit the tastebuds with sharpness.

'The hot and sour vermicelli salad (hot and sour are the flavours of every month in Thailand) from the vegetarian section was not as good as I had anticipated. The omelette with onion was just that. We had some boiled rice and completed the meal with that delicious fruit with a flavour something like lychee, mangosteen.'

If you still feel none the wiser or braver, the staff at Chiang Mai are helpful and courteous and, as at almost any restaurant, genuine curiosity and appreciation will pay off.

CUISINE: Thai	*Also vegetarian dishes*
OPEN: Mon to Sun	
MEALS: 12 to 2.50; 6 to 11.15 (Sunday till 10)	

CHICAGO RIB SHACK

1 Raphael Street, Knightsbridge Green, SW7
01-581 5595

Bob Payton (*q.v.*) aims to bring the real thing in ribs to London and to this end has installed ovens in the kitchen that are wood-fired to bring you that hickory-smoked down-home gen-u-ine flavour of barbecued spare ribs. His characteristic thoroughness of approach has paid off. In a survey I did of rib restaurants in London (they are on the increase) the Rib Shack's ribs won out. They are the item to stick with for the barbecued chicken, the barbecued beef sandwich and the salad bowl all disappointed. The only side dish you should not miss is the moreish Hillary's onion loaf, a rectangular tangle of deep-fried onion rings. The room is agreeable; you would never guess it was converted from a Bejam frozen food store. The jokes on the menu and round the room are egregious and the robot-like staff – trained to utter only certain phrases and responses in a distressingly unspiritual litany – can get you down, but basically it is good fun and heaven for children and the greedy. Coca-Cola is served in the proper bottles and those interested in more uplifting drinks should note that there is a full-on licence meaning you may drink alcohol without eating. Bob Payton is to be congratulated for hammering on at the authorities until they granted him this concession.

CUISINE: American	*Also vegetarian dishes*
OPEN: Mon to Sun	
MEALS: 11.45 am to 11.30 pm	
AVERAGE PRICE: £12	

CREDIT CARDS: None

SEATS: 250

MUSIC: Piped

CHUEN CHENG KU

17 Wardour Street, W1
01-437 1398

A seething cathedral of Cantonese cooking facing the two main streets of Chinatown; it is argued that the dim sum pushed on trolleys are the best here (some favour New World in Gerrard Place which is under related management). When eating à la carte, or after 6 pm when dim sum cease to be served, try not to be daunted by the long menu and thus feebly settle for familiar items for the interesting cooking lies in their treatment of pieces of animals you may never have contemplated. You may still not want to think about tripe but deep-fried and served with shiny, slightly sweet sauce it can be good. Pork belly is a cut of which the Chinese are very fond and it provides an unctuous quality when casseroled with, for example, eel. Some customers speak well of duck cooked with lemon where the citrus flavour teeters on the edge of being over-powering. Despite the fact that the premises seat 400 on three floors there are often queues particularly at weekend lunchtimes when Chinese families are out and about shopping and noshing. Go in any time, just as the Chinese do, and assuage hunger, dissatisfaction, heart-break or whatever with a bowl of soup, some dumplings, a noodle assembly or a one-dish meal of roasted meat with rice and green vegetable.

CUISINE: Cantonese

OPEN: Mon to Sun

MEALS: 11 am to 11.45 pm

AVERAGE PRICE: £12. Set Menu: £5.25

CREDIT CARDS: Access, Amex, Visa, Diners

SEATS: 400

PRIVATE ROOM: 100

CIBOURE

21 Eccleston Street, SW1
01-730 2505

I reviewed Ciboure most enthusiastically soon after it opened in the summer of '82. The chef Richard Price had worked, most noticeably, at Lichfield's in Richmond and he had successfully transported the notion of a royale (almost a custard) of leeks and mushrooms and impressed me by a garnish of pears sliced pearly thin laid on barely cooked spinach on which sweetbreads were couched. If this sounds very *moderne* to you, you are a perceptive reader, and the style goes on, though with four years' more practice. Reports, as they say in other guides, continue to be enthusiastic. My very favourite PR man (in London) eats there regularly and often takes advantage of the set-price lunch (priced, it must be noted, excluding VAT which seems so unfair as to be almost illegal). Bruce Oldfield the dress designer has been interviewed there in the English *Elle* magazine on the grounds that it is a usual haunt of his. Perhaps his trim shape is not only due to the body conditioning class where I used to see him before I gave up the ghost aspirations, but to the fact that he describes the food as 'nouvelle tubby' whereas my PR friend talks regretfully of small portions. Dishes well spoken of are mousse of foie gras with gooseberry chutney, fillet of venison in a lemon and walnut sauce, the lamb in a sorrel sauce. The decor is slightly bloodless – the feeling that a home without children can have – but there is attention to detail and acknowledgement of what goes to make a special meal.

CUISINE: French	*Also vegetarian dishes*
OPEN: L: Mon to Fri; D: Mon to Sat	
MEALS: 12 to 2.30; 7 to 11.30	
AVERAGE PRICE: £28. Set Menu (2 courses): £11 (lunch)	
CREDIT CARDS: Access, Amex, Visa, Diners	
SEATS: 36	
Wheelchair access	

CINECITTA ROMA

76 Welbeck Street, W1
01-935 2794

In this guide because there are few places where you can eat and also dance without paying exorbitant prices. Here in the wild decor, supposedly representing various film sets, you can dance to the disco and eat the pizza/pasta food without spending much. It is open only on Thursday, Friday and Saturday evenings but can be booked privately other nights and a rather more enterprising menu arranged. It is part of the Spaghetti House Group.

CUISINE: Italian	*Also vegetarian dishes*
OPEN: Thurs to Sat	
MEALS: 9 pm to 1.30 am	
AVERAGE PRICE: £10 (2 courses)	
CREDIT CARDS: None	
SEATS: 150	
MUSIC: Disco	
DANCING	

♥ CLARKE'S

124 Kensington Church Street, W8
01-221 9225

Sally Clarke has worked in California helping Michael McCarty set up Michael's Restaurant in Santa Monica. Before that she did a Cordon Bleu course in Paris. Her menu ideas and her policy of a no-choice evening meal is probably the closest we come in London to the sort of food that gets described as 'Californian cuisine'. Basically what this means is an emphasis on creativity and originality in flavourings and garnishes and a certain simplicity, e.g. barbecueing as a mode, in the cooking process. Some typical dinner menus will get the concept across: clam and mussel soup made with chillis and roasted red peppers, skewered leg of lamb grilled with sweet potato, parsnip and pumpkin sliced and baked in cream, an English cheese served with home-made biscuits, apple, walnut and spices wrapped in wafer thin pastry and served warm; tart of black mushrooms, garlic saucisson and fresh thyme, fresh red mullet fillet served char-grilled on a bed of parsley pasta with strips of various vegetables, an English cheese, baked Cox's apple filled with dried fruits macerated in rum with crème fraîche from Kent. This sort of dinner menu costs £17, a price that includes service, VAT and tea or coffee with chocolate truffles. From 10 to 11 pm a supper menu is served for £12 – the evening's menu minus the main course but with perhaps a salad with the cheese or some embellishment to the first course. At lunchtimes when the menus are similar in style but simpler in terms of accompaniments to the main course there is a small choice and a difference in price depending on whether you have two or three courses. Clarke's has been successful from the start, as well it should be, for the food is always appealing and often delicious. The surroundings are pretty and the waitresses attentive and keen. Details like the carefully selected cheeses from British and Irish smallholdings, the three kinds of bread – including a great onion bread – made daily on the premises, the house aperitif of blood oranges and champagne and the fairness and squareness of the deal all add up to a praiseworthy and likeable formula. My only reservation is to do with the aspect of no choice. Everyone eating the same dish seems more like a dinner party than a restaurant outing where coveting someone else's choice is part of the thrill, and the natural assumption that the menus are planned according to daily marketing is shattered by the list of the week's menus posted outside. Wines are sensibly chosen with some interesting French regional bottles, Californian choices and one English wine.

CUISINE: *Eclectic*

OPEN: *Mon to Fri*

MEALS: *12.30 to 2; 7.30 to 9.45; 10 to 11*

CLOSED: *Bank Holidays, Christmas, New Year and 2 weeks in August*

LA CLOCHE

304 Kilburn High Road, NW6
01-328 0302

L a Cloche, The Lantern and Pigeon are all owned by Yugoslav Peter Ilic and all run to the same sensible formula: one (restrained) price for first courses, one for main courses, vegetables and desserts, so your choice from the eclectic menu is not governed by considerations like can I afford the beef, or should I have the chicken. Naturally, the prices and the scheme appeal to the young and impecunious and there is usually a pleasantly raffish and disorganized atmosphere. There is an emphasis on healthy eating with some good composed salads, dishes like tabbouleh (cracked wheat salad) and soups based on pulses and seaweed. Sometimes portions seem skimpy and some dishes misfire, but it is hard to be too judgmental in the circumstances. I liked the choux pastry stuffed with crab and draped with a hollandaise sauce, was less keen (at The Lantern) on a pastry parcel containing pieces of duck. On the whole expensive ingredients cannot successfully be served cheaply so it is wiser to opt for, say, a casserole or a dish heavily into vegetables. These restaurants suit gatherings well, particularly The Lantern, where a large central table is ideal for parties, but rather less terrific fun for the rest of the diners. Desserts are simple, house wine the appropriate choice. The latest venture of Peter Ilic is a restaurant called Just Around the Corner where you are served a meal of several courses but little choice. You elect to pay for the food and for your drinks what you think it is all worth. I think it is a dotty, discomfiting idea, but should it appeal to you the address is 446 Finchley Road, NW2 (01-431 3300).

CUISINE: *Eclectic*   *Also vegetarian dishes*

OPEN: *Mon to Sun*

MEALS: *12 to 3; 7 to 12*

CLOSED: *Christmas Day and Boxing Day*

AVERAGE PRICE: *£12*

CREDIT CARDS: *Visa (The Lantern only)*

SEATS: *58*

THE CONNAUGHT HOTEL RESTAURANT AND GRILL

♥   *Carlos Place, W1*
01-499 7070

Quite simply, the Connaught Grill is the place I would choose if asked out by someone for whom money was no consideration. I mean, rather than someone for whom their company's money was no consideration, since one of the good things about the Grill is that it never seems papered by expense accounts. The service is as stately as a quadrille and chef Michel Bourdin has hit exactly the right note in combining French food with Grand Hotel. The dishes of the day are British classics like oxtail and Irish stew – probably the best British food in a London restaurant – but the main burden of the menu is haute cuisine mercifully unsullied by recent fashion; dishes with all the elegance of couture clothes. The last meal I had in the Grill began with something I seldom resist, scrambled eggs with truffles served in a case of feuilleté pastry. After that came saddle of hare with purées of chestnuts and vegetables. Game of all kinds is extremely well handled at the Connaught. The main dining room, which has its own charm, largely entrenched in the polished wood panelling and widely spaced tables, has a different pricing system from that in the Grill. The main course price includes that of the other courses (unless you choose an item with a supplement). The menu changes in part daily. The dessert trolley has wonderful nursery puddings like port jelly. Aficionados find it hard to decide where is the better bread and butter pudding – here or at the Dorchester Hotel. Mark-up on the wines is without much restraint but the advice from the sommelier is sound if you are planning to indulge in a great bottle. For a visitor to London planning a treat of a meal, The Connaught would be top of my list of suggestions. Fine food these days is similar the Western world over so you look to other areas for differentiation, areas like tradition and dignity.

Restaurant
CUISINE: French/English

OPEN: Mon to Sun

MEALS: 12.30 to 2.30; 6.30 to 10.15

AVERAGE PRICE: £35

CREDIT CARDS: Access

SEATS: 80

Wheelchair access

Grill Room
CUISINE: French/English

OPEN: Mon to Fri

MEALS: 12 to 2; 6 to 10.15

AVERAGE PRICE: £41

CREDIT CARDS: Access

SEATS: 36

Wheelchair access

CORNEY AND BARROW

118 Moorgate, EC2
01-628 2898

When this wine bar and restaurant owned by long-established city wine merchants opened in 1983 there was much publicity for the architecture and design, the inspirations of Julyan Wickham, the chap responsible for the club Zanzibar. It is rather stunning and it would not be inappropriate to pop in for a quick glass of something here before going on to see the new Lloyds building. Also it is a relief to get away from the Sweeney Todd environment that most city places affect. A wide and handsome staircase takes you down from the ground floor champagne bar and wine shop into the bar and restaurant. Aspirants to the title Busy Executive could have one course at the bar and also be seen to use one of the cordless phones or study the Press Association newswire. You would want to have a flourishing expense account to tackle a three course meal at the tables. City restaurants have to make their money in fewer hours and the outcome is all too clear on the bill. However, the food here is good; modern without being precious and robust enough for those who want to make lunch the meal of the day. The menu at the time of writing features among the first courses warm gâteau of carrot with a cream herb sauce, french lettuce salad in walnut oil dressing and scampi and, among the main courses, escalope of turbot soufflé on a Noilly Prat sauce, roast best end of lamb with a rosemary flavoured sauce and grilled sirloin steak Bercy. Not surprisingly the wine list is long, strong on claret, burgundy and champagne. The formula clearly has worked, for two new branches have opened at 44 Cannon Street, EC4 (01-248 1700) and 109 Old Broad Street, EC2 (01-638 9308). Note the evening hours and consider too the proximity of the Moorgate restaurant to the Barbican Arts Centre.

CUISINE: *Franglais*	
OPEN: *Mon to Fri*	
MEALS: *11.30 to 3; 6 to 8*	
AVERAGE PRICE: *£27*	
CREDIT CARDS: *Access, Amex, Visa, Diners*	
SEATS: *75*	
PRIVATE ROOM: *(20)*	

COSMO

4–6 Northways Parade, Finchley Road, NW3
01-722 1398

This restaurant is not included because of its haute cuisine but because there are few places in London where you can find rheinischer sauerbraten, raisin sauce, red cabbage, and continental dumpling (£4.75) and even fewer that have been going since 1939 at the same address. The Cosmo is a great favourite with Jewish refugees, many of whom settled around Swiss Cottage and West Hampstead. There is lemon tea, coffee with whipped cream and pastries to sit over in the café part of the premises, bordered in the front window by plants which I think are called mother-in-law's tongues. The restaurant side has suitably dignified waiters, other dishes along the lines of the above and daily specials which change weekly. On the whole the food is carefully cooked and is certainly sustaining. Places like Cosmo provide much needed contrast to the fast food joints and 'theme' pubs cum brasseries spreading everywhere.

CUISINE: German/Continental	*Also vegetarian dishes*
OPEN: Mon to Sun	
MEALS: 12 to 10.30	
AVERAGE PRICE: £13. Set Menu (1 main course): £2.25	
CARDS: Access, Amex, Visa, Diners. Luncheon Vouchers	
SEATS: 45	

CRANKS

8 Marshall Street, W1
01-437 9431

Cranks vegetarian restaurants are like some of one's relations: nice to know they are there but you don't necessarily want to visit them all that often. Originally established in 1961 near the Marshall Street premises, Cranks was defiantly named but in their latest book, *Entertaining with Cranks*, they quote the

Christmas cracker motto, 'A crank is a little thing which starts a revolution', and indeed vegetarianism has a quite different status now compared to 25 years ago. Something of the homespun, hand-reared, crafts-man-potted style clings to Cranks, however, and the dishes tend to deal you rather healthy blows of beneficence. Bucolic good taste is very much in the offing with the varnished pine tables and scrubbed complexions and ceramic bowls to hold the salads, vegetable risottos, savoury casseroles, lentil rissoles, cheese flans and the like. Much as I espouse the cause of unadulterated eating no one will persuade me that pastry is anything but leaden made with wholemeal flour. Yoghurt and fruit makes a better dessert, one rather less likely to make you regret the whole idea of going healthy. For vegetarians who wish to make a proper evening of it, note there is waiter service from Tuesday to Saturday evenings and often live music. Other Cranks branches are at 9–11 Tottenham Street, W1 (01-631 3912) where they do the sort of breakfast that gives a proper start to the day and at 11 The Market, Covent Garden, WC2 (01-379 6508), handy if you just want to graze on sprouted aduki beans while shopping.

CUISINE: Vegetarian	
OPEN: Mon to Sat	
MEALS: 10 am to 11 pm (Mon till 8.30)	
CLOSED: Christmas Day, Boxing Day and Bank Holidays	
AVERAGE PRICE: L: £7; D: £13	
CREDIT CARDS: Access, Amex, Visa, Diners	
SEATS: 170	
MUSIC: Guitarist 2/3 evenings a week	

THE CRITERION
BRASSERIE

222 Piccadilly, W1
01-839 7133

There is something about catering chains that manages to dim the sparkle of the most glittering premises and the latter could hardly be more dazzling than the Criterion, which is the recently restored Marble Hall originally designed by Thomas Verity in 1874. There are wonderful examples of mosaic work including a glinting gold ceiling. However, the owners are Trust House Forte and the food, though French in name, seems ever compromised in delivery. That said, the building itself, once the epitome of the chic place to be seen at, is well worth experiencing and your oeuf Porte Maillot and andouillette de Troyes grillé and tarte aux pommes might catch the reflections of some of the architectural excitement.

CUISINE: French	*Also vegetarian dishes*
OPEN: Mon to Sat	
MEALS: 11 to 3; 6 to 11	
AVERAGE PRICE: £18	
CREDIT CARDS: Access, Amex, Visa, Diners	
SEATS: 100	
MUSIC: Pianist in the evenings	

Sir Terence Conran

One of the first business enterprises of Terence Conran was a restaurant called The Soup Kitchen. His restaurant involvement since has been in designing them, doubtless furnishing many with Habitat merchandize, opening The Neal Street Restaurant (*q.v.*), the restaurant at Heal's (*q.v.*), in-store cafés in the Habitat chain. Now with his connection to British Home Stores he is, he proudly told me, the largest restaurateur in Britain. It will be interesting to see what changes will be wrought in meals for those shoppers so keen on low-price lighting and good Cheddar cheese. Sir Terence's manifest enthusiasm for food has been passed on to his wife Caroline, author of many cookery books, some with a special slant on English food, and to their son Tom and daughter Sophie who are presently running a catering company called Tom's Happy Palate. Their youngest son Ned is still at school.

LA CROISETTE

168 Ifield Road, SW10
01-373 3694

When I first went to this restaurant in January 1975 I likened a meal there to a brief holiday in the south of France, so warm and welcoming was the Provençal print decor, so sparklingly fresh the fish. What was also winning was the generosity of the set-price meal; more like eating in the home of a prolific cook than in a restaurant. Ten years later they are not wooing with quite such ardour as offering sautéed brown shrimps, slivers of pissaladière, rillettes and slices of salami even before the first courses arrive, but the hospitable spirit remains and that sense of relaxation that a set-price menu induces quickly sets in. La Croisette was the first restaurant opened by Pierre Martin and Alberto Bracci who went on also to succeed with Le Suquet, Le Quai St Pierre and L'Olivier. The formula seems so simple – first-rate ingredients, French style – yet how few places get it right. Pierre is one of the nicest chaps I know in this business and that cannot be discounted as an ingredient. The platter of shellfish is an arresting first course and it does have an enlivening whiff of the briny but it can prove too much if you are intending to eat your way through to dessert on the menu. The main course fish dishes are usually subtly sauced and the salads are well composed. Wine is obviously viewed as an adjunct rather than an aim in itself. It is as well to stay with the Muscadet. Tables are crammed together in the basement room so in sunny weather try to book one of the few in the garden. A good place for a celebratory sort of meal.

CUISINE: *French/Fish*	
OPEN: *L: Wed to Sun; D: Tues to Sun*	
MEALS: *12.30 to 2.30; 7.30 to 11.30*	
CLOSED: *2 weeks at Christmas*	
AVERAGE PRICE: *£27. Set Menu: £20 (inc. kir, cheese and coffee)*	
CARDS: *Amex*	
SEATS: *55*	
TABLES OUTSIDE: *(10)*	

DAQUISE

20 Thurloe Street, SW7
01-589 6117

L ike Cosmo (*q.v.*), Daquise is one of those places that you are thankful stand solid and calorific in the face of American imports and minimalist chic. It is a Polish café open from breakfast onwards that satisfies needs like chlodnik soup, borscht, stuffed cabbage, zrazy, kasha, hot beetroot and creamy cakes and moods like melancholia, gnawing hunger and nostalgia. The premises occupy ground floor and basement. The staff are suitably lugubrious. One of the many nice things about Daquise is that it attracts solemn men in homburgs but also coaxes away French Lycée students and budding shorthand typists from the hamburger bars and pizza parlours. The set-price two course lunch menu is a bargain – in quality and width.

CUISINE: *Polish*	
OPEN: *Mon to Sun*	
MEALS: *10 am to 11.30 pm (breakfast till noon every day)*	
AVERAGE PRICE: *£8. Set Menu (2 courses): £2.90 (lunch)*	

Dim Sum

Dim sum (sometimes called tim sum), I read, means a touch of heart or dot the heart and certainly these sweet or savoury, steamed or deep-fried dumplings and other assemblies have dotted the heart of perspicacious Londoners who appreciate their delectability and good value. Drinking tea, the appropriate accompaniment, two people could make quite a meal out of £8. Basically, dim sum are small parcels with different wrappings such as won ton skin, rice-flour bun, noodle dough, beancurd skin, pastry, shredded yam, pancake etc. The savoury fillings based on meat, prawns and vegetables are usually vigorously seasoned. The Cantonese restaurants of Chinatown are the place to look for dim sum during the day until about 5.30 pm when they cease to be served. Making dim sum is a skilled job and special chefs are recruited for it. For this reason Chinatown is a better hunting ground than elsewhere, where a restaurant might buy the product deep-frozen. Two exceptions to this rule are *Lee Ho Fook, 5 New College Parade, Finchley Road, NW3* and *Kam Tung, 59–63 Queensway, W2.* If you go to a restaurant that serves dim sum from trolleys it is correct form to lift the lids of the steamer baskets and peer in to see if you like the look of the contents nesting there in groups of three or four. (The hazard with trolley or menu is getting a sweet dim sum when your mouth was prepared for savoury.)

A dim sum menu will include some of the following. Har kow is steamed shrimp dumpling with a wrapping of noodle dough; siu mai is steamed minced pork in won ton skins (these two are usually ordered in tandem); kai pau is a steamed dumpling filled with chicken and Chinese mushrooms; mei kai is sticky rice enclosing meat steamed in lotus leaves, worth ordering as a base for other mouthfuls; woo kok is a deep-fried yam croquette with a meat filling; fun kwor refers to a crescent shaped pastry which can be filled either with vegetables or pork and coriander. Also usually available are steamed beef meat balls, spare ribs with garlic and black bean sauce chopped into ½in lengths, ducks' feet flavoured with star anise with a patty of meat attached by bean curd skin (wonderful, I promise), chickens' feet, char siu pau which is a rice-flour bun, slightly sweet and cloud-like, filled with roasted pork, and the more expensive cheung fun, canneloni-shaped rolls with a slippy shiny dough wrapped round beef, pork or chicken, to be eaten with a generous splash of soya sauce.

DON PEPE

99 Frampton Street, NW8
01-262 3834

Considering the number of Spaniards working in London restaurants, some of them chefs of 'French' restaurants, it is odd how limited is the choice of Spanish restaurants and how mediocre the existing ones are. It is as if package holidays have not only spoilt the Costa Brava and the Costa del Sol but everyone's expectations of Spanish food as well. And there is some culinary law along the lines that food rises to meet customers' demands; evangelists are thin on the ground among restaurateurs. Don Pepe, to my mind, comes closest to providing reasonably authentic Spanish food in central London (Rebato's, a bit further out at 169 South Lambeth Road, SW18 (01-735 6388) is another contender) but you are closer to the Spanish experience by staying in the bar, eating tapas and choosing from their fairly comprehensive list of reasonably priced Spanish wines than by eating in the restaurant and choosing their veal escalope milanese – shades of the chef's previous job? There are attempts to provide the indigenous dishes – the merluza a la gallega (Galician-style hake), the chicken in a Rioja sauce and the paella. The last might well be improved by ordering it in advance for lunch rather than dinner. First courses are a better story, particularly the tripe in a spicy sauce and the fabada asturiana(white beans casseroled with salt pork and sausages) but having recently stayed a week in San Sebastian (a great centre of gastronomy) I cannot really raise a great deal of enthusiasm even for these. The bar, which occupies a large area, is patronized by Spanish men, the sort who, as a woman, make you feel you should be at home crocheting some gloomy bit of lace. The set lunch is good value and every evening but Monday there is live guitar music in the late evening.

CUISINE: Spanish	
OPEN: Mon to Sun	
MEALS: 12 to 2.30 (Sun till 1.15); 7 to 12.15 (Sun till 10)	
AVERAGE PRICE: £22. Set Menu: £6.50. Children's Menu (Sun lunch): £4	
CREDIT CARDS: Access, Amex, Visa, Diners	
SEATS: 60	
MUSIC: Guitarist after 9 pm Tues to Sun	

THE DORCHESTER HOTEL TERRACE AND GRILL

Park Lane, W1
01-629 8888

Anton Mosimann, the chef now managed by the Mark McCormack group, has become, in a way, a separate entity from the restaurants he runs. His demonstrations at Lyn Hall's cookery school La Petite Cuisine which at the moment of writing have become a travelling roadshow, his television appearances when he goes up to the north of England to dine with a truck driver and then invites him back to cook at The Dorchester, his virtuous cookery book *Cuisine Naturelle* are all more entertaining than a meal at the hotel, be it in the fancy Terrace room with a band playing in the evenings or in the rather feudal Grill room. Since chefs have become superstars, and Anton in his polite, quiet Swiss–German way has jumped on the bandwagon as gleefully as any, this dichotomy is apt to happen, particularly in the scenario of an hotel where your best intentions can be thwarted by the behaviour of management or staff. Inept service has certainly taken the edge off superb food when I have dined recently at The Terrace as has the music more suited to a Home Counties' golf club Christmas dance. Also, hotels spell big bills and it is galling now that the original cellar has been sold off, to pay so much over the top for choices from a badly cobbled together new list. However, Anton is unarguably a dedicated and skilled chef and also a great organizer. His brigade respect him and it is said that the kitchen is a harmonious place. Since nouvelle cuisine would seem to have made cousins of us all and the same dishes are served at the same level of establishment all over the world, it is probably more to the point to skip over the dishes like tronçon de turbot, soufflé aux écrevisses and the magret de canard grillé Nossi-Be (with green peppercorns) and see where the austerity of no fat, no sugar, no flour, no alcohol, the foundations of cuisine naturelle, takes us. It can lead to a great poached fillet of beef served with various raw vegetables cut in julienne strips and differently dressed, or a dramatic dish of oyster sausages served with a yellow and black sauce coloured with saffron and the ink of squid, or a stunning lobster consommé with coriander leaves garnished with lobster shaped vegetables, enoki mushrooms and lobster eggs. One of the best dishes of Anton's that I have eaten was one served in his own dining room: poached veal tongue served with grated horseradish and fresh green lentils from a supplier he had found in Kent. The man and his restaurants are not synonymous, which is perhaps as he wants it. The Grill is dedicated to English food but

cooked by chefs as opposed to housewives. The set-price menu, which includes half a carafe of wine at lunchtime, is good value and chicken pie cooked by The Dorchester kitchens is a helluva different ball game from the pie you get in the pub. This is the place to try Anton's bread and butter pudding. It is worth remembering The Grill when you want to show off English food to others.

The Terrace	
CUISINE: French	Also vegetarian dishes

OPEN: D only: Mon to Sat

MEALS: 6 to 11.30

AVERAGE PRICE: £38. Set Menus: £29 and £32

CREDIT CARDS: Access, Amex, Visa, Diners

SEATS: 100

MUSIC: Pianist 8 to 9, then live band till 1

The Grill	
CUISINE: English	Also vegetarian dishes

OPEN: Mon to Sun

MEALS: 12.30 to 3; 6.30 to 11 (Sun 7 to 10.30)

AVERAGE PRICE: £33. Set Menu: £16.50

CREDIT CARDS: Access, Amex, Visa, Diners

SEATS: 85

Wheelchair access

LA DORDOGNE

5 Devonshire Road, W4
01-747 1836

L a Dordogne is a neighbourhood bistro (neighbourhood if you live in Chiswick, that is) that merits a wider catchment area – though I am not sure I could make out a case for much beyond Shepherd's Bush. A notable quality is its reasonable prices with first courses starting at £1.20 for fresh vegetable soup and rising to £1.40 for avocado with Roquefort mousse or a salad served with hot chicken livers. Fillet of turbot cooked en papillote with a julienne of fresh vegetables and bacon tasted good but was sloppily presented. I doubt that the civet of lamb was a civet in the sense of the sauce being thickened with blood but the introduction of fresh mint was *une bonne idée*. It wouldn't seem to take much extra trouble to make fresh vegetables of the day appropriate to the dish they are garnishing; sprouts sit uneasily beside fish. When La Dordogne opened in 1985 there was a certain *frisson* about the fact that the chef had once worked for President Mitterrand in the kitchens of the Elysée Palace. Now a new chef has been promised – could he be from M. Chirac's establishment? – and La Dordogne is aiming for a Michelin star. I hope the prices don't rocket for these are at present a large part of the charm. The owner obviously cares deeply and the gourmet dinners organized each month are worth checking out. They will also cater for private parties.

CUISINE: French	
OPEN: L: Mon to Fri; D: Mon to Sat	
MEALS: 12 to 2.30; 7 to 11 (Fri and Sat till 12)	
AVERAGE PRICE: £18	
CREDIT CARDS: Access, Amex, Visa, Diners	
SEATS: 38	

DRAGON GATE

7 Gerrard Street, W1
01-734 5154

Despite the British tolerance, even fondness, of spicy food – as in sorting-the-men-from-boys sort of vindaloo demanded at Indian restaurants – Szechuan food from south-west China, hot with fegara pepper, has not made the impact in London it has in New York. There has never been a vogue for it and consequently there are few restaurants that do more than include a few Szechuan dishes, often designated by a symbol of leaping flames, on their menus. Dragon Gate is considerably more dedicated to the region and most of their long list of dishes are authentically Szechuan which doesn't mean that your meal will be unrelieved punches to the palate. Tea-smoked duck, for example, the natural centrepiece for a Szechuan meal, has subtle flavours, the results of various cooking processes including the use of jasmine tea, camphor wood chips and rice to fuel the smoking process. Fish-fragrant, meaning the ingredients used for cooking fish applied to something else, is another Szechuan mode and is the description for a dish of shredded pork which they serve here with aubergine. If you like tripe, or if you want to like tripe try it as served here with chilli in chilli oil and you'll put behind you for ever that namby-pamby English version using milk and onions. I like very much dumplings which they call pelmeni (more of a Russian term) and serve in a red pepper sauce. This is the obvious place to try hot and sour soup and it kicks off the set-price menu. A nice gesture is the roasted peanuts and pickled cabbage that are placed on the table when you sit down and which serve the purpose of alerting your taste buds to what is to follow. As with most restaurants in Chinatown, decor and service are adequate but little more than that.

CUISINE: Szechuan	Also vegetarian dishes

OPEN: Mon to Sun

MEALS: 12 to 2.30; 5.30 to 11.15 (Fri and Sat: 12 to 11.15, Sun: 12 to 12)

CLOSED: Christmas

AVERAGE PRICE: £15. Set Menus: £5 and £7 (dinner)

CREDIT CARDS: Access, Amex, Visa, Diners

SEATS: 100

PRIVATE ROOM: (10–14)

MUSIC: Piped Chinese

DRAKES

2a Pond Place, SW3
01-584 4555

D rakes, which has been going for over ten years, might well have been the outcome of some astute market research. You study an SW3 clientele, create an atmosphere that is ersatz country house with beams, candelabra, sheepskin rugs and hunting pictures and provide unalarming food strong on puds called things like Bliss and Tipsy Sussex Squire. It is the sort of formula that if handled by a brewery chain would have ghastly results but in the hands of a family (the Moss family) works satisfactorily. It is one answer to where to go for English food even if we must now allow that avocado with prawns is a typically British dish. Rather more enterprising first courses are venison pâté with cranberries, baked quails' eggs on a bed of spinach with Cotswold sauce and creamed sorrel and leek soup. A feature of the dining room is the revolving spit behind a glass panel on which spins duck, leg of lamb, pork and game in season. It is probably a rather more appetizing sight than a contribution to flavour, but they are popular items. Alternatives are also, rightly, straightforward. As well as chops, steaks and poached and grilled fish there is a game pie called poacher's pie. The English have always been strong on puddings and also savouries so the soft roe on toast is a welcome inclusion. Earl Grey tea is served as well as coffee, which comes with fudge; it is a concept thoroughly worked out. Drake's is best of all, perhaps, for Sunday lunch when this sort of food is consummately appropriate. Note the full-on licence which means you may drink at the bar, while leafing through the scattered copies of *Country Life*, without eating in the restaurant.

CUISINE: *English*

OPEN: *Mon to Sun*

MEALS: *12.30 to 2.15 (Sun till 2.45); 7 to 11 (Sun till 10.30)*

AVERAGE PRICE: *£23. Set Menu: £7.55 (lunch)*

DUKE'S HOTEL RESTAURANT

33 St James's Place, SW1
01-491 4840

This is one of London's more discreet and charming hotels, established in 1908 (having previously been London chambers for nobility) in an Edwardian building surrounding a courtyard off St James's Street. It would be a pleasure to stay in, I should think, and has an unexpectedly romantic, small and calmly decorated dining room. The menu is simple in layout but the cooking reveals considerable skill on the part of the chef, Anthony Marshall, previously at The Dorchester and The Savoy. Good use is made of seasonal ingredients and I remember a well-made spinach and wild mushroom salad and there is an interesting dish of chicory parcels filled with brill served on a light red wine sauce. The soups are imaginatively composed, for example clear lobster soup infused with coriander and a cream of watercress soup. No doubt they satisfy the sedate clientele. As well as a list of grills among the main courses, there are dishes more complicated but not so convoluted as to distress those who dislike their food 'mucked about'. A table d'hôte lunch includes the daily dish from the trolley which can be a roast or a pie. Trifle and bread and butter pudding figure among the desserts. The service has old world courtesy. The last time I ate at Duke's was with a woman friend and our treatment was impeccable which is noteworthy since many hotel waiters are horrified, even slightly repelled, by the sight of two women eating together. The more expensive wines tend to reveal the bargains on the list.

CUISINE: French/English   Also vegetarian dishes

OPEN: *Mon to Sun*

MEALS: *12.30 to 2.30; 6 to 10 (Sun 7 to 10)*

AVERAGE PRICE: *£27. Set Menus (Lunch): £13
(2 courses), £15.50 (3 courses)*

CREDIT CARDS: *Access, Amex, Visa, Diners*

SEATS: *34*

PRIVATE ROOMS: *(12 and 45)*

EATON'S

49 Elizabeth Street, SW1
01-730 0074

About ten years ago Santosh Bakshi, a chef from Inigo Jones, and two other members of their staff opened Eaton's. They built up a strong local following and both the dishes and the customers now could be described as regulars. But for those who during the decade have grown over-familiar with dishes like the fresh herring fillets with pickled cucumber, apple and sour cream and the pork escalope filled with red cabbage and raisins (dishes also once served at Inigo Jones) there is a supplementary à la carte menu that changes each week. The dishes are what might unkindly be called dinner party food – paupiette of smoked salmon with soft cheese, shallots, paprika and sliced avocado, a main course of suprême of chicken with a white wine, cream and paprika sauce – but in their very style they are reassuring evidence that not everyone is swayed by the vagaries of food fashion. And they are popular. In part this must be ascribed to the reasonable prices which for some reason include a 12½% service charge but not VAT at 15%, an anomaly that is allowed on a menu shown inside the restaurant but not one displayed outside. The dining room is long and narrow with a skylight at the back. It is a sedate restaurant for sedate people.

CUISINE: *French/Continental*

OPEN: *Mon to Fri*

MEALS: 12 to 2; 7 to 11.15	
AVERAGE PRICE: £19	
CREDIT CARDS: Access, Amex, Visa, Diners	
SEATS: 40	
MUSIC: Taped classical	

ELEGANZA

70 High Street, Stoke Newington, N16
01-254 1950

I f you read this guide carefully you might notice that geographical fairness is not its underpinning. However, if you live in or near Stoke Newington or happen to be passing through, it is worth considering the quite inappropriately named Eleganza. For one thing their prices are about one third less than in similar Chinese restaurants nearer central London and for another, there seems to be a pride in what they do. The food is basically Peking and with 24 hours' notice they will prepare the duck authentically (as opposed to deep-frying it). 'Special Dishes' is a rather touching misnomer pointing you towards various chop sueys and chow mein. If you like the predictable dishes the set menus will relieve you of that tedious task of ordering. Otherwise, you can have a slightly more lively meal à la carte. Service is grave and polite.

CUISINE: Peking	
OPEN: L: Mon to Sat; D: Mon to Sun	
MEALS: 12 to 2.15; 6 to 11.45	
AVERAGE PRICE: £16. Set Menus: £4.50–10	
CREDIT CARDS: Access, Amex, Visa, Diners	
SEATS: 55	

ELEVEN PARK WALK

11 Park Walk, SW10
01-352 3449

An actress friend who admitted that she really liked eating out in order to look at other people named Eleven Park Walk as one of the places she favoured. It is a strength of certain Italian restaurants that they provide a set on which well-dressed people can parade (Meridiana, San Lorenzo, Cecconi's are a few other examples) and despite this restaurant being a basement, the cool decor does nicely set off designer clothes. The waiters are friendly and speedy and understand the language of the pepper mill. To fit into your Azzedine Alaia you probably need to have crudités con bagna cauda followed by carpaccio (thinly sliced raw beef). This style of eating is much favoured by the clientele and there are helpful dishes like grilled raddichio and the king prawns with salad but it seems a pity to ignore the home-made fettucine with smoked salmon (though pasta and smoked salmon are not my idea of a horse and carriage), the ricotta-stuffed ravioli, the crespelle with four cheeses and the more homely main courses like bollito misto and the osso buco. Since the eating, in many people's minds, is almost incidental to the event, it is praiseworthy that standards remain as high as they do. The owners run the Covent Garden Pasta Bar in Henrietta Street, WC2, useful in the area and also run with style.

CUISINE: Italian	*Also vegetarian dishes*
OPEN: Mon to Sat	
MEALS: 12.30 to 3; 7 to 12	
CLOSED: Bank Holidays	
AVERAGE PRICE: £19	
CREDIT CARDS: Amex	
SEATS: 120	
PRIVATE ROOM: (30)	
MUSIC: Taped jazz, classical	

THE ENGLISH HOUSE

3 Milner Street, SW3
01-584 3002

An obvious answer to where to go for English food? Possibly, if you like your food and surroundings elaborate or, to put it another way, gussied-up. Michael Smith, author of many fine cookery books on English food, old and new, and authority on food in history, is the creator of the menu. Whilst some food notions and combinations stand the test of time, others, you feel, might have been allowed mercifully to fade away. Fruit with meat is an English concept that apparently puzzles the French and they might be even more mystified by fruit with fish as in the orange mayonnaise accompanying a crab mousse. Rack of lamb, you might think, might be all the better for not having a coating of cheese and almonds. However, Olde Englishe comes into its own with the puddings, the strength of English cuisine. Something called Chocolate Pye is a real self indulgence. Michael Smith is also a dab hand at interior design and although if The English House were your house, you might end up running screaming into the garden driven crazy by the frills and furbelows, the style is fine for a restaurant and in a sense the dining room is a very romantic room. Malcolm Livingstone is a dedicated manager but he also dedicates some of his time to The English Garden, a not altogether dissimilar restaurant just off the King's Road. I can quite see the rationale behind The English House but if I were going there it would be with foreign visitors in tow, in order to re-inforce some of their preconceptions about the English but also to show them that we don't *always* eat boiled beef and overcooked carrots.

CUISINE: English	*Also vegetarian dishes*
OPEN: Mon to Sun	
MEALS: 12.30 to 2.30 (Sun till 2); 7.30 to 11.30 (Sun till 10)	
AVERAGE PRICE: £27. Set Menus: £9.50 (lunch) and £13.50 (Sun dinner)	

CREDIT CARDS: *Access, Amex, Visa, Diners*

SEATS: 35

PRIVATE ROOMS: *(12 and 6)*

L'EPICURE

28 Frith Street, W1
01-437 2829

This is a restaurant that does not appear in self-styled gastronomic guides presumably because it is no longer the mode to flame items over spirit lamps and slosh in alcohol and cream. Perversely I have come to value the style as recourse from the anxieties of modern food and health obsessions. Also I admire the fact that L'Epicure stubbornly carries on in much the same way they were doing 30 years ago with a chef who has been in the kitchen almost as long. The flaming gas lights outside the restaurant are a landmark in Soho and it will be a sad day when these premises become a brasserie, sushi bar or Creole restaurant (which happens to be the new vogue). This is not to say that you mustn't pick your way carefully through the menu or ignore the dishes of the day, which have more of a chance of not being stiff with cholesterol. Just to give you an idea of the experience, here are a few dishes, all of them prepared with gueridon service: crêpe aux crevettes à L'Epicure (prawns sautéed in butter with brandy and lobster sauce, served in a thin pancake); homard Newburg (lobster sautéed in butter, flamed with Madeira wine, with egg yolks and cream, served with rice); sauté de pintard au Chartreuse (boned guinea fowl sautéed in butter flamed with yellow Chartreuse, reduced with cream); and of course you must finish with crêpes Suzette. The interior is pleasantly tatty with that mad wiring peculiar to old Soho restaurants. The prices are relatively old-fashioned and half-portions are available. The menu concludes with a quotation from Epicurus with which I concur: 'Of all things which wisdom provides to make life entirely happy, much the greatest is the possession of friendship.'

CUISINE: French

OPEN: L: Mon to Fri; D: Mon to Sat

MEALS: 12 to 2.30; 6 to 11.15

CLOSED: Bank Holidays

AVERAGE PRICE: £15–22

CREDIT CARDS: Access, Amex, Visa, Diners

SEATS: 50

EQUATORIAL

37 Old Compton Street, W1
01-437 6112

Singapore is a place so devoted to food and the influences there so diverse that the likelihood of true authenticity in London is slight – at least until they turn all NCPs into areas for foodstalls – but at Equatorial they try hard and it is possible to discern from the long menu some of the strands that make up the weave of non-ya food, the term applied to the blending of Malay and Chinese styles. Coconut and peanut are two flavours that it is almost mandatory to like if you are going to enjoy Malaysian food and also some dishes are alarmingly chilli-hot. I happen to like coconut and not peanut and so appreciate the laksa, a soothing broth in which various ingredients float, but fail to understand the appeal of gado-gado which is a cooked vegetable salad coated in a peanut sauce. Chicken in coconut (ayam opor) is good too. The noodle dishes are irresistible and they tend to be a better bet than the rice-based assemblies such as nasi goreng. Sambal refers to a usually fiery sauce or side-dish but they strike me as a necessary enlivening ingredient in some of the bland soupy dishes. Satay – skewers of barbecued beef, pork and chicken – is probably the best known dish of South-East Asian cooking and they are well done here. Desserts are weird and rather wonderfully vulgar looking. You could try, for example, the shaved ice and syrup with red beans, sweet corn and jelly, unless lack of demand has led to its demise. A party of six is about the right number to take to the Equatorial. Ask for one of the tables in the basement. House wine is quite well chosen but old Malay hands prefer the Tiger beer.

CUISINE: Singaporean/Malaysian	Also vegetarian dishes

OPEN: Mon to Sun

MEALS: 12 to 3; 6 to 11.15 (Sat and Sun 12 to 11.30)

AVERAGE PRICE: £12. Set Menus: £4.10 (lunch) and £9.50 (dinner)

CREDIT CARDS: Access, Amex, Visa, Diners

SEATS: 70

PRIVATE ROOM: (20)

L'ESCARGOT

48 Greek Street, W1
01-437 2879 (Restaurant)
01-437 2679 (Brasserie)

L'Escargot Bienvenu, as it used to be called, was a French restaurant which achieved what some- one once described as a 'faded gentility'. Twenty years ago, when I was working as a copywriter for JWT, I used to love being taken there for lunch. Going to lunch was something copywriters in those days spent a lot of time planning. I loved the faded gentility, the lampshades made of table napkins with snail shells at the corners weighting them down and the good list of Alsace wines. Now that Nick Lander has re-vamped and re-launched the premises as L'Escargot, signs of the times are the food being cooked by a young English chef, Martin Lam, the snail shells now appearing as chocolates and also woven into the border of the carpet, and the wine list – which is a model wine list – offering some interesting Australian and Californian bottles among the choices. L'Escargot is popular with what is inelegantly referred to as the media crowd. On the ground floor is a brasserie which, at lunchtimes at least, behaves as it should and resists taking bookings (except for parties of more than five). Upstairs there are two dining rooms decorated in greeny shades which some find a bit queasy. Upstairs there is also Elena the manageress, a warm-hearted Italian woman who Nick Lander cleverly lured from Bianchi's where she had mother-henned the same customers who have transferred their allegiance to be with her and, it must be admitted, to receive rather better food. Martin Lam prepares a seasonal menu with plats du jour that are the fish dishes. His style is the kind personified by dishes like salad of sun-dried tomatoes, mangetout, avocado and celery, warm salad of crispy duck with Chinese vegetables, seafood terrine en gelée followed by perhaps rack of English lamb served with a hot onion tartlet, fricassee of farmhouse chicken with saffron sauce or a vegetarian assembly like galette of wholewheat pancakes filled with aubergines, mushrooms and spinach. My experience is that the fish dishes are often the more successful and sometimes you gain by avoiding the 'modern' approach and composing a meal along the lines of hot leek tart with farmhouse cheddar followed by medallions of Scottish beef served with a seed mustard sauce. A basement kitchen could be blamed for a slip between saucepan and lip, but slips there sometimes are. For this reason, and because I like eating lightly and relatively cheaply, I prefer the brasserie. If you want just two small dishes, say a gâteau of chicken livers with cointreau followed by a hot apple and stilton strudel, it seems allowable. In the evenings there is a pianist and if you have to wait for a table the bar is a nice place for lounging. All restaurateurs or anyway all restaurateurs with very few exceptions, should be made to study the wine list composed and written by Jancis Robinson MW, which edifyingly presents wines by grape variety as well as by identifiable needs like light fruity whites and dry flinty whites, attaches useful but brief notes and has a section called Classic wines for when you want to treat yourself with nothing above £30, which seems to me a realistic definition of a treat.

Restaurant
CUISINE: French   *Also vegetarian dishes*

OPEN: L: Mon to Fri; D: Mon to Sat

MEALS: *12.30 to 2.30; 6.30 to 11.15*

CLOSED: *Bank Holidays, Christmas–New Year*

AVERAGE PRICE: *£23*

CREDIT CARDS: *Access, Amex, Visa, Diners*

SEATS: *92*

Brasserie
OPEN: *L: Mon to Fri; D: Mon to Sat*

MEALS: *12.15 to 3, 5.30 to 11.15*

AVERAGE PRICE: *£16*

CREDIT CARDS: *Access, Amex, Visa, Diners*

SEATS: *85*

PRIVATE ROOMS: *(15–30 and 30–52)*

MUSIC: *Singer every night*

L'EXPRESS

16 Sloane Street, SW1
01-235 9869

Joseph Ettedgui, who owns various fashionable clothes shops including the Kenzo boutiques and Joseph Tricots, started work in London as a hairdresser and would seem to want to be a restaurateur. His ownership of Le Caprice was not a success but it did impose the Eva Jirinca effect. Eva Jirinca is the architect with whom he has collaborated in designing his cool, uncluttered shop interiors. This café in the basement of Pour La Maison, serving espresso coffee, brioches and croissants all day at the bar and salads and sandwiches and small dishes at the tables, is popular and successful and a place to see or be seen or indeed just to get good coffee, which is not an easy task in London. His latest venture, 'unpretentiously', he says, called Joe's Café at 126 Draycott Avenue, SW3 (01-225 2217) is open all day for snacks like carpaccio at £9 and a club sandwich at £7 and in the evening for dinner with a dull menu and similarly inflated prices. At the moment of writing it is too early to see if Joe's Café succeeds in this form but it will be an interesting but depressing phenomenon if it does.

LA FINEZZA

62–64 Lower Sloane Street, SW1
01-730 8630

I took my mother here on my birthday soon after the restaurant had opened and she loved it. It is an elegant establishment decorated in shades of cream and grey with the tablecloths a lemon yellow and the mirrors crackled and speckled so even those who are not birthday girls get a pleasing reflection. The manager has dealt with racier crowds at Mr Chow and Montpeliano but seems now content in these more sedate surroundings. The antipasti are fairly unimaginative and the selection of smoked and boiled Italian hams and salamis is probably the best bet. If your appetite can handle it, it would be jollier to start with pasta e fagioli soup which is a speciality of the chef and which I know to be good from his early days at the Trattoria Terrazza. Granchio, crab in a sauce of black beans, herbs and tomato is an interesting notion though not so successful a dish as the Chinese version minus the tomatoes. The most distinctive parts of the menu are offal, which includes brains and sweetbreads, and the list of game, though it worryingly features partridge and pheasant all year round. The rabbit might be worth trying. Prices reflect the up-market approach but no tiles, no rush-seated chairs, no racket can be desirable.

CUISINE: Italian	Also vegetarian dishes

OPEN: Mon to Sat

MEALS: 12 to 2.30; 7 to 11.30

AVERAGE PRICE: £27

CREDIT CARDS: Access, Amex, Visa, Diners

SEATS: 86

Fish & Chips

For a while the great British fast food looked as if it was
going to be buried under the avalanche of hamburger
bars, pizza parlours, taco stands, doner kebab kiosks
and Chinese and Indian take-away counters, in part
because of its relative expense due to the rise in costs
of fish, potatoes and oil. However, being British, fish
and chips rallied and now dotted throughout London
there are some high-class establishments that buy
their fish daily from Billingsgate, or have it delivered
from ports, and change the frying oil regularly enough
to achieve a fresh flavour and crispy chips and batter.
Some people favour a batter made with matzoh meal
and this can be found at *Nautilus, 27–29 Fortune Green
Road, NW6 (01-435 2532)* and *The North Sea Restaurant,
7–8 Leigh Street, WC1 (01-387 5892)*. Apart from *Geale's*
and *Sea Shell* (see entries), I would also recommend *The
Fryer's Delight, 19 Theobald's Road, WC1 (01-405 4114)*,
Seafresh Fish Bar, 80–81 Wilton Road, SW1 (01-828 0747),
*Windmill Fish Bar, 211 Kennington Lane, SE11 (01-582
5754)*, *Upper Street Fish Shop, 324 Upper Street, N1 (01-359
1401)*, *Maxwell's of Ealing, 177 Haverstock Hill, NW3
(01-586 9277)* and *Sea Shell, 424–426 Kingsland Road,
E8 (01-254 6152)*. Don't assume, however, from this
positive paragraph that every fish and chip shop will
be good. Shoddy ones are extant.

LA FONTANA

101 Pimlico Road, SW1
01-730 6630

I go to La Fontana in November when Signor
Pavesi brings over the white truffles from Alba.
Other restaurateurs do it, but none with such
tenderness for the pricey little tubers as he. He serves
them shaved on to a risotto which is prepared in the
restaurant over a flame or, even better in my opinion,
on tagliatelle. The scraps go into a sauce for carpaccio
(thin slices of raw beef), and if you asked you could also
have truffles on scrambled egg. I met Bernard Levin
one year in La Fontana and asked whether he had the
risotto or the tagliatelle. 'I have the risotto for the first

course, the tagliatelle for the main course,' he replied firmly. La Fontana is different in style from most of London's Italian restaurants; rather more middle-aged in decor and with greater commitment to authenticity in the cooking, the best of which is usually found in the dishes of the week. Bollito misto often features there, as do interesting game preparations in season which, tactfully, they are at much the same time as the truffles. I was impressed to see a dish of tripe with butter beans. The decor has been re-vamped recently but the overall impression is still of an old-fashioned plushy red. The waiters' styles vary from brusqueness to the sympathy of a psychiatric nurse. Signor Pavesi is almost invariably present and his beautiful daughter graces the front desk. There are some interesting Italian wines. The clientele tends to look considerably more soberly well-heeled than at the average trattoria.

CUISINE: Italian	
OPEN: Mon to Sun	
MEALS: 12 to 2.30; 7 to 11.30	
CLOSED: Bank Holidays	
AVERAGE PRICE: £18	
CREDIT CARDS: Amex, Visa, Diners	
SEATS: 42	
MUSIC: Piped classical and pop	

FONTANA AMOROSA

1 Blenheim Terrace, NW8
01-328 5014

Considering that the large terrace overlooking a pretty residential and neighbourhood shopping street is one of the more interesting facts about this Italian restaurant, it seems perverse of the management to take their holidays in the last two weeks of August and the first two weeks of September. However, there are other assets: the family-run quality and some of the owner's own creations added to an otherwise conventional list, namely the risotto of rice mixed with lentils, the chicken livers scrambled with eggs, the rollatina alla Giuseppina, the white beans cooked with virgin olive oil and the dessert of vanilla-scented apple mousse. It would seem to be a good place for a party based on the experience of a man friend of mine who went there for lunch with some business colleagues, joined in a wedding party, sang opera along with the tapes and came home at 7 pm.

CUISINE: Italian	Also vegetarian dishes
OPEN: L: Tues to Sun; D: Tues to Sat	
MEALS: 12.30 to 2.30; 7 to 11.30	
CLOSED: mid August to mid September	
AVERAGE PRICE: £15	
CREDIT CARDS: Access, Amex, Visa, Diners	
SEATS: 40	
TABLES OUTSIDE: (50)	
PRIVATE ROOM: (25–30)	
MUSIC: Piped Italian	

FOXTROT OSCAR

79 Royal Hospital Road, SW3
01-352 7179

This is a cleverly conceived place, that is apart from the name, which I think has some RAF connotation but I must admit to not feeling galvanized to research any further. The menu is on a blackboard and has definite appeal for those whose palates are jaded or their appetite sated; Foxtrot Oscar is a haunt of chefs and restaurateurs. Their tastes, famously nursery or retarded, are gratified by the kedgeree, sausage and mash, Loch Fyne kippers and puddings like treacle tart. Sloanes, another element of the clientele, like the muffin with smoked salmon and caviar and the enterprising composed salads, such as the one featuring smoked goose, and the savouries like mushrooms on toast. There are also club sandwiches, burgers and plain grills. It is possible to put together a sketchy or a complete meal and the staff are easy-going about what you choose to do. There are some better than basic wines. Downstairs is subterranean in feel but calmer than the ground floor where there is a well-attended bar. Children not only welcomed but under-age drinkers can try a Buck Rogers or an ET cocktail.

CUISINE: Eclectic	*Also vegetarian dishes*
OPEN: Mon to Sun	
MEALS: 12.30 to 2.30; 7.30 to 11	
CLOSED: Bank Holidays	
AVERAGE PRICE: £13	
CREDIT CARDS: Access, Visa	
SEATS: 55	
PRIVATE ROOM: (30)	
MUSIC: Piped jazz, popular and Radio Caroline	

FRERE JACQUES

37 Long Acre, WC2
01-836 7823

This notably pretty restaurant with one of the best sites in London is owned by Kennedy Brookes (*q.v.*). Use it for the downstairs bar which provides an unusual service in London, a menu of small, reasonably priced fish dishes, marinated salmon, various seafood cocktails, oysters, mussels and so forth. Follow with cheese. Upstairs is just a fairly expensive restaurant with main courses often seeming pre-assembled and others oddly conceived. For example, give yourself this test: guess which is the appropriate ingredient in the ones they list for salade marina: green pepper stuffed with rice, pine-apple, prawns and pine kernels?

CUISINE: Fish	*Also vegetarian dishes*
OPEN: Mon to Sat (upstairs closed Sat lunchtime)	
MEALS: 12 to 3; 6 to 11.30	

AVERAGE PRICE: £20	
CREDIT CARDS: Access, Amex, Visa, Diners	
SEATS: 70	
MUSIC: Piped	

FRITH'S

14 Frith Street, W1
01-439 3370

F rith's is so definitely, consciously, palpably, full of good intentions that anything but hearty praise would seem churlish. But before describing its strengths I must say it can be somewhat prissy and I prefer Frith's for lunch rather than dinner. Carla Tomasi is the chef and though even noticing that she is female would seem, by definition, sexist, it is gratifying to register that she is part of a small but growing band of women chefs and restaurateurs. Her cooking is inventive and subtle, sometimes original, sometimes over-intricate but worthy of the restaurant's own description of 'new British'. The pricing system of a menu from which you may choose two courses or three courses (cheese carrying a supplement) at sums that include cover charge, VAT and coffee – which is served with luscious home-made truffles – encourages you to give the menu the attention it deserves. Marketing is obviously done with enthusiasm and dedication and thus there can be dandelion leaves in the salad, golden carp as a main course, fresh currants as a garnish, spiced plums taking the mickey out of a plum sauce, purple basil used as a contrast with fish. The menus change seasonally and always include a dish of the day. Interestingly, Carla Tomasi's approach can be usefully compared with that of Sally Clarke (see Clarke's). The vegetarian dishes are by no means poor relations of the meat and I remember an excellent roulade of aubergines, goat's cheese and herbs. Desserts are excellent and some, with an understanding of most people's preoccupations, contain no sugar or sweetener, e.g. a mousse of blood oranges with orange cream. The cheeses are from Pierre Androuet and are served with home-made oatcakes or walnut bread. The owner, Claudio Quarticelli, is devoted to the restaurant business but his ministrations occasionally seem intrusive. The wine list is sensible and has more than the usual supply of half-bottles. The decor is plain; tech not high-tech.

CUISINE: Eclectic	Also vegetarian dishes

OPEN: L: Mon to Fri; D: Mon to Sat

MEALS: 12 to 2.30; 6 to 11.30

AVERAGE PRICE: £20–£22. Set Menus: £14 (2 courses); £16 (3 courses)

CREDIT CARDS: Access, Amex, Visa, Diners

SEATS: 70

PRIVATE ROOM: (16)

FUNG SHING

15 Lisle Street, WC2
01-437 1539

I look at my fact sheet of research on Fung Shing and find both the owner and the chef different from the ones listed in the current *Good Food Guide*. Such is the problem with writing about Chinatown's restaurants which are built on shifting sands from which no Westerner could hope to build castles. However, though the enthusiasm for Fung Shing has wavered occasionally since the restaurant opened in summer '84 re-vamped in style, it is without doubt one of the more interesting in the Gerrard Street/Lisle Street area. Thorough coverage by restaurant reviewers means that a European clientele is attracted, which can tend to make standards wobble. The list of specials delivers dishes that are not too *recherché*. It includes minced quail wrapped in lettuce leaves, a dish that is beginning to rival Peking duck in popularity. The scallops which are steamed and served with garlic or with black bean sauce are quiveringly fresh. Sea bass is an excellent centrepiece for a group of four or more. If you wish to get away from the standard choices, try the braised dishes or the one-pot assemblies, whose long simmering often with the flavour of star-anise incorporated provide welcome relief from the stir-fry or deep-fry side of Chinese food. The staff are helpful on the whole, and if you are serious it is worth ringing up to consult over ordering some dishes in advance. Chinese friends of mine use Fung Shing for lunch when the experience is probably more authentic than in the evening.

CUISINE: Cantonese	*Also vegetarian dishes*
OPEN: Mon to Sun	
MEALS: 12 to 11.30	
AVERAGE PRICE: £8–£12. Set Menus (for two): £14 and £16	
CREDIT CARDS: Access, Amex, Visa, Diners	
SEATS: 90	
PRIVATE ROOM: (30)	
MUSIC: Piped	

THE GALLERY BOAT

Cumberland Basin, 15 Prince Albert Road, NW1
01-485 8137

About the time this guide is published Mr Wong should be taking delivery of a new and more streamlined boat for his floating Chinese restaurant. The old one (formerly the Barque and Bite) was pleasantly tatty, many cracks, you felt, papered over by the Laura Ashley fabric, and it afforded a chance of eating well on the water – not a strong point in London. As you nibble sesame prawn toasts, spare ribs and other predictable items from the mainly Peking menu you can watch ducks bobbing or, sometimes, when they are draining the canal, stare at a lot of mud. It seems appropriate to eat fish and the steamed scallops are good and, if you feel like lashing out, so is the lobster. I like the special mixed noodles which have a very fair proportion of prawns, liver and mixed vegetables to pasta, and also the lemon chicken which the kitchen will make on request. The staff are usually jolly and Mr Wong is a benign, if constantly anxious-looking presence. A visit to The Gallery Boat makes a good treat for children, for it is axiomatic that all children like Chinese food and gangplanks.

CUISINE: Peking	*Also vegetarian dishes*
OPEN: Mon to Sun	
MEALS: 12 to 2.30; 6 to 11.30 (Sat and Sun: 12 to 11.30)	
CLOSED: Bank Holidays	
AVERAGE PRICE: £22. Set Menus: £9, £10.50 and £15	
CREDIT CARDS: Amex, Diners	
SEATS: 90	
PRIVATE ROOM: (20–25)	

THE GARDEN

616 Fulham Road, SW6
01-736 6056

Wholefood shops seem to have muddled and muddied the already rather dubious notion of what is wholefood. It should not mean paying more than you do in a supermarket for brown rice, cosmetic sized bottles of olive oil, unnecessary food supplements, nor some ersatz meat loaf made out of soya. The interpretation The Garden chooses is humanely reared (and killed) poultry and game, fish and, in so far as possible, vegetables and fruit grown without chemical fertilizers and pesticides. The result is a restaurant where vegetarians and others can eat together, no hassle. Now that other restaurants, bowing to the pressure, are including imaginative vegetarian dishes on their menus, The Garden seems less unique but what is nice is how seamlessly the dishes mesh, and since it is a set-price menu there is no discrimination of cost. First courses might be grilled stuffed mushrooms, dolmades or deep-fried Brie croquettes, main courses vegetable aviyal (a Southern Indian, faintly spicy dish), spinach loaf with tarragon sauce, chicken and mushroom pie and game in season. Puddings include cosy things like crumble and the sensible offering of

Greek yoghurt with honey. The service is gentlemanly. There is a pleasant air of someone's beliefs being put into practice.

CUISINE: Vegetarian plus
OPEN: D only: Mon to Sat
MEALS: 7.30 to 11
CLOSED: Bank Holidays and 2 weeks August
AVERAGE PRICE: £16. Set Menu: £10.50
CREDIT CARDS: Access, Amex, Visa, Diners
SEATS: 26
TABLES OUTSIDE: (24)
MUSIC: Piped

GASTRONOME ONE

311 New King's Road, SW6
01-731 6381

The 1985 *Good Food Guide* awarded Gastronome One their accolade of Young Chef of the Year for Bruno Loubet's cooking. They then left the restaurant out of the listings in the 1986 edition on the grounds the chef had changed. As the rightfully indignant owner Matthew Wallis has said it would be unlikely that he would find a hopeless chef to take over and indeed he claims, but he would, wouldn't he, that Thierry Aubugeau who has worked at the Michelin three star restaurant Lameloise in Chagny and at Fouquet in Paris and at Le Gavroche in London is as good if not better. Bernard Levin has written a book called *Enthusiasms*. One of them is for good food and he recently disclosed to me his latest discovery: Gastronome One. Lack of continuity bedevils restaurant guides but this restaurant would seem not to be an example. In appearance it is a neighbourhood place with the main dining room in the basement and what it provides is imaginative and capable French cooking at palatable prices. To my mind there are rather too many signals of the new cooking: pink peppercorns which are not truly peppercorns with marinated salmon, exotic fruits garnishing duck, an onion marmalade accompanying a terrine of pigeon, but I suppose I am more bombarded by these things than others and so react more strongly. I like the use made of skate (a favourite fish) in a salad with dill and en feuilleté with a red wine sauce, and of monkfish in a blanquette with mushrooms, braised with green peppers or sautéed with strips of endive. Though this would seem to indicate a concentration on fish there are tempting meat dishes such as the saddle of hare with a pepper sauce, the filet d'agneau au jus des truffes and (another favourite of mine) confit de canard. They make an issue of their desserts and rightly so since they have a chef pâtissier and thus can avoid the dreaded rumble of the trolley. I am not mad about the sound of Délice 'After Eight' but perhaps it goes down well in that part of the world (just past World's End). The wine list is ambitious but I can't point you to any bargains. Gastronome One is a thought when you do not want to fork out for the accepted shrines of gastronomy but you want a meal with style.

CUISINE: French	
OPEN: L: Mon to Fri; D: Mon to Sat	
MEALS: 12 to 2; 7 to 10.30	
CLOSED: August and Christmas–New Year	
AVERAGE PRICE: £24. Set Menus: £9 and £11 (lunch); £11 and £13 (dinner)	
CREDIT CARDS: Access, Amex, Visa, Diners	
SEATS: 70	
PRIVATE ROOM: (12–14)	

LE GAVROCHE

43 Upper Brook Street, W1
01-408 0881

Three Michelin stars remains the Holy Grail of French chefs. It is pretty pointless for chefs of other cuisines to strive for it, since the French set up the system predicated on the assumed superiority of French cooking. Albert Roux (see entry under Roux Brothers) at Le Gavroche was the first person in England to be awarded three Michelin stars (in the guide book of 1982). Thereafter his brother got his third star at The Waterside Inn (see Worth a Drive). Those who have done the grand gastronomic tour in France know what three stars signifies: millions of francs spent on decor, a waiting staff like a small private army, a chic wife who will receive or at least who can be glimpsed from time to time, menus and other related artefacts on sale in the foyer, as often as not the chef absent because he is demonstrating in Tucson, Arizona or renegotiating his contract with Tefal saucepans, a large bill. It was not until Le Gavroche moved from relatively simple premises in Lower Sloane Street (now Gavvers, *q.v.*) to this luxurious basement in Mayfair close by the American Embassy that the three stars were conferred. However, Albert Roux is no self-publicist. He is in the kitchen the majority of the time and, according to chefs who have worked for him, a great inspirer and educator. The food is not tricksy nor nouvelle. It is expensively prepared food – in terms of chef's time taken and the finest produce bought – for rich people; if haute cuisine is your goal, you will be on the winning side. However, you go to Le Gavroche for the food and the dancing-in-attendance service, not for the atmosphere which is just expensive interior design (by David Mlinaric) nor to see or be seen unless you happen to know or want to know expense account business people, many of them from abroad. A large proportion of the dishes remain constant, some – like papillotte de saumon fumé Claudine (smoked salmon wrapped around a mousse of smoked salmon and smoked trout, glazed with fish aspic) – and soufflé suissesse (a soufflé lapped in cream and glazed with melted cheese) – seeming to be in some sort of time warp, but there is a certain justified confidence in stalwartly offering the same creations, establishing (in their words) a New Classic Cuisine. For reasons of liveliness and economy, it is to the point to choose the set-price menu at lunchtime, which is almost a bargain, or the Menu Exceptionnel (for a minimum of two people) in the evening where that felicitous combination of highly professional skills brought to bear on quite straightforward ingredients is often in evidence. Desserts are beautiful and it is worth experiencing as many *bonnes bouches* as possible by ordering l'assiette du chef. The wine list has some treasures but at bank vault prices. The English sommelier is helpful and you should be frank about what you wish to spend which can range from about £10 to several hundred, but at about £20 there are some treats. The problem with restaurants like Le Gavroche and other temples of gastronomy is that you approach them expecting too much and then almost inevitably feel disappointed because you have not been transported to another sphere of being. For this reason, I would visit here when money is no object or when you have set aside a certain sum, say £120 for two, because you have decided that eating in a three-star Michelin restaurant is what you want to do with it.

CUISINE: French
OPEN: Mon to Fri
MEALS: 12 to 2; 7 to 11
CLOSED: Bank Holidays
AVERAGE PRICE: L: £38; D: £60. Set Menus: £19.50 (lunch); £30 (dinner, 5 courses)
CREDIT CARDS: Access, Amex, Visa, Diners
SEATS: 60
PRIVATE ROOM: (20)

GAVVERS

61–63 Lower Sloane Street, SW1
01-730 5983

Gavvers is proof that big business can work to the benefit of all. Owned by the Roux brothers (*q.v.*) and once the site of Le Gavroche, it now pleases customers immensely with its sensible all-in menu price which includes an aperitif, three courses, coffee, half a bottle of wine, tax and service and trains up staff for the glossier end of the Roux operation. Whether or not the spread of *sous-vide* (vacuum packed) dishes which the Roux empire are also backing with, soon, a restaurant in the City devoted to them, will affect the standards, only time will tell, but at the moment the majority of dishes are the work of chef Denis Lobry and they are most satisfactory. They range from rustic, as in the boudin noir with apples, to nouvelle, as in the sensitive handling of fish. You will be pleased that there is no temptation to forgo desserts for they are usually delicious, and the sorbets true to their origins. The wine included in the meal is appropriate to the style of the meal and it seems a pity to spoil the neatness of the deal by buying above it. That this is a formula of the future is rather distressingly hammered home by blow-ups of photographs of the Big Brothers staring down at you in the rather cramped room. The management likes to turn over the tables once so a later meal tends to be more relaxed than one starting early.

CUISINE: French

OPEN: D only: Mon to Sat

MEALS: 7 to 11

CLOSED: Bank Holidays and 1 week at Christmas

SET MENU: £18.25

CREDIT CARDS: Amex, Diners

SEATS: 65

♥ # GAY HUSSAR

2 Greek Street, W1
01-437 0973

The Gay Hussar is a Soho institution and the owner, Victor Sassie, a great restaurateur of the old school. Many many years ago, unlike his contemporaries who went to train in France, Victor, from his home town of Barrow-in-Furness, went to Budapest to work in the kitchens of Karoly Gundel. He brought Hungarian food back to London and the Gay Hussar remains by far the best restaurant to offer dishes of this misunderstood and often underrated cuisine. (If you entertain any doubts about that last phrase, buy *The Cuisine of Hungary* by George Lang.) The menu is long and features dishes you will not find elsewhere, which is not just praise from a restaurant critic with a jaded palate, they are dishes anyone would value: smoked goose, which is home-smoked, cold pike with a beetroot sauce and a wonderful cucumber salad, roasted fillet of hare, quenelles of carp, breaded calves' feet, shredded marrow in a dill sauce, cherry soup (which I have to admit I do not like) and many substantial assemblies using lentils, pulses, tarhonya (egg barley), kasha, and dumplings that can be so delicious when as carefully made as they are here. With such a long menu there are naturally some dishes better than others and it is wise to be guided by the waiters or, best of all, by Victor himself, although in a continuing effort to retire he is not around quite as much as he used to be. Victor's interest in (left-wing) politics and literature is reflected in the clientele, particularly at lunchtime, when you might see authors, MPs and trade unionists taking advantage of the very reasonable set-price menu. The wine list shows some historic Tokays but also some result of the recent export drive applied to Hungarian wines. The decor is red and plushy, the banquette seats plump with whispered indiscretions. No children.

CUISINE: Hungarian

OPEN: Mon to Sat

MEALS: *12.30 to 2.30; 5.30 to 10.30*

CLOSED: *Bank Holidays*

AVERAGE PRICE: *£20. Set Menu: £9.50 (lunch)*

CREDIT CARDS: *None*

SEATS: *50*

PRIVATE ROOM: *(10)*

GEALE'S

2 Farmer Street, W8
01-727 7969

Geale's was established in 1919 by the grandmother of the present owner and it has been treating that British staple, fish and chips, with the respect it deserves all the time. Fish is delivered daily from the ports and, correctly, it is the focus of the meal. Despite a certain fashionability and its popularity with BBC staff, accessories such as first courses and puddings are rudimentary. Chips are good. What is surprisingly elaborate is the choice of wines and you may start drinking, say, a bottle of Muscadet while you queue, which is another British institution alive and well here. There is a take-away counter with the entrance in Hillgate Street. A roof terrace comes into its own in fine weather but note that Geale's is closed for most of August.

CUISINE: *Fish and chips*

OPEN: *Tues to Sat*

MEALS: *12 to 3; 6 to 11.30 (Sat till 11)*

CLOSED: *Last 3 weeks in August*

AVERAGE PRICE: *£7*

CREDIT CARDS: *Access. Luncheon Vouchers*

SEATS: *100*

OUTSIDE TABLES: *(20+)*

PRIVATE ROOM: *Roof garden*

GONBEI

151 King's Cross Road, WC1
01-278 0619

'Gone by' is what you might have done half a dozen times before noticing this Japanese restaurant, which is one of a growing band apparently appealing to a younger and more impecunious clinetele than the stiffly formal, pricey places that opened up this cuisine in London. There is a sushi bar serving a quite wide selection of the fashionable nuggets of vinegared rice topped by slices of raw fish. There is yakitori, items threaded on skewers and grilled, and familiar assemblies such as tempura. I like the miso soup and also the deep-fried bean curd which is topped with a shredded vegetable that literally trembles with delicacy. Buckwheat noodle dishes (soba) are both economical and good. Gonbei (along with Ajimura and Ikkyu) is a good place to get to grips with Japanese food; the staff are helpful, the surroundings simple and you are not, as can happen, made to feel foreign – a gaijin – clumsy and crass.

CUISINE: *Japanese*	
OPEN: *D only: Mon to Sat*	
MEALS: *6 to 10.30*	
AVERAGE PRICE: *£16*	
CREDIT CARDS: *None*	
SEATS: *24*	

♥ GREAT NEPALESE TANDOORI RESTAURANT

48 Eversholt Street, NW1
01-388 6737

There are several Nepalese restaurants in London. They differ from Northern Indian restaurants most significantly in their use of fermented vegetables in pickles and the dried meats and vegetables that in Nepal are a necessary part of the diet in the harsher months. Also they serve pork. A visit to a Nepalese restaurant makes a refreshing change from what has become in so many cases a standardized list of dishes served at Indian restaurants and the Great Nepalese, to my mind, has the most diverting menu. It is also a jolly place. Among the first courses are masco bara, a black lentil bread, fried and puffy, served with a spicy sauce, mamocha which are dumplings and kalezo ra chyau, chicken liver bhutuwa with mushrooms. In the main courses, when they say mutton they seem to mean mutton and as this is often more flavourful than lamb and better able to stand up to vigorous spicing it is worth trying, say, the dumba curry, although it can be tough. The Nepalese Set can give you a mutton curry, black dhal, aloo bodi tama (which is fermented bamboo shoots cooked with potatoes and black-eyed beans), achar (pickle), spinach and a dessert. There is duck curry and tandoori duck and for the less adventurous, tandoori grills, birianis, and the various curries you might find elsewhere. The special Nepalese vegetable dishes are worth attention and with the breads, plain and stuffed, dahi (yoghurt) and achar, they would make a good vegetarian meal. Purists could drink lassi. Others fired with the fighting spirit might try the Nepalese coronation rum.

CUISINE: Nepalese	*Also vegetarian dishes*
OPEN: Mon to Sun	
MEALS: 12 to 2.45; 6 to 11.45	
AVERAGE PRICE: £10	
CREDIT CARDS: Access, Amex, Visa, Diners	

GREEN COTTAGE
AND GREEN COTTAGE II

9 New College Parade, Finchley Road, NW3
01-722 5305
122a Finchley Road, NW3
01-794 3833

Green Cottage is an authentic Cantonese restaurant useful in the area, especially at lunchtime, for one-dish meals of barbecued meats, rice and green vegetables. The service is not noted for its charm but at the same time the place has not succumbed to the new chi-chi of Chinese, much in evidence in the Finchley Road.

Green Cottage II is a surprising offspring in that it is expensive, stylishly decorated, and self-styled the first wholly vegetarian Chinese restaurant in Europe. The Chinese vegetarian tradition, they say, goes back 2000 years and this may account for what health-conscious customers would nowadays consider very retrograde notions like liberal use of MSG and bright orange food colouring. Also, just as the nut cutlet has rightly faded, so should dishes such as 'goose', 'duck', 'fish' and 'sweet and sour pork' which turn out to be made from bean curd and gluten. Straightforward, sensitively prepared vegetable dishes would be more welcome. Those dishes using bean curd as bean curd and various dried mushrooms are good, and there is a vegetable sausage that I liked. From the start, Green Cottage II has been busy and popular. It offends no dietary laws which is to the point in north London, and the suave decor with the rather strange arts-and-crafts-movement tall chairs gives the feeling of a special night out, but so does the bill.

Green Cottage
CUISINE: Cantonese   *Also vegetarian dishes*

OPEN: Mon to Sun

MEALS: *12 to 11.30*

CLOSED: *Christmas*

AVERAGE PRICE: *£9. Set Menus: £8, £10 and £12*

CREDIT CARDS: *None*

SEATS: *70*

Green Cottage II
CUISINE: *Chinese vegetarian*

OPEN: *Mon, Wed to Sun*

MEALS: *12 to 3; 6 to 11.30*

CLOSED: *Christmas*

AVERAGE PRICE: *£16. Set Menu: £8*

CREDIT CARDS: *Access, Amex, Diners*

SEATS: *80*

THE GREENHOUSE

27a Hays Mews, W1
01-499 3331

The Greenhouse is owned by David and Margaret Levin who own The Capital Hotel (*q.v.*) and the wine bar Le Metro (*q.v.*). Medium is a word that comes to mind when considering The Greenhouse: medium in prices, medium sort of ambition in the food, medium sort of decor, small-to-medium wine list. It is perhaps revealing of something in the human psyche that it is usually necessary to book sometimes a day or two in advance for a table at The Greenhouse. The chef, Nigel Davis, is English and the food basically English with accepted assimilations. Interesting dishes are first courses of ox tongue ravigote, hot ham mousse with creamy mushroom sauce, shrimp bisque and main courses of medaillon of venison with blackberry sauce, pink kidneys with shallots, skate with black butter and capers. Anglophiles among the many tourists who appreciate the restaurant's whereabouts, enjoy the treacle tart and the rice pudding with strawberry jam. The name is slightly misleading as you could throw stones without breaking too many windows and the jumble of decor is more dining room than conservatory.

CUISINE: English	Also vegetarian dishes

OPEN: L: Mon to Fri; D: Mon to Sat

MEALS: 12 to 2.30; 7 to 11 (Sat 7.30 to 11)

AVERAGE PRICE: £23

CREDIT CARDS: Access, Amex, Visa, Diners

SEATS: 80

♥ GREEN'S CHAMPAGNE AND OYSTER BAR AND RESTAURANT

36 Duke Street, SW1
01-930 4566

B efore espousing this place I must tell you that my sister Beth Coventry is chef in the restaurant half of the premises, which opened in 1985 following on from the success of the bar with its excellent oysters (opened by Peter Manzi, world champion oysterman), crab, lobster, prawns, cold beef, etc., which still runs alongside, with a pianist to provide moody music in the evenings. The aim of the restaurant is to provide straightforward English food, a commodity that is peculiarly hard to come by in London. To augment the cold shellfish there is a menu of the day, both at lunch and at dinner, featuring a soup and items such as potted shrimps, The Marquess of Queensberry's cod's roe pâté, shepherd's pie, English sausages, kedgeree, steak and kidney pudding, grills, oxtail, game in season – and fish cakes. Fish cakes both made with white fish and fresh salmon are inordinately popular and in themselves almost constitute a raison d'être for Green's. Steamed English puddings, tarts, pies and home-made ice cream continue the Best of British approach. The service is quick and professional, sometimes almost Dickensian in style. There are seats at the bar for more casual meals. Green's in The Royal Exchange in the City is a long-established wine company and the wine list has good bottles and reasonable prices. The decor is club-like which attracts pin-striped gents and the racing fraternity, but the restaurant is also often used by ladies lunching; it is a haven in the tourist season when you long to hear an English accent, in the chatter and in the food.

CUISINE: *English*

OPEN: *Mon to Fri*

MEALS: *12.30 to 3; 6.30 to 10.30 (Bar: 11.30 to 3; 5.30 to 8)*

CLOSED: *Bank Holidays*

AVERAGE PRICE: *£23*

CREDIT CARDS: *Access, Amex, Visa, Diners*

SEATS: *100 (75 in evening)*

PRIVATE ROOM: *(28)*

GRIMES

6 Garrick Street, WC2
01-836 7008

When it opened Grimes had the subtitle 'the cold fish café' which sounds sadder than the sad café but, in the winter anyway, the phrase is dropped and there are more hot dishes to supplement the oysters, smoked salmon, potted prawns, crab salad, smoked eel and gravad lax, and plates of assorted cold fish that were originally the mainstay of the menu. I like very much the idea of Grimes, fish straightforwardly served in pleasantly pared down but quite eccentrically decorated surroundings; it adds up to something very English. The first time I went there, I was full of enthusiasm, the next time, the cooking was indifferent and the bill was shocking. My Godmother told me yesterday that she had a lovely meal there. In other words, it seems subject more than most to the ups and down suffered by restaurants but Piers Sturridge, the owner, is an experienced restaurateur, and so I feel just confident enough to include it in the guide. Fish soup with rouille, bouillabaisse, scallops on spinach with beurre blanc sauce, fresh tuna steaks in a provençale sauce are some of the hot dishes. The wine list has some interesting affordable bottles. There are a few meat dishes, if you have a renegade in the party.

CUISINE: Fish	*Also vegetarian dishes*
OPEN: L: Mon to Fri; D: Mon to Sat	
MEALS: 12 to 3; 5.30 to 11.30	
AVERAGE PRICE: £16	
CREDIT CARDS: Access, Amex, Visa, Diners	
SEATS: 58	
TABLES OUTSIDE: (8)	
PRIVATE ROOM: (35)	
MUSIC: Piped popular and classical	

HEAL'S RESTAURANT

196 Tottenham Court Road, W1
01-636 1666 or 631 1921 (direct line)

Sir Terence Conran is a man who concentrates on, among other things, his stomach and so when he bought Heal's department store he set about installing a good restaurant, which miffed some because it forced out Cranks. He was lucky in getting Lorna Wing to run it as her ideas on food and food presentation are sympathetic and stylish. In the morning various teas, espresso coffee and filter coffee, chocolate and fresh orange juice are served with croissants, brioches and scones. Greek yoghurt with honey is also offered. At lunchtimes the menu changes each week and it might have a theme – such as Japanese – or it is more likely to be an eclectic selection featuring, for example, first courses of onion flan, steamed mouli with watercress mayonnaise, scrambled eggs with smoked salmon, followed by penne with ricotta and nut sauce, calf's liver with bacon, chicken tikka with cucumber raita and poppadums, oriental duck breasts with stir-fried vegetables, and desserts that are slightly less round the world in 80 ways. The first lunch that I enjoyed at Heal's included an ace chicken bouillabaisse and mussels in a creamy sauce flavoured with Pineau de Charentes. The tempura included among its deep-fried items a bundle of tiny carrot sticks tied with a strip of seaweed – a prop in a Japanese version of Good King Wenceslas. The wine list is more serious than you might expect in a furniture shop and there are several interesting aperitifs. Afternoon tea is served, but not dinner. Incidentally, Lorna Wing organizes imaginative outside catering, something as scarce as hen's teeth.

CUISINE: Eclectic	*Also vegetarian dishes*
OPEN: Mon to Sat	
MEALS: 10 to 5.30 (Thurs: Happy Hour 5.30 to 7)	
CLOSED: Christmas and Bank Holidays	
AVERAGE PRICE: £16	
CREDIT CARDS: Access, Amex, Visa, Diners	
SEATS: 80	
MUSIC: Piped classical and jazz	
Wheelchair access	

HENRY J. BEAN'S BUT ALL HIS FRIENDS CALL HIM HANK BAR AND GRILL

197 King's Road, SW3
01-352 9255

F orget the daft name which presumably passes for a sense of humour with Bob Payton (*q.v.*) and keep this converted pub (formerly The Six Bells) in mind when you have children to entertain. They serve food children like – hamburgers, chilli con carne, deep-fried potato skins, chocolate cheesecake and pecan pie – and they have a large garden with swings. The system of ordering is atavistically comforting for children who have ever had shoes bought for them in the children's shoe department of John Lewis – you take a number and wait for it to appear and then collect your goods. Because this was a pub, there is a full-on licence, meaning that you do not have to eat in order to drink and many grown-ups take up this option. In the evenings there is a pianist. They claim to serve the best burger in the town and certainly my eldest daughter gave it, the smokehouse burger, her seal of approval.

CUISINE: American	
OPEN: Mon to Sun	
MEALS: 11.30 to 11 (Sun 11.45 to 10.30)	
AVERAGE PRICE: £10	
CREDIT CARDS: None	
SEATS: 150	
TABLES OUTSIDE: (100)	
MUSIC: Pianist in the evenings. Taped	

♥ # HILAIRE

68 Old Brompton Road, SW7
01-584 8993

Without beating around the bush, I think I would rather eat Simon Hopkinson's food than that prepared by anyone else. This is because it is not three star food with its hyperbole (either a *reductio ad absurdum* or a return to granny food where mashed potatoes cost what you used to pay for truffle) but appetizing food cooked with utter dedication – probably the sort of thing Bocuse *et al*. eat in their time off. It is as English as it is French, partly because it is cooked by an Englishman, but also because a menu might include a risotto milanese with Parma ham, gravad lax and a sweet-cured herring accompanied by dill and horseradish mousse, and steamed clams with dashi (Japanese soup stock). The French influence can be felt in offerings like mousse of pleurottes (oyster mushrooms) with mustard sauce, tripes lyonnaise, breast of pheasant with apples and Calvados, fromage de tête de veau, demi-pigeon rôti aux girolles fraîches. There are also plain dishes like a boudin noir aux pommes and a steak au poivre because it is not all the time that one wants to be fashionable over a meal. Hilaire is the only jewel in Kennedy Brookes' crown and they are soon to lose chef Simon Hopkinson to Sir Terence Conran who will be setting him up in the first floor restaurant of the Bibendum building in Fulham Road which he has bought in conjunction with Paul Hamlyn. Who knows what the price structure there will be, so go quickly to Brompton Road to take advantage of the set-price lunch or dinner (both hedged about with rather too many supplements) and the skills of someone who is more obsessed with food than I am.

CUISINE: Eclectic	
OPEN: L: Mon to Fri; D: Mon to Sat	
MEALS: 12.30 to 2.30; 7 to 11.30	
AVERAGE PRICE: L: £15; D: £24. Set Menus: £10.50 (lunch); £18.50 (dinner)	
CREDIT CARDS: Access, Amex, Visa, Diners	
SEATS: 40	
PRIVATE ROOM: (20)	

HILTON HOTEL ROOF RESTAURANT *(Lunch)*
Park Lane, W1
01-493 7800

On a clear day you can see Farnham (almost) from this restaurant on the 28th floor which, about three years ago, the Hilton sensibly decided to give over to set-price meals at lunchtime. The buffet offers an adequate and sometimes more than

adequate selection of cold meats, cold fish, terrines, salads and marinated vegetables. The plates are not tea plates as so often happens at these 'eat as much as you please' places and the waiters are helpful with the other courses. A half-bottle of wine is included in the price. It is a romantic place to meet. There is also a Sunday brunch which is fun.

CUISINE: International	
OPEN: Mon to Fri, Sun	
MEALS: 12 to 2.45 (Sun 9.30–2.30). Set Menu: £14.50 inc. ½ bottle wine	
CREDIT CARDS: Access, Amex, Visa, Diners	
SEATS: 100	
Wheelchair access	

I CHING

14 Earl's Court Road, W8
01-937 7047

This restaurant belongs to the same ownership as the Chinese restaurant Zen (*q.v.*) and in some ways I prefer the menu as there is emphasis on offal and game and a real effort to go beyond the dishes with which any devotee of Chinese restaurants will be all too familiar. The preface to the menu stresses the kitchen's concern with health, and indeed with the rise in popularity of austere Japanese food and the Vietnamese cuisine with its many raw herbs and vegetables, customers are becoming increasingly aware of the pools of oil, the blankets of cornflour and the bombs of MSG involved in Chinese food, not to mention the deliberate fattiness of meat like belly of pork, which although wonderful must make the heart beat a little more hesitantly. There is little escape from frying techniques in the first courses, other than in the Imperial Hors d'Oeuvre. Satay made with fillet of rabbit and the steamed fresh scallops are probably the healthiest bet. Stuffed whole guinea fowl with eight treasures makes an interesting party dish. I know lobster served with braised noodles is wonderful because I have tried it more than once. I Ching whole fish is a pretty idea with a witty contrast of textures; the head and tail deep-fried, the flesh sautéed. Sometimes the descriptions are more delectable than the reality. This was true for me with the duck's kidney quick fried (tough) with melon seeds and the guinea fowl fillet sautéed with celery and garnished with deep-fried 'fragrant' bones, though these last were diverting to gnaw upon. Bho-jai refers to dishes braised in a sealed pot and I liked very much indeed the shin of beef with golden needles and dried mushrooms prepared this way. There is much I haven't tried and much not mentioned here. Helpful, interested service makes it an ideal place for experimentation and discoveries such as whether you like wind-dried sausage when it is stir-fried with oysters. (I do.)

CUISINE: Chinese	*Also vegetarian dishes*
OPEN: L: Sat and Sun; D: Mon to Sun	
MEALS: 6 to 12 (Sat and Sun 12 to 12)	
AVERAGE PRICE: £16	
CREDIT CARDS: Access, Amex, Visa, Diners	
SEATS: 75	
PRIVATE ROOM: (10–12)	
MUSIC: Piped	

IKEDA

30 Brook Street, W1
01-629 2730

Those aware of the subtleties of Japanese food rate Ikeda and its sister restaurant One Two Three, 27 Davies Street, W1 (01-409 0750) very highly in the spectrum of Japanese restaurants. At the premises of Ikeda used to be Michael Chow's restaurant Game and the sense of fashionability and fun has clung on. The best seat is in the front stalls, i.e. up at the bar where watching the chefs preparing sushi and other assemblies is entertaining and gratifying the way watching anything done supremely well always is (that was after all the basis for The Generation Game). Even watching the staff clean up at the end of service had me enthralled. At both restaurants prices can best be kept in check by staying with the set-price menus. Lunch is about half the price of dinner. The Japanese themselves are keen patrons of Mr Ikeda's restaurants.

CUISINE: Japanese	*Also vegetarian dishes*
OPEN: Mon to Fri	
MEALS: 12.30 to 2.30; 6.30 to 10.30	
AVERAGE PRICE: L: £15; D: £29. Set Menus: £7.50 and £9.90 (lunch); £18.60 and £25 (dinner)	
CREDIT CARDS: Access, Amex, Visa, Diners, JAL, JCB	
SEATS: 36	
PRIVATE ROOM: (8)	

♥

IKKYU

67 Tottenham Court Road, W1
01-636 9280

What is appealing about this Japanese restaurant is that it seems more like downtown Tokyo than the sort of credit-card-humbling, personalized-bottles-of-Chivas Regal, impenetrable-to-Westerners style of Japanese restaurant that predominates. It is unusual in having a chef who is willing to deviate from tradition and combine a mélange of disciplines. The basement premises are simply decorated with a bar taking up one third of the room and some tables screened. Yakitori – food grilled on skewers – comprises one part of the menu and a mixture, including grilled vegetables which are reasonably priced, makes a good start to the meal. Deep-fried beancurd in ginger sauce is another thought. The sashimi is perhaps not the most polished that you could find in London but it is reasonably priced. Among the main courses I particularly like is rolled five vegetables which is an omelette wrapped around lightly cooked vegetables, sliced into pinwheels and served with a dipping sauce. The salad of three kinds of seaweed with prawns and squid would be beneficial (think of the iodine and the trace minerals). Fresh fruit is the best and I, believe, the only dessert. Sake sits ready-heated in a dispenser making one little carafe after another a temptation. The staff are friendly and in what seems a bizarre gesture of comradeship towards Western customers the chef lists meat and potatoes on the menu.

CUISINE: Japanese	*Also vegetarian dishes*
OPEN: L: Mon to Fri; D: Mon to Fri and Sun	
MEALS: 12.30 to 2.30; 6 to 11	
AVERAGE PRICE: £16	
CREDIT CARDS: Access, Amex, Visa, Diners	
SEATS: 60	

INIGO JONES

14 Garrick Street, WC2
01-836 6456

In all the media razzmatazz that accompanies the activities of chefs these days, relatively little attention is paid to Paul Gayler, chef at Inigo Jones, which only demonstrates, I think, that culinary talent is not the issue at stake. He is one of the most accomplished of the chefs who have recently risen to prominence and I have felt more sympathetic to the style of nouvelle cuisine here than almost anywhere else. However, these warm feelings are more warmly elicited at lunchtime, addressing myself to the set-price menu, for the prices at Inigo Jones hit the roof, and though that is of a former stained-glass factory with features that lend an ecclesiastical air, the surroundings are not up to the bill. This is based on the premise, to which I adhere, that there is a limit to what food should cost. The set-price menu is also served as a pre-theatre supper so it gives you another chance to try dishes such as spiced leg of duckling and offal with onion marmalade or a vegetable tempura followed by, say, veal sweetbreads with ginger sauce and beetroot, a ragoût of rabbit in red wine and fresh noodles or roast wood pigeon with a pepper and wine sauce. The vegetables served are not just the standard chorus line, as so often happens in this sort of meal, but geared to suit the main dish you choose. The pace does not let up either with cheeses – a selection from Pierre Androuet in Paris – or desserts, a list printed on a separate card that in combining and contrasting flavours matches the skill evidenced in what has come before. From time to time there are promotional menus such as one for asparagus or one for game and always there is a vegetarian 'Menu Potager', which avoids nut roast or macaroni cheese with dishes like glazed vegetables in a creamed truffle and herb sauce and a puff pastry case layered with wild mushroom purée and fresh asparagus. The wine list is interesting but marked up with the same carefree abandon as the menu. Inigo Jones is a puzzlement. Here is some of the best cooking in London, pedigree service, a chef whose understanding of the palette of flavours, textures and colours, seems instinctively brilliant, yet the word on Inigo Jones is not much bruited about. It is like a ravishingly beautiful woman – who has no sense of humour.

CUISINE: French	Also vegetarian menu
OPEN: L: Mon to Fri; D: Mon to Sat	
MEALS: 12.30 to 2.30; 5.30 to 11.30	
CLOSED: 2 weeks at Christmas	
AVERAGE PRICE: £40. Set Menu: £14.75 (lunch and 5.30 to 7)	
CREDIT CARDS: Access, Amex, Visa, Diners	
SEATS: 65	
PRIVATE ROOM: (30–35)	

JACQUES

130 Blackstock Road, Finsbury Park, N4
01-359 3410

The owner, Jacques Hubert, is a Frenchman straight from central casting but even if Gallic-garlic chat does not impress you, the cooking, which is surprisingly ambitious, might. It is perhaps fairer to call the place a bistro in terms of the food but as far as the licence goes, it is a wine bar (which means no spirits served). Two young French chefs send dishes from the kitchen – sometimes at erratic intervals – like a home-made langoustine bisque, a chicken liver pâté served with onion marmalade, moules marinière, grilled fillet of brill with cockles and prawns, best end of lamb cooked with herbs and honey and steak au poivre. There is obeisance towards nouvelle cuisine with, for example, a hot goat's cheese on croûton with salad and a vegetable terrine served with a tomato coulis, but somehow it is not wearisome. The special, which is breast of duck with green peppercorns, avoids being a cliché but only by an unnecessarily rich sauce containing brandy, port and cream. The vegetables are wholesome and all is served with an old-fashioned generosity. Jacques confesses to a diverse and glamorous culinary past. The end result is a sit. com. small French restaurant. Note that on Sundays a traditional English breakfast with papers and champagne is served at lunchtime.

CUISINE:	*French bistro*
OPEN:	*L: Wed to Sun; D: Tues to Sun*
MEALS:	*12 to 3 (Sun till 2); 7 to 10.45 (Sun till 10.30)*
CLOSED:	*Christmas week and 2 weeks in summer*
AVERAGE PRICE:	*£16*
CREDIT CARDS:	*Access*
SEATS:	*45*
PRIVATE ROOM:	*(8)*
MUSIC:	*Piped classical and French*

AU JARDIN DES GOURMETS

5 Greek Street, W1
01-437 1816

This restaurant is owned by a wine merchant, Joseph Berkmann, who sold the other establishments in his group to Kennedy Brookes (*q.v.*) by whom he is retained as a wine consultant. The great wine list with some classic bottles, difficult even to buy at auction these days, is the point of Au Jardin des Gourmets but that is not to denigrate the chef, a trainee of Paul Bocuse, for it would be hard to produce food to outshine, say, a '45 Haut-Brion. However, if you do order a drinking treat, my advice is to stay with simpler orders like a rack of lamb, leaving your palate alert and single-minded. A set-price lunch and dinner helps you justify extravagance on the wine. A restaurant of this name has been at this address for over 50 years and although, to my mind, the last redecoration lacked style, it remains a pleasant room with some curvaceous art nouveau artefacts. The wood-panelled first floor rooms are somewhere to keep in mind when organizing private parties.

CUISINE: French

OPEN: L: Mon to Fri; D: Mon to Sat

MEALS: 12.30 to 2.30; 6.30 to 11.15

CLOSED: 1 week at Christmas and Bank Holiday lunchtimes

AVERAGE PRICE: £24. Set Menu: £12

CREDIT CARDS: Access, Amex, Visa, Diners

SEATS: 90

PRIVATE ROOMS: (12 and 20)

JOE ALLEN

13 Exeter Street, WC2
01-836 0651

Joe Allen has lost some of the novelty it had when it opened in 1977. Since then other easy-going establishments with American-inspired food and agreeable staff have come into being, but Joe Allen hangs on to a theatrical crowd which continues to distinguish it from other Covent Garden establishments – its closest rival perhaps being the Café Pélican (*q.v.*). The blackboard menu offers much the same as it did nine years ago: black bean soup, large salads garnished with bacon, croûtons and avocado served in wooden bowls, fried chicken, ribs, chilli, chopped steak, grilled fish. The lunch dishes of eggs with hash browns, eggs Benedict and the like served from noon strike me as the best way of approaching this style of food, but of course the daytime crowd is not as glitzy as in the evenings. Although there is no hamburger as such offered on the menu, you can ask for one and there are those who say it will be the best hamburger in town. The staff who used to be notable for their efficiency and solicitude now tend to be tetchy, as if their brush with stars has left a dusting of artistic temperament. At any time it is wise to book, but there is a long bar where you can wait until a table in the large room becomes vacant. The decor – bare brick walls with framed theatrical posters, red gingham cloths on the tables – is apparently the same as at the New York Joe Allen and the Paris Joe Allen. When you have got a good formula, stick to it. See also Orso's.

CUISINE: *American*	
OPEN: *Mon to Sun*	
MEALS: *noon to 12.45 am (Sun till 11.45)*	
AVERAGE PRICE: *£15*	
CREDIT CARDS: *None*	
SEATS: *250*	
MUSIC: *Pianist from 9 pm*	

JOY KING LAU

3 Leicester Street, WC2
01-437 1132

F our floors of Cantonese food in relatively stylish, cool surroundings, Joy King Lau is keenly supported by the Chinese community. Since I prefer to order dim sum from the menu rather than bob up and down like a yo-yo peering into baskets on trolleys, I often come here for a cheap and satisfying lunch or 'tea'. It is handy for the cinemas of Leicester Square.

CUISINE: Chinese
OPEN: Mon to Sun
MEALS: 11 am to 11.20 pm (Sun 10 to 10) Dim sum: 11 to 5.30
AVERAGE PRICE: £13. Set Menus: from £5.50
CREDIT CARDS: Amex, Diners, Carte Blanche
PRIVATE ROOM: (40–50)
Wheelchair access

JULIE'S WINE BAR

137 Portland Road, W11
01-727 7985

I t is the premises that are the USP (advertising jargon meaning unique selling point) of Julie's. Gothic rooms originally decorated by Julie Hodges, she who set the style of Biba, a courtyard garden, and a bomb shelter of a private room with a table that seats twenty, in a part of London that has become gentrified and almost rustic, distinguishes the restaurant part of Julie's from neighbouring eating places – of which there are now many. However, I cannot warm to the food which is over-blown dinner party in style and almost egregiously eclectic – wind-dried goose and duck breasts, Swabian noodles on field mushrooms, smoked leg of lamb with French leaves – and seldom quite as delicious in expectation as you might imagine. It is also, in common, I suppose, with almost any other restaurant, not cheap. The part of Julie's to use is the wine bar which is equally atmospheric, romantic too, and serves perfectly agreeable little lunches and suppers and a proper English tea with scones and cakes. Customers whose heyday was in the Sixties rather touchingly hang around. It is a good place to arrange to meet someone you don't know well but would like to know better.

CUISINE: Wine Bar and Afternoon Tea   *Also vegetarian dishes*

OPEN: Mon to Sun

MEALS: 11 to 11

AVERAGE PRICE: £14

CREDIT CARDS: None

SEATS: 75

KALAMARAS MEGA

76–78 Inverness Mews, W2
01-727 9122

KALAMARAS MICRO

66 Inverness Mews, W2
01-727 5082

John Fowles, author of *The Magus*, set in Greece, when offered a Greek restaurant meal in London (I used to be married to his publisher) would say in a disapproving tone that of course the so-called Greek restaurants in London are all run by Cypriots. That this is often to the benefit of the food, and therefore to the customers, did not seem to him the point. However, Stelios Platanos who runs these now almost historic restaurants in a little mews off Queensway, is Greek – as Greek as can be after running restaurants in London for twenty years or so and assuming the mantle of Zorba of the kitchen. In his two establishments, one licensed, the other not, you will not even find pitta bread which, it goes without saying, is heretical; worse than Cypriot, Turkish. What you *do* find is a menu that is probably incomprehensible, however many holidays you have spent on the islands of Kos or Paxos, and the pliant waitresses will have to explain it to you. This is part of the 'charm'. The first courses tend to be considerably more diverting than the main courses where the meat has an almost school dinner quality. Consistent popularity has led to a blunting of the edges of detail: e.g. the fried aubergines that are served with skordalia (sauce of breadcrumbs, garlic and olive oil) fried ages before being served, making them tough and leathery. Dishes of octopus and squid, or better still, *soupies* (cuttlefish) are usually good and there can be felicitous combinations of vegetables like artichoke hearts and broad beans flavoured with lemon. There are, indeed, many dishes that get away from the one kebab, two kebab, three kebab, four, formula and on a summer's night with a few tables set out in the mews and the cooking smells filtering from the kitchens, you can imagine, if only for a minute or two, that you are in Greece, in a Greek town anyway.

Mega
CUISINE: Greek	*Also vegetarian dishes*

OPEN: Mon to Sat
MEALS: 6.30 to 12
CLOSED: Bank and Public Holidays
AVERAGE PRICE: £16
CREDIT CARDS: Access, Amex, Visa, Diners
SEATS: 96
PRIVATE ROOM: (12–28)
MUSIC: Piped Greek
Wheelchair access

Micro
CUISINE: Greek	*Also vegetarian dishes*

OPEN: Mon to Sat
MEALS: 7 to 11
CLOSED: Bank and Public Holidays

AVERAGE PRICE: £11. No Licence (bring your own, no corkage)

CREDIT CARDS: Access, Amex, Visa, Diners

SEATS: 80

MUSIC: Piped Greek

Wheelchair access

KEN LO'S MEMORIES OF CHINA

67–69 Ebury Street, SW1
01-730 7734

For years and years in the realm of food Ken Lo has acted as interpreter from East to West and West to East. Born in Foochow, he came to study English Literature at Cambridge and first became involved with food when, as assistant consul in Liverpool at the time of the Pacific war, he helped to start welfare centres and restaurants for wounded Chinese seamen. His first book on Chinese food was published in the 1950s and since then many books have been published by many publishers and Mr Lo, with his indefatigable energy, must be credited with easing many Westerners into the art of cooking Chinese. Part of the restaurant premises are given over to a cooking school and Mr Lo also runs a Chinese Gourmet Club whose members can attend various meals and banquets organized in London and have first dibs at places on his tours of China. He would also want you to know that he still plays at Senior Wimbledon. Ambitiousness or perhaps just eager-beavering dents the inscrutability, and to my mind Ken Lo's restaurant is more of a success as a marketing operation than a source of the finest Chinese food. Although the menu lists some original-sounding dishes, unless you order 24 hours in advance, a meal here, particularly a set meal, to my mind, has little to distinguish it from other up-market Chinese establishments. Some items read temptingly – Shantung hand-shredded chicken in a garlic sauce, pomegranate prawn balls and mange-tout – and if you are eating as a couple you should order à la carte, for they only appear in the more expensive set menus. Regionality is well defined, with one set meàl, menu A, planned as 'a gastronomic tour of China', complete with salt-and-pepper pork choplettes (*sic*) from Metropolitan China. Ken Lo's is popular with Oriental businessmen entertaining and being entertained and for quick executives there are two menus for 'quick executive luncheons'. The dining room is stylishly designed with screens affording some privacy and the standard of service reflects Mr Lo's understanding of the West. At the moment of writing Mr Lo is soon to do a televised tour of China, in the company of paying guests, taking in his birthplace and other old haunts. Maybe it will also serve to make the memories more precise.

CUISINE: Chinese	*Also vegetarian dishes*
OPEN: Mon to Sat	
MEALS: 12 to 2.30; 6.30 to 11	
CLOSED: Bank Holidays	
AVERAGE PRICE: £27. Set Menus: £14.50 and £15.50 (lunch); £18.50 (8 course dinner)	
CREDIT CARDS: Access, Amex, Visa, Diners	
SEATS: 120	
PRIVATE ROOM: (12–20)	

KETTNERS

29 Romilly Street, W1
01-434 1214

Peter Boizot owns the Pizza Express chain. Whether or not those pizzas are the best – various restaurants and chains have their devotees – he is a force for the good in his promotion of live jazz, his work for the Soho Society, his contributions to the Venice in Peril Fund (10p sent for every Pizza Veneziana ordered) and for keeping the plushy decor of Kettners more or less intact and serving fast food there.

You sit in Edwardian surroundings in the heart of Soho that speak of big bills yet pay a very reasonable sum for pizzas, hamburgers or, for vegetarians, chilli senza carne. There is also a champagne bar with a good selection of *marques*, fairly priced. Now, if only he would turn the whole place into a stylish, romantic and individualistic hotel . . .

CUISINE: Italian//American	*Also vegetarian dishes*
OPEN: Mon to Sun	
MEALS: 11 am to midnight	
CLOSED: Christmas Day	
AVERAGE PRICE: £8	
CREDIT CARDS: Access, Amex, Visa, Diners. Luncheon Vouchers	
SEATS: 200	
PRIVATE ROOMS: (several, for 2–50)	
MUSIC: Pianist nightly and lunchtime Thurs to Sun	

KHAN'S

13–15 Westbourne Grove, W2
01-727 5420

This is the sort of restaurant guides eschew – perfunctory service, erratic quality of food, occasional long waits for a table – but outside of Southall it is the one place that reminds me of eating out in India once you have left the safety of luxury hotels. The back room with its trestle tables, which you are obliged to share, where food is slapped down with no ceremony whatsoever is particularly evocative and whilst you may have no wish to bring to mind the experience of a rudimentary restaurant in Delhi, it is worth noting that the food is cheap and can be good. The front room with its tall pillars like stylized palms is very pretty but somehow one always seems to be hustled towards the back even though a system of no bookings should mean that you get lucky sometimes. Khan's was once highly fashionable – it is still throbbingly busy.

CUISINE: Indian	Also vegetarian dishes

OPEN: Mon to Sun
MEALS: 12 to 3; 6 to 12
CLOSED: Bank Holidays
AVERAGE PRICE: £7
CREDIT CARDS: Access, Amex, Visa, Diners
SEATS: 200

KOTO

75 Parkway, NW1
01-482 2036

I love Japanese food and this restaurant is close to where I live so I have visited it perhaps (unfairly) more often than I would a comparable establishment in Blackheath. But I feel, therefore, confident in uttering the dreary comment that standards are variable. Dinner has been better than lunch. Prices are relatively reasonable. The assorted hors d'oeuvre (zensai) are £1.70. Sunomo (deep-fried bean curd swimming in a soya sauce broth) is £1.20. Other first courses including the grilled skewer of chicken called yakitori hover round these prices. The main courses feature tempura, grilled meats and fish, some with a teriyaki sauce, sukiyaki, shabu-shabu and yose nabe. There is also sashimi and sushi including an egg and vegetable variety rolled in nori (toasted seaweed) at prices considerably less than you would pay in the West End, but somehow what with one rice and another noodle the bill mounts up to more than you think you should pay in such a simplistic environment. Traditionalists can sit in the little room upstairs on tatami mats but the inherent discomfort (to stout Westerners) is not justified by what you might call the meal experience. As with most Japanese restaurants, the set meals are something of a bargain. The last time I ate at Koto, the grilled fish seemed as though it had come from the deep blue freezer. Staff are friendly in that dazed way the Japanese have.

CUISINE: Japanese	Also vegetarian dishes
OPEN: Mon to Sat	
MEALS: 12.30 to 2.30 (Sat from 12); 6 to 10.30	
AVERAGE PRICE: £16. Set Menus: £4.50–£6 (lunch); £11–£14 (dinner)	
CREDIT CARDS: Access, Amex, Visa, Diners	
SEATS: 45	
PRIVATE ROOMS: (16 and 8)	

LAL BHAG

51 Kilburn High Road, NW6
01-624 5289

The owner, Mr Haque, once worked at Geetanjli in Brook Street, an eccentric but occasionally great Indian restaurant, sadly now no more. He has injected some originality into the Lal Bhag menu and under the heading Specialities there are various dishes I would recommend: Bengal duckling which can be a bit lean but benefits from its marinade of herbs and spices; quails (all the go nowadays in Indian restaurants) in a rich sauce; mahee-surma, fish (often pomfret) grilled in the tandoori oven. Fish figures more often than on most Indian menus. Try also the moali ramna, which is fish in a delicate creamy sauce. The special curry dishes tend to have sauces, grainy with ground almonds and mild with egg yolk and cream or yoghurt but for those who like sweat beading the brow to prove that they are having an Indian meal there is chicken chilly mossala (*sic*) and an extra hot preparation, lamb morchee. Breads are well made and the puri forms part of a good first course, prawn puri. Lassi – a yoghurt drink – comes sweet or salty or flavoured with mango. The inevitable cocktails and a pink and green decor only detract from the food. The buffet is an economical, but less interesting way, of approaching the menu.

CUISINE: Indian	Also vegetarian dishes
OPEN: Mon to Sun	

MEALS: *12 to 2.45; 6 to 11.45 (Sun 12 to 11.45)*

AVERAGE PRICE: *£11. Set Menus: £4.50–£7.50*

CREDIT CARDS: *Access, Amex, Visa, Diners*

SEATS: *44*

LANGAN'S BAR AND GRILL

7 Down Street, W1
01-491 0990

Opened by Peter Langan (see Langan's Brasserie), in partnership with Lubin and Myers of Theme restaurants, the Bar and Grill, which bears absolutely no resemblance to Irish establishments so called, is the ground floor and basement of the small, highly decorated Hotel 7 Down Street much frequented by pop stars. Langan has imposed his style with interesting pictures, including an early Hockney of Himself, and flattering lighting. The chef, David Bickford, is from the Brasserie and the menu in a sense is a scaled down version of the one offered there. When I visited I found it curiously stolid given the clientele the place attracts but perhaps it is a relief to find few traces of the 'modern' approach or, with the exception of a spinach, endive and bacon salad with a warm dressing, none of the fashionable dishes for the glitzy non-hungry like carpaccio and steak tartare and marinated fish. There is a small choice and it changes daily but in case they are on the menu when you visit, I enjoyed the trout quenelles with a fresh herb sauce and the half pheasant with oyster mushrooms. The desserts are particularly good and a selection served for two is a sybaritic experience. Something tells me that the ground floor is the place to be. The Bar and Grill sops up some of the overflow from the Brasserie but it has a pulse of its own which can be set racing when Langan imitates the illustration on the menu. The food is reasonably priced, the wines unreasonably in several instances.

CUISINE: *French/English*   *Also vegetarian dishes*

OPEN: *Mon to Sun*

MEALS: 12 to 2.45; 6 to 12 (Sun 7 to 11)

AVERAGE PRICE: £20

CREDIT CARDS: Access, Amex, Visa, Diners

SEATS: 80

PRIVATE ROOM: (40)

LANGAN'S BISTRO

26 Devonshire Street, W1
01-935 4531

These premises housed the original Odin's where, though it might be hard to believe now, Peter Langan once cooked. It has become a cheaper version of Odin's decorated with Langan's inimitable style that always includes an interesting collection of paintings, prints and photographs. Oriental paper umbrellas cover the ceiling. The tablecloths are brown paper. It is immensely popular and gets booked up well in advance which can only mean that what I recently noticed as an insidious increase in prices – over-priced accoutrements such as vegetables, salad, desserts, coffee – is outweighed by the imaginative cooking which is modern French in style complete with puréed vegetables, fish terrines and salades tièdes. The menu changes frequently. Mrs Langan would probably no longer recognize her chocolate pudding but it continues to be sought after by chocoholics. Getting my kicks in other ways, I prefer the sorbets to complete the meal. Langan's Bistro is the sort of place you wish there were more of in London.

CUISINE: French

OPEN: L: Mon to Fri; D: Mon to Sat

MEALS: 12.30 to 2.30; 7 to 11.30

AVERAGE PRICE: £21

CREDIT CARDS: Amex

SEATS: 40

♥ LANGAN'S BRASSERIE

Stratton Street, W1
01-493 6437

Pierre Martin (*q.v.*) said about Langan's Brasserie that it is the sort of restaurant that only happens once in every 50 years. It is indeed hard to imagine another confluence of circumstances such as large Mayfair premises like the old Coq d'Or being on the market, a partnership of Irish recklessness and élan and beady showbiz as exemplified in Peter Langan and Michael Caine and, just in time to make the place work, the dedicated services of a dedicated chef such as Richard Shepherd. It is he who can run a kitchen that turns out over 500 meals a day selected from a menu of about 60 choices in the first course and main course alone. To say, as some have said, probably me included, that Langan's is La Coupole of London is not accurate. First, it is not a brasserie – it adheres to restaurant hours – and secondly it is considerably more dramatic than La Coupole. The large bar and long main dining room subtly lit with a combination of art nouveau lamp brackets and spotlights provides a cat-walk for every customer to be appraised and the combination of the art on the walls and the artifice on the faces – famous or followers of fashion – makes every meal a happening. I am ambivalent about the menu. It is too long, in a sense, for the purpose since most people are unwilling to devote the time to reading it when they could be looking around or into their companion's cleavage but on the other hand it is its sturdiness, its thorough quality, that lifts Langan's above mere trendiness. Dishes like the bisque of crevettes, the croustade d'oeufs de cailles, oeufs poché au haddock fumé, soufflé d'épinards sauce anchoise, langue de boeuf braisée sauce madère choux rouge, deep-fried wing of skate sauce tartare, pojarski de veau à la crème et champignons, bratwurst sausage with mashed potatoes and onions, carré d'agneau rôti aux herbes de Provence and desserts like profiteroles sauce chocolat, baba au rhum, rice pudding, apple pie with fresh cream, poire Belle Hélène among many, many others provide the sensible underpinning which allows fantasy to flourish. It strikes me as an achievement that has yet properly to be recognized for its worth. It goes almost without saying that no one has managed to copy it. There are critics of the food but if they were honest with themselves they would admit that it wasn't for the perfect béarnaise that they went to Langan's and if other demands went unfulfilled that is not entirely the fault of the restaurant. Prices are reasonable for food and wine. Oddly, though it is fashionable, it is also a people's restaurant.

CUISINE: French	*Also vegetarian dishes*
OPEN: L: Mon to Fri; D: Mon to Sat	
MEALS: 12.30 to 2.45; 7 to 11.45 (Sat 8 pm to 12.45 am)	
AVERAGE PRICE: £22	
CREDIT CARDS: Access, Amex, Visa, Diners	
SEATS: 275	

THE LANTERN

23 Malvern Road, NW6
01-624 1796

See La Cloche.

LAST DAYS OF THE RAJ

22 Drury Lane, WC2
01-836 1628

The sloppiness that comes with popularity has not by-passed this restaurant but it is included as a sort of landmark in the London Indian restaurant scene. Started in 1980 by the Bengali Workers' Action Group backed by Camden Council, it had a lot of publicity, a lot of success and subsequent offshoots like Amin Ali's Red Fort and Lal Qila (busy Mr Ali was featured on television's *The Money Programme*) and the Bayleaf Tandoori in Highgate. Apparently the prawn puri (now appearing at a local Indian near you) first made its appearance here. It is a circle of fried puffy bread topped with prawns in a spicy sauce. I also first tasted here lamb chops Indian-style which I thought much better than lamb chops any other way. The fish dishes are usually well prepared, the Raj special being based on trout. For those with a sweet tooth the dessert called frinee made with ground rice, pistachio nuts and rose water is of interest. Perhaps the competition in Covent Garden e.g. Taste of India in Catherine Street, Bhatti's in Great Queen Street, will make the front of house pull up its puttees.

CUISINE: Indian	*Also vegetarian dishes*
OPEN: Mon to Sun	
MEALS: 12 to 2.30; 6 to 11.30	
CLOSED: Bank Holidays lunchtime	
AVERAGE PRICE: £12. Set Menu: £6.90 (Thali)	
CREDIT CARDS: Access, Amex, Visa, Diners	
SEATS: 50	
PRIVATE ROOM: (40)	
MUSIC: Piped	

LAUNCESTON PLACE RESTAURANT

1a Launceston Place, W8
01-937 6912

Other guides are careful, priggish even, about not passing judgements on restaurants that have not been visited. However, *au fond*, I am a journalist and I want to be as up to date as publishing schedules will allow. The careers of the people involved in Launceston Place Restaurant make me feel confident about writing about it before the doors have opened to the public. The owners are Simon Slater who has been involved recently with 192 (*q.v.*) and Nick Smallwood who previously was the very efficient manager of L'Escargot (*q.v.*). They have taken over premises, formerly Casa Porelli, that had a strong local following, and I don't think the basically English food cooked by Sebastian Snow and his sous-chefs who were at L'Escargot will alienate them, nor the fairly priced set-price meals. Looking at the proposed menu I like the sound of pumpkin and saffron soup, crispy chicken wings with lamb's lettuce and sweet rocket, coddled eggs with anchovy and Melba toast and terrine of trout and halibut in aspic from among the first courses. The main courses that grab me are roast guinea hen with elderflower fritters, butterfly lamb chops with crab apple and mint jelly and calf's liver with fried onions and bubble and squeak. It seems to me that a well-judged amount of Englishness has seeped in. Desserts include cherry tart with clotted cream and banana flummery. When you read this you will be able to judge whether I was right to stick my neck out. I'm not worried.

CUISINE: English plus	Also vegetarian dishes

OPEN: L: Mon to Sun; D: Mon to Sat

MEALS: 12.30 to 2.30; 6.30 to 11.30

AVERAGE PRICE: L: £12; D: £20. Set Menus (available until 8 pm): £7.50 (2 courses) and £9.50 (3 courses)

CREDIT CARDS: Access, Visa

SEATS: 55 (including conservatory)

PRIVATE ROOM: (15)

LAURENT

428 Finchley Road, NW2
01-794 3603

In culinary matters, countries tend to reap what they sow in the realm of imperialism. To illustrate this simplistic theory simplistically, we have Indian restaurants and the French have Vietnamese establishments and even in provincial towns in France it is possible to find the Algerian dish couscous or merguez sausages. Couscous has not made much impression on London, which is why Laurent is of note. A simple neighbourhood restaurant with an uninspired basic bistro menu, it features as the speciality couscous either vegetarian or with meat, the second version coming as Complet or Royal, where a lamb chop and brochette are served as well as lamb stew and merguez sausage. If semolina speaks to you of school puddings, try it steamed over broth as for couscous, moistened with stew and peppered with the hot sauce harissa. It is a comforting dish. To start choose brik à l'oeuf, a sheet of paper-thin pastry folded diagonally across an egg and deep-fried. Go one better than the house wine which could be usefully employed in writing secret messages. The Moroccan red or rosé is both reasonable and an appropriate accompaniment. The service at Laurent is a family affair and has charm.

CUISINE: North African	*Also vegetarian dishes*
OPEN: L: Mon to Sun; D: Mon to Sat	
MEALS: 12 to 2.30; 6 to 11	
CLOSED: Bank Holidays and first 3 weeks in August	
AVERAGE PRICE: £12	
CREDIT CARDS: Access, Visa	
SEATS: 34	
MUSIC: Piped European	

LEITH'S

92 Kensington Park Road, W11
01-229 4481

P rue Leith is a force to be reckoned with in the catering world. Having started a catering company, Leith's Good Food, in 1961 from a bed-sit in Earl's Court she has gone on to open a restaurant, a cooking school, a much enlarged outside catering company and done a stint on the board of British Rail with, sadly, few visible results. She also contributes a regular cookery column to *The Guardian* and writes books, some of them in conjunction with Caroline Waldegrave, her partner in the school. As you might imagine Ms Leith is not a constant presence in her eponymous restaurant but she has an excellent manager in Jean Reynaud and she does passionately care. Leith's, which opened in

1969, was designed by Nathan Silver and the rather strange interior for Victorian houses – carpets on the ceiling, tinted mirrors and upholstered office chairs on castors – has worn well, in part because it is *hors de combat* in terms of design fashion. So too in a way is the menu with its hors d'oeuvre trolley and its dessert trolley but that, Ms Leith tells me, is what the customers want. When in the light of the new cooking she banned the hors d'oeuvre trolley and its passengers like kipper pâté and avocado mousse, regular customers got up a petition and campaigned for its return. It could be that a (high) set price for a meal, the price depending on your choice of main course, produces a demand for tangible value for money, e.g. having a little bit of everything from the dessert trolley rather than the delicious clean-tasting hot orange and lemon soufflé. Leith's duckling, an Aylesbury bird crisply roasted and garnished with almonds, celery and orange peel is another firm favourite. Barbary duck was substituted for a while but another complaint – Leith's customers are avid letter writers – put paid to that. Other options, such as the plaited salmon and sole fillets with a sorrel sauce, and the breast of pheasant with pheasant mousse do reflect changes in culinary attitudes since the late sixties. There is a nice sense of theatre about a dinner at Leith's – it is a whole evening out and one that can take place on a Sunday – but recent competition has somewhat eclipsed the style, but it is there if you want an old-fashioned tuck-in. Businessmen apparently often do. The wines are marked with the same enthusiasm Prue Leith brings to everything she embarks upon.

CUISINE: International	*Also vegetarian menu*
OPEN: D only: Mon to Sun	
MEALS: 7.30 to 11.45	
AVERAGE PRICE: £35. Vegetarian Menu: £20.50	
CREDIT CARDS: Access, Amex, Visa, Diners	
SEATS: 90	
PRIVATE ROOMS: Three (10, 20 and 30)	

LEMONIA

154 Regent's Park Road, NW1
01-586 7454

Having to book quite a few days ahead for a table on Saturday evening in a Cypriot restaurant in a residential area of London would seem to indicate unusually good food at fair prices, and it does. The Evangelou family, who also run a delicatessen, run the place with enthusiasm and flair and the cooking strays interestingly away from the formula applied to most Greek/Cypriot places. There are few restaurants (if any), for example, that serve the homely soup trahana made from dried coarse wheat mixed with yoghurt or goat's milk: very nutritious. The usual dips – taramasalata, hoummus and the aubergine-based melidzanosalata – are well prepared. Main course dishes vary between the long-stewed, sometimes to very good effect as with the lamb with onions, and the charcoal-grilled, the quails making a nice light course. I like their way with sweetbreads: slightly sharpened with wine. I like their way with customers: cheerful and accommodating. To sample a bit of most dishes order the good value meze. In summer a sliding roof can be rolled back in the ground floor conservatory, but book well ahead for that, too, on a promising day. If you fail to get a table at Lemonia, you could try the sister restaurant, Daphne, at 83 Bayham Street, NW1 (01-267 7322) which has its own virtues, a pretty interior and a roof terrace that is fun to book for parties.

CUISINE: Greek	*Also vegetarian dishes*
OPEN: Mon to Sat	
MEALS: 6 to 11.30	
AVERAGE PRICE: £10. Set Menu: £5.50 (Meze)	
CREDIT CARDS: None	
SEATS: 85	
TABLES OUTSIDE: (20)	

Limehouse

In my parents' day, the Chinese Experience involved a rather daring trip down to Limehouse in the East End. It was the nearest, I suppose, in London to going to slum it in Harlem. The presence of Chinese seamen round the docks meant that some Cantonese restaurants had sprung up. Eventually a group emerged with names that played on the word 'friends' but now some friends, for example the Good Friends, are not such good friends; are, in fact, not connected with the others. As a contrast to the more sophisticated food available in Gerrard Street, Lisle Street and thereabouts it is still diverting to go to Limehouse. The food is not from the chop suey era but it has a more simplistic style. The development of studios, offices and expensive housing at Limehouse and the move of Rupert Murdoch's group of newspapers to Wapping might well work a change, so go soon in case the change is not for the better, to: *Good Friends, 139 Salmon Lane, E14 (01-987 5541)*; *New Friends, 53 West India Dock Road, E14 (01-987 1139)*; *Young Friends, 11 Pennyfields, E14 (01-987 4276)*; *Chinatown, 795 Commercial Road, E14 (01-987 2330)*. It is important to ring to make a reservation. Some of the restaurants will not accommodate casual visitors.

LOU PESCADOU

241 Old Brompton Road, SW5
01-370 1057

Pierre Martin (*q.v.*) has been quoted as saying that he wanted to open a large brasserie, but with these premises, formerly an African restaurant called Toddies, the word bistro is more applicable. Also the opening hours, although generous in the evenings with a closing time of 2 am which attracts a lot of French mafia in the catering business, are not those of a brasserie, i.e. all day long. The theory is that a one-course meal could be adequate both for you and for them. It might be a pizza niçoise or some fresh pasta with seafood or clams or an omelette paysanne or a substantial fish soup or a bowl of mussels accompanied by a pitcher of wine or a beer or glass of cider. In fact, as with similar user-friendly intentions in London restaurants, it seems more tactful to have a two- or three-course meal with a bottle of wine. The fish or meat is well caught and well bought and simply grilled. Plats du jour, e.g. osso buco, are also offered. The tarte aux pommes minute is a delicious dessert and an idea to copy at home. On a circle of the thinnest puff pastry a layer of overlapping slices are laid, sprinkled with sugar and dotted with butter and baked briefly and fiercely, then splashed with Calvados and served with cream. The wine list is sensibly brief and the champagne cheap enough to make it a tempting alternative or aperitif. At the moment the laudable policy of no bookings holds and I hope it is true when you read this.

CUISINE: French	
OPEN: Mon to Sun	
MEALS: 12 to 3; 7 to 2 am	
AVERAGE PRICE: £16	
CREDIT CARDS: Access, Amex, Visa, Diners	
SEATS: 55	
TABLES OUTSIDE: (20)	

MA CUISINE

113 Walton Street, SW3
01-584 7585

I must confess to not having visited Ma Cuisine for a very long time because the notion of booking days or weeks ahead is alien to me and the combination of fine cooking, reasonable prices and small premises makes it necessary. I feel I discovered Ma Cuisine. In April 1975 when wandering down Walton Street on a clothes buying spree with my friend Vera I said, 'Look, here's a new restaurant, let's try it.' Guy Mouilleron, who had been working as head chef at The Café Royal, had just opened his kitchen and we were the only customers in the restaurant. I was impressed then by the food but apologetic to readers of *The Evening Standard* about the prices – I estimated that a three-course meal for two with wine would come to about £10 excluding service. Mouilleron is no longer in the kitchen, that is now the domain of Jean-Claude Aubertin, and £10 would not buy one person two courses (unless you had the vegetable soup and the boned leg of chicken with roasted cloves of garlic), but Ma Cuisine continues to attract loyal custom and also one Michelin star. They have achieved that level of successful French restaurant where you close at the weekends. The cooking is inventive, modern but not skimpy. The premises which, to put no finer a point on it, are cramped, are decorated in that French style that put the kitsch into kitchen. I wonder if there is still a clock that looks like a copper saucepan. I hope so.

CUISINE: French	*Also vegetarian meals on request*
OPEN: Mon to Fri	
MEALS: 12.30 to 2; 7.30 to 11	
CLOSED: Bank Holidays, Christmas and 4 weeks in summer	
AVERAGE PRICE: £26	
CREDIT CARDS: Amex, Diners	
SEATS: 30	

MAGNO'S BRASSERIE

65a Long Acre, WC2
01-836 6077

Magno Coliades once ran a successful restaurant in Lindos, that sophisticated and (some would say) spoiled resort in Greece. Success in Long Acre has led to the Café du Jardin and a chic and expensive champagne bar and restaurant in the city, Le Champenois, which adheres to the new city formula, self-serving architectural detail and green peppercorns with the stockbroker's sirloin steak. Convincing French food is served here but its popularity can make the experience of eating it less than sublime. A modern menu, e.g. dishes like feuilleté with wild mushrooms, marinated raw fish dotted with pink and green peppercorns, a sausage of chicken served with Roquefort sauce among the first courses, escalope of chicken with crayfish and magret de canard in the main courses, is enhanced by plats du jour which include fish dishes that can be as enterprising as red mullet, bass and carp poached in wine and served cold, and grilled John Dory topped with a crab gratin made crunchy with sesame seeds. Vegetables and salads are priced separately. The pat on the back for Magno's is for their pre-theatre menu served between 6 and 7.30 pm which includes two interesting courses, glass of wine and coffee. They want the table back by 8 pm, however, so it's as well to have some entertainment, public or private, planned for afterwards.

CUISINE: French	
OPEN: L: Mon to Fri; D: Mon to Sat	
MEALS: 12 to 2.30; 6 to 11.30	
CLOSED: Bank Holidays	
AVERAGE PRICE: £22. Set Menu: Pre-theatre: £7.45	
CREDIT CARDS: Access, Amex, Visa, Diners	
SEATS: 50	

MALABAR

27 Uxbridge Street, W8
01-727 800

This is unlike most other medium price Indian restaurants in several ways: the location in a particularly twee part of Notting Hill Gate (or Campden Hill to stretch a point, which I am sure residents would want me to), the decor which is pleasant but plain and the dishes that are an attempt to produce real Indian food which is home-cooked food. I have been twice to eat at Malabar and both times ended up choosing more or less the same dishes: the devilled chicken livers cooked with yoghurt, the sliced venison marinated in tamarind (in season), the fish curry which is only available on Fridays, and the kayla foogath, green banana cooked with spices and ginger, which loses its point if the banana is not green which it wasn't the last time I tried it. Vegetables, on the whole, are enterprising: e.g. the barbecued aubergine and the marrow fried in butter and herbs. The tandoori oven is put to good effect with the Malabar king prawns and the lamb tikka. In the main courses the selection is sensibly limited and I am tempted by the gosht masala, lamb in a creamy sauce spiked with mint, and the stick prawns cooked on a skewer and served with a lemon sauce. Rice is basmati which is as it should be, and breads are well made. For dessert try mango fool or kulfi, the ice cream made with reduced-down milk, almonds and pistachio nuts. Drink lassi or a combative wine like one from Alsace. Service is pleasant, if harried. Malabar is rightly popular, so make sure to book.

CUISINE: Indian	Also vegetarian dishes

OPEN: Mon to Sun

MEALS: 12 to 3; 6.30 to 11.30

CLOSED: 4 days at Christmas

AVERAGE PRICE: £13. Set Menus: £17 for two (Mon to Sat); Vegetarian thali: £8; Sun lunch buffet: £4.75

CREDIT CARDS: Access, Visa

SEATS: 54

MUSIC: Piped if requested

THE MANDALAY

100 Greenwich South Street, SE10
01-691 0443

Before getting frightfully excited about visiting what the owners say is the only Burmese restaurant in Britain, note that they are only open on three evenings. This is because Gerald Andrews (evidently Burmese despite the name) is a freelance quantity surveyor and Suzy Andrews teaches PE. On these three evenings however they are keen to pass on their enthusiasm for Burmese food, which is not dissimilar to Thai cuisine though the curries tend to be dry-cooked, depending on a soupy accompaniment (hincho), based on either tomato, potato or marrow as sauce for them and the rice. The first courses give you a chance to sample in limited quantity some of the main dishes. Gravy kow suar are noodles in a delicate chicken-based sauce, creamy with coconut and topped with what seemed like crushed prawn crackers. Bhudi jow is marrow or courgette deep-fried in batter and served with a chilli and garlic dip. Sebaur, the traditional Burmese curry, refers to a particular blend of spices and a garnish of onions and tomatoes. Applied to prawns, as I tried it, it was good. Food is cooked to order so service can be slow. The dining room is the ground floor and basement of the Andrews' house. Once you decide to go with the family-run feeling, you are in for a rewarding, albeit slightly precious, evening.

CUISINE: Burmese	Also vegetarian dishes

OPEN: D only: Thurs, Fri, Sat
MEALS: 7.30 to 10.15
CLOSED: 2 weeks at Christmas and 1 week at Easter
AVERAGE PRICE: £14
CREDIT CARDS: Access, Visa
SEATS: 32

♥ # MANZI'S

1–2 Leicester Street, WC2
01-734 0224

This is one of my favourite restaurants and I wish there were more like it. It is a functional, jolly place in an area better known for the tatty or the tawdry. There is an oyster bar running down one side of the ground-floor room (the only room to be in). A straightforward and fairly priced menu of fish dishes is served at tables covered in gingham cloths. The simpler dishes such as skate or grilled plaice or sole are probably the best bet though I have enjoyed the hot eels and the mussels. Waiters are brisk and efficient and if you have the foresight to book, the hours make it a sound choice for after the movies or theatre. Manzi's is family run and is part of an hotel about which I have always

144

entertained fantasies of lost weekends, or anyway fishy ones.

CUISINE: Fish	
OPEN: L: Mon to Sat; D: Mon to Sun	
MEALS: 12 to 2.40; 5.30 to 11.40 (Sun till 10.40)	
CLOSED: Bank Holidays	
AVERAGE PRICE: £18	
CREDIT CARDS: Access, Amex, Visa, Diners	
SEATS: 125	

MARTIN'S

88 Ifield Road, SW10
01-352 5641

John Armstrong is the chef at this peachy little restaurant favoured by the richer residents of South Kensington/Chelsea. His cooking in the modern style is sound, even sometimes surprisingly good as when, lulled into slightly bored passivity by the mention of dishes like croustade d'oeufs de caille Maintenon, tresse de saumon et turbot aux St Jacques (ever since watching a chef laboriously plaiting and re-plaiting strips of fish and then hardly cooking them at all I have been off this dish) and magret de canard aux herbes de Provence, I was surprised and delighted by the liveliness of flavour in the dish of the day, timbale of crab. A warm chicken mousse enclosed large pieces of crab and the sauce set off the marriage perfectly. However the same meal also delivered a widgeon too undercooked for even the most ardent follower of nouvelle cuisine and dotted with pine kernels that just seemed irritating. The owner Martin Caldicott has worked in the wine trade and the list is worthwhile but zealously marked up. One reason for this, Caldicott confided, is that it is hard to make profitable a small restaurant open only in the evenings. Indeed he was looking for new larger premises and whither he goes I imagine John Armstrong, who is a partner, goes too. He is a chef worth following.

CUISINE: French	
OPEN: D only: Mon to Sat	
MEALS: 7 to 11	
AVERAGE PRICE: £27. Set Menus: £15.50 (2 courses) and £18.50	
CREDIT CARDS: Access, Amex, Visa	
SEATS: 34	
TABLES OUTSIDE: (4)	

MAXIM

155 Northfield Avenue, W13
01-567 1719

This is a smart and ambitious Peking restaurant where you might not expect to find it, though the approach via Ealing seems well paved with Chinese restaurants. It is a mother and son operation with Mrs Chow in charge of the kitchen. Occasions like Christmas and New Year's Eve inspire them to create special menus and it is always possible to order in advance a hot-pot meal – very reviving in winter – or a Peking duck, properly air-dried and roasted as opposed to fried. The menu, sensibly I suppose, is in the main a list of the dishes familiar to and appreciated by Westerners, but Mrs Chow after a visit to her mother in China a few years ago did lash out with some scallops cooked in sake and frogs' legs Chinese style – a fitting dish since China is from where they are often imported these days. Unless you live in Hanwell or Ealing, Maxim might be quite a drive and because they seem to prefer that you do, it is wise to book. Tony Chow (the son) can claim to

have opened the first Chinese wine bar, Maxim Wine Bar, 7 Boston Parade, W7 (01-567 9708) and by the time you read this has probably followed it with Maxim Wine Bar, Knights Arcade, 143 Knightsbridge, SW1.

CUISINE: Peking	*Also vegetarian dishes*

OPEN: L: Mon to Sat; D: Mon to Sun

MEALS: 12 to 2.30; 6.30 to 12 (Fri and Sat till 12.30)

AVERAGE PRICE: £11. Set Menus: £6 (lunch) and £13 (dinner)

CREDIT CARDS: Access, Amex, Visa, Diners

SEATS: 150

PRIVATE ROOM: (30–35)

MUSIC: Piped, traditional Chinese

MAXIM'S DE PARIS

32 Panton Street, SW1
01-839 4809

This seems worth mentioning as a phenomenon. Now we have designer labels, in this case Pierre Cardin, stuck on to restaurants, in this case the much vamped-up premises of what used to be Stone's Chop House. The expensive food is usually creditably made and the service can, at times, flatter the word formal, but in my view if you want to eat at Maxim's it is in Paris in the rue Royale. Reasons to use the London premises: one, the private room for parties; two, from 5.30 pm for a drink and a *bonne bouche* in the bar.

CUISINE: French	*Also vegetarian dishes*

OPEN: L: Mon to Fri; D: Mon to Sat	
MEALS: 12 to 2.45; 6 to 11.45	
AVERAGE PRICE: £40. Set Menu £17.50 (lunch and 6–7.30)	
CREDIT CARDS: Access, Amex, Visa, Diners	
SEATS: 120	
PRIVATE ROOMS: Four (10–180)	
MUSIC: French, 9.30 to 1 am	
DANCING	

LE MAZARIN

30 Winchester Street, SW1
01-828 3366

Chef René Bajard was formerly head chef at the three-star Michelin Le Gavroche (*q.v.*) and the brothers Roux have backed him in this enterprise. The premises were previously Tapas. Snicky-snacky dishes of various nationalities were served and the cellar-like premises that seemed to be all corridors and no rooms were not unsuitable. Alas, now even despite a second attempt at interior decoration that has replaced slime green walls with pink and the stag-at-bay prints with Ronald Searle cartoons, the effect remains bargain-basement haute cuisine. Excellent, reasonably priced food – which is what you get – would not jar anywhere but the style of service – showing each order before it is served, handing customers the napkins between a silver spoon and fork, just seems absurd and irritating. However, so good is the deal that customers seem happy to bear a high noise level and the palpable toing and froing of waiting staff, some of it seemingly purposeless. The set menu which changes every evening is £15.50 and includes three courses, tax and service. There are house wines at £3.70 a half, making a meal for one £19.20 inclusive. M. Bajard seems happiest cooking meat dishes and a first course I tried recently of poulet fermier au basilic would have sat more happily in the main course position. However, the mousseline de canard au porto was sublime; a classically good dish. The use of herbs is emphatic and done to good effect with the noisettes d'agneau à l'estragon and to a slightly less extent in the magret de canard rôti au thym. There are always fish dishes and I remember at an early test meal a good rendition of that nouvelle cuisine classic, escalope of salmon with sorrel. The vegetable garnish, understandably given the intricacy of the meal otherwise, tends to be standard and often an easily pre-prepared timbale. Desserts are beautifully made as are the little extras such as the *amuse-gueules* before the meal and the petits fours with coffee. In addition to the daily menu there is a five-course no-choice Menu Gastronomique for £22.50 where you might be inclined to stray from the sound house wines, a Muscadet and a Brouilly, on to the list of expensive relatively young burgundies and clarets. To see and to savour what an inspired and classically trained French chef can do without paying through the nose, try Le Mazarin.

CUISINE: *French*

OPEN: *D only: Mon to Sat*

MEALS: *7 to 11.30*

Set Menus: *£15.50 and £22.50*

CREDIT CARDS: *Amex, Diners*

SEATS: *45*

♥ # MELANGE

59 Endell Street, WC2
01-240 8077

In London this comes nearest to the sort of place where in other cities, like Paris and Amsterdam, students would hang out. Indeed the proprietors, Freddie and Raksha Zuidjik, with between them degrees in Art, Economics, Catering and Hotel Management, have lived in Amsterdam, Paris, Switzerland (accounting for the hotel management no doubt) and London. The name is an apposite one both for the food and the decor which is fairly amateur 'paint magic' with examples of stippling, scumbling, rag-rolling, dragging and every other kind of louche behaviour applied to covering a wall or chair. Lacing and jibbing, where canvas is concerned, is also in evidence. The food is inventive in an untidy way and good value. It ranges from nouvelle combinations using exotic fruits, through Japanese influence to prosaic dishes like sausages and mash. The more formal dining room is upstairs. Downstairs they are happy for you to snack. The service is usually charming and diverting in appearance. It is one of the more heart-warming places in Covent Garden.

CUISINE: Eclectic	Also vegetarian dishes
OPEN: L: Tues to Fri; D: Tues to Sat	
MEALS: 12 to 2.30; 6 to 11.30	
CLOSED: 2 weeks at Christmas	
AVERAGE PRICE: £15	
CREDIT CARDS: Access, Amex, Visa, Diners	
SEATS: 40	
PRIVATE ROOM: (23–30)	
MUSIC: Piped jazz	

MENAGE A TROIS

15 Beauchamp Place, SW3
01-589 4252

Chef Anthony Worrall-Thompson gets on some people's nerves. Convinced of his own brilliance he darts round the world from Bombay to Sydney to Phoenix, Arizona promoting Ménage à Trois and his own concept of a meal which, to use his less than felicitous phrasing, is composed of starters and puddings – 'no inter-course'. This idea came to him when he noticed his girlfriends, ever dieting, would order two first courses and then having been so restrained indulge in a sybaritic pudding. Detractors of the system – usually men – say that all it means is that you end up paying main course prices for a scaled-down dish, but although they are not cheap, assemblies like a julienne of duck magret with duck foie gras and oyster parcels served with a truffle vinaigrette, and a ragout of scallops and lobster cooked with dill in dry vermouth and courgettes, asparagus and tomato on a spinach bed are not skimpy in terms of quantity or value, given the produce. In fact the formula could be said to be a game of eenie, meenie, minie mo with luxury ingredients and when combinations like breast of wood pigeon with snails and wild mushrooms and lardons and croûtons and a confit of garlic seem too chaotic, it is tempting to opt for the vegetarian creations. The menu is long, divided into raw, cold, warm and hot dishes, traditional first courses, fish and shellfish, meat, poultry and game, salades tièdes and hot and cold puddings. I admire what Tony Worrall-Thompson is doing which seems to me to be injecting fun and glamour into haute cuisine, but perhaps more importantly I have also seen and tasted evidence of highly skilled cooking, more often no doubt from chef David Wilby than Himself. The surroundings are pretty, the waitresses are pretty and on the whole the customers are pretty. It is more a women's restaurant; men's bottoms seem to spill uncomfortably over the edges of the seats. The wines have been bought with the same eye to no-expense-spared-for-quality as the food ingredients. I am a firm believer in the relationship of energy to success and Mr W-T has plenty of the former, enough of the latter and a kind heart to boot.

CUISINE: Eclectic	*Also vegetarian dishes*
OPEN: Mon to Sat	
MEALS: 11.30 to 3; 7 to 12.15	
AVERAGE PRICE: £22	
CREDIT CARDS: Access, Amex, Visa, Diners	
SEATS: 76	
MUSIC: Pianist	

LE METRO

28 Basil Street, SW3
01-589 6286

Opened by the next door Capital Hotel (*q.v.*) Le Métro is the very model of a wine bar. It opens for breakfast every day, a meal that can usefully punctuate Knightsbridge shopping. At meal times they serve good pâtés or perhaps a home-made brawn with salad, fish terrines, salades composées, for example one with sautéed chicken livers, marinated tuna, skate au beurre noir, blanquette de veau (a dish I love) just to name a few choices from the changing menu. A Cruover machine dispenses fine wines by the glass though the selection is less noble than at the start. A glass of vintage red can be accompanied by some well-chosen cheeses. There are advantages to a place such as this that relies on the buying power of a classy hotel with an energetic and ambitious chef and at Le Métro the customers reap the rewards. I am all for their policy of not accepting bookings at lunchtimes. The svelte manageress deals nimbly with queues.

CUISINE: wine bar French	
OPEN: B: Mon to Sun; L: Mon to Sat; D: Mon to Fri	
MEALS: 7.30–2.45 (Sat till 2.30, Sun 8–11); 5.30–10.15	
AVERAGE PRICE: £14	
CREDIT CARDS: Amex	
SEATS: 56	

MINAR

323 King Street, W6
01-741 2380

In the Little India that is King Street – except that in India you wouldn't find so many restaurants in the whole of Bombay – Minar stands out with its cool restrained architect-designed interior and its well set out menu. After returning from a gastronomic trip to India in the company of some Michelin-starred

French chefs (who remained resolutely unimpressed), I visited Minar determined to allow Indian breads the role they are properly accorded: where we might nibble tentatively on one naan, Indians will put away several kinds of bread including a handful of chapatis during a meal. As well as rotis and naans, plain or stuffed, Minar also offers the delicious paratha lachedar, a particularly light wheat bread, layered and slightly salted with butter, and kulcha, a leavened bread stuffed with onions, potatoes, egg and fresh coriander. Ace among the first courses is the Punjabi dish of spiced chick peas and potatoes that they call channa chatpati. The onion bhaji that I tried seemed freshly made, not knitted from a mix as can be the case these days. The tandoori cooking includes fish (trout) but the dishes I have tried, on the grounds that they must be those of which they are proudest, were from the list headed Specialities of Minar. The slightly sour murg jalfarezi – chicken marinated in lemon juice and vinegar before cooking – was good. The navratan kofta, a dish of fried grated marrow, rather spongy and disappointing. Vegetables are well attended to. Desserts include a home-made kulfi, an ice-cream made by emphatically reducing milk and flavouring it with almonds and pistachios, and ras malai, curd cheese balls flavoured with cardamom, soaked in condensed milk – you have to be rather childish to like Indian sweets. Fresh mango in season is an alternative. Friends whom I have pointed in the direction of Minar have been contented; I think you will be.

CUISINE: Punjabi/Indian	*Also vegetarian dishes*
OPEN: L: Mon to Sat; D: Mon to Sun	
MEALS: 12 to 2.45; 6 to 11.45 (Sun till 11)	
AVERAGE PRICE: £18	
CREDIT CARDS: Access, Amex, Visa, Diners	
SEATS: 38	

♥ # MON PLAISIR

21 Monmouth Street, WC2
01-836 7243

About eighteen years ago when I was walking out with the chap I subsequently married, it was to Mon Plaisir he would very occasionally take me – the style, proper French bistro and the restrained prices just about justified, in his mind, not eating at home. In those days Mon Plaisir was owned by the Viala family who ran it with a delightful simplicity and rare authenticity. Alain Lhermitte who now owns Mon Plaisir has had the sense to change little in the way of decor beyond expanding into a back room which has a fireplace. The fly-blown posters on the walls and the dusty-looking plants in the window remain. Plats du jour are displayed on a blackboard and the strengths of the menu, namely the steak-frites, the cheeseboard with properly dressed salads and the casserole dishes, are also consistent. There is a real French feel, underlined, sometimes quite aggressively, by the service. The wines complement the menu in that they are adequate, not wildly ambitious. If you fail to get a table at Mon Plaisir – the popularity of the place has never flagged – a former member of staff has opened round the corner a not at all dissimilar restaurant: Mon Marché, 63 Endell Street, WC2 (01-836 2320).

CUISINE: French   *Also vegetarian dishes*

OPEN: L: Mon to Fri; D: Mon to Sat

MEALS: 12 to 2.15; 6 to 11.15

AVERAGE PRICE: £17. Set Menu: £7 (lunch)

CREDIT CARDS: None

SEATS: 55

PRIVATE ROOM: (26)

MUSIC: Piped French

MONSIEUR THOMPSON'S

29 Kensington Park Road, W11
01-727 9957

The owner Dominique Rocher is a great prosely-
tizer (naturally enough) for his restaurant and
he had the grace recently to admit to charging
rather too enthusiastically for the food and wines.
Perhaps he saw a kind of drift across the road to 192
(*q.v.*). There are now set-price menus which make a
meal in this attractive restaurant more of a proposition,
particularly if you use it as a neighbourhood bistro
which was its original strength. Regulars included
writers Lady Antonia Fraser, Emma Tennant and
Philip Roth. Chef Aram Atanasyan originally trained
at the Crillon in Paris and the style of the cooking is
modern French. Thus walnut oil might dress first
course salads and salmon trout and mackerel be served
raw but marinated and enlivened with fresh coriander.
There are more robust choices too, e.g. a pistou aux
crustaces, using the provençal flavourings of basil,
garlic and pine nuts with shellfish. Among the fish
dishes on an autumn menu is the tempting sounding
couscous de la mer served with a sharp sauce rouille.
Children or the childlike who hate to be tricked by
unexpected ingredients will appreciate the menu style
at Monsieur Thompson's which spells out the detail of
the garnish for each dish, as in: fan of roast Barbary
duck in a light caramelized sauce, *Garnish:* chicory and
tomato and courgette gratin; saddle of best English
lamb with a slightly peppered sauce bound with red-
currant jelly, *Garnish:* shredded Savoy cabbage, bacon
and baby onion. A gratin dauphinois also accompanies
all meat dishes. Desserts are keyed to the seasons and a
meal taken from the dishes described above might be

completed by a roast almond cake flavoured with rum or a gratin of pears accompanied by a sorbet flavoured with Poire William. The wine list offers a wide choice but does not connive with the set-price menus to keep the bill in check. I like Monsieur Thompson's. There is the crackle of romance in the air.

CUISINE: French	*Also vegetarian dishes*
OPEN: Mon to Sat	
MEALS: 12.30 to 2.30; 7.30 to 10.30	
AVERAGE PRICE: £22. Set Menus: £8 and £10 (lunch); £13 (dinner)	
CREDIT CARDS: Access, Amex, Visa, Diners	
SEATS: 55	
TABLES OUTSIDE: (10)	
PRIVATE ROOM: (40)	

MR KAI OF RUSSELL SQUARE

50 Woburn Place, WC1
01-580 1188

There are now three restaurants under this ownership whose trademarks are aggressively smart service (much of it from no-nonsense ladies in cheongsams), elegant decor and daft names for the dishes. Under the heading The Culinary Art of Mr Kai, it says on the menu 'We invite you to join Mr Kai on his gastronomic travels in the footsteps of Kai Lung, selecting dishes from our menu to suit your mood as the philosopher chose tales from his wallet to suit the occasion.' The credit card from your wallet will have tales to tell after a meal in any one of the restaurants but if you can swallow facts like The Encirclement of the Surprised Piglet means dumplings stuffed with minced pork and that The Career of the Charitable Quen-Ki-Tong, First Period, refers to dishes based on bean curd, then you are in for, at least, a competently cooked meal and at best a meal demonstrating sophisticated skills applied to good quality raw materials. The Distress of the Abandoned Prawn and suchlike nonsense more or less fades out after the first courses and the main courses are easy to interpret, though the phrase 'price variable' should be checked out before embarking on the more interesting Recommended Specialities such as the steamed winter melon and the braised shark's fin. Although under the subtitle The Refreshment of the Abstainer they maintain that they are happy for you to follow the Chinese custom and drink tea throughout the meal the staff are in fact much cheered if you drink several bottles of wine and will pour assiduously to encourage you to do so. I find this branch of Mr Kai the most sympathetic, the least geared to business entertaining. The other branches are Mr Kai of Mayfair, 65 South Audley Street, W1 (01-493 8988) and Tang Dynasty, 19 New Cavendish Street, W1 (01-935 3570).

CUISINE: Peking	*Also vegetarian dishes*
OPEN: Mon to Sun	
MEALS: 12 to 2.30; 6.30 to 11.30	
CLOSED: Bank Holidays	
AVERAGE PRICE: £20. Set Menus: £8, £12 and £15	
CREDIT CARDS: Access, Amex, Visa, Diners	
SEATS: 150	
PRIVATE ROOMS: Three (10–24)	

MR KONG

21 Lisle Street, WC2
01-437 7341

I n terms of its style, ambitiousness and, indeed, many of its specialities, Mr Kong can be compared to Fung Shing (*q.v.*), so much so that there was a story, no doubt a fib, going round that said that the same chef alternated between the two kitchens. With space on three floors there is more chance of getting a table at short notice at Mr Kong. Once installed, address yourself to the list of specialities, because they are the most interesting but also because the long laminated list of Peking and Cantonese dishes might baffle you into the suggested set menus which would be a pity. Some dishes I have particularly liked are the satay eels – fillets of eel threaded on to a wooden skewer and cooked over charcoal, sautéed venison with ginger wine, stuffed dry bean curd skin with steamed stuffed prime vegetable (practically a meal in itself), the casserole of stewed duck with yam, and the rather spectacular sautéed scallop and king prawns Szechuan style in 'bird's nest'. There are other rather more commonly found assemblies such as the fried mussels with chilli and black bean sauce and the minced quail and oyster served with lettuce leaves. Nouvelle touches, such as lychee with chicken and mango with fillet steak, probably work (I have not tried them) but avoid the ultimate daring for Chinese, their flirtation with creamy sauces; for thousands of years they have been right to avoid dairy products in their food. Go to Mr Kong in a spirit of adventurousness – I leave it to you to discover what is the last of the miscellaneous dishes, boiled geoduck.

CUISINE: Chinese	*Also vegetarian dishes*
OPEN: Mon to Sun	
MEALS: 12 to 1.45 am	
CLOSED: Christmas	
AVERAGE PRICE: £13. Set Menus: £5.50–10.50	
CREDIT CARDS: Access, Amex, Visa, Diners	
SEATS: 130	
PRIVATE ROOM: (50)	
MUSIC: Piped	

MUMTAZ

4–10 Park Road, NW1
01-723 0549

This qualifies for the title of the prettiest Indian restaurant in London (although I prefer the style of the Bombay Brasserie) and the food can be extremely good, but the service is offhand and the last time I reviewed Mumtaz in the paper I concluded by saying, 'every breath you take, every move you make they'll be charging you' so hefty seemed the bill, so larded with high prices for breads, rice, vegetables etc. Ram, the owner (he who started selling cheesecloth Indian shirts and went on to open and close Régine's nightclub in what was Derry & Tom's) naturally took exception but readers of *The London Standard* have written of similar experiences. I leave it, then, as a warning, but would encourage you to try the specialities, particularly raan, a spiced and roasted piece of lamb on the bone, and the murgh massallam. Louise Nicholson, who wrote the consummate guide to India, *India in Luxury*, rates the Mumtaz.

CUISINE: Indian	*Also vegetarian dishes*
OPEN: Mon to Sun	
MEALS: 12 to 3; 6 to 11.30	
AVERAGE PRICE: £17. Set Menu: Sun lunch buffet: £9.75 (£6.75 for under-12s)	
CREDIT CARDS: Access, Amex, Visa, Diners	
SEATS: 100	

LE MUSCADET

25 Paddington Street, W1
01-935 2883

I first went to Le Muscadet, owned by François Bessonnard who once had a well-padded French restaurant in Kensington called Le Bressan, after seeing the film *La Balance*. All French movies make me want to rush to a café or brasserie and although the Belleville setting of that cop flick might have required couscous to follow, our dinner of French bourgeois food completed the evening perfectly. Herrings with potatoes in an oily dressing, boudin noir with a tart purée of apples, blanquette de veau and cassoulet are typical dishes (all of those well done when I tried them). The blackboard gives plats du jour. Details such as the cheeses from Philippe Olivier in Boulogne and sorbets from Madame Yvonne Troutot, ace sorbet maker, make a satisfactory meal all the more so.

CUISINE: *Traditional French*	*Also vegetarian dishes*

OPEN: *L: Mon to Fri; D: Mon to Sat*

MEALS: *12.15 to 3; 7.15 to 11 (Sat till 10.30)*

CLOSED: *Bank Holidays, 3 weeks in August and 2 weeks at Christmas*

AVERAGE PRICE: *£15*

CREDIT CARDS: *Access, Visa*

SEATS: *30*

MUSIC: *Piped*

NAYAB

9 Park Walk, SW10
01-352 2137

Park Walk – considerably easier to walk to than park in – sees restaurants come and go and the basement of No 9 has housed a few recently. It is hoped that Nayab is a stayer as it is a cut above most Indian restaurants for the freshness of the food and the pleasantness of approach; ready and willing to serve every day with last orders at midnight. They make use of fresh herbs in the sauces such as the one that coats the chicken green masala and when I last ate there both the breads and the vegetables – I chose a dish of tiny perky bhindi – were well made. The decor is cool. No longer must customers watch the flocks by night.

CUISINE: *Indian*	*Also vegetarian dishes*

OPEN: *Mon to Sun*

MEALS: *12 to 3; 6 to 12*

CLOSED: *Bank Holidays*

AVERAGE PRICE: *£13*

CREDIT CARDS: *Access, Amex, Visa, Diners*

SEATS: *46*

NEAL STREET RESTAURANT

26 Neal Street, WC2
01-836 8368

Antonio Carlucci who is married to Priscilla Conran, the sister of the owner Sir Terence Conran (*q.v.*), is passionate about food and he is the manager of the Neal Street Restaurant. His passion, which in part takes the shape of acquiring interesting raw materials such as forest mushrooms or white truffles from Piedmont, somehow seems to get filtered by the menu which changes only occasionally and in part. I am all for doing just a few things and doing them well but it seems to bore the chef, Santiago Gonzales. I was disappointed by the game ravioli which others have enthused about but, on the other hand, a simple grilled calf's kidney was absolutely delicious. There are studiously down-to-earth dishes like steak and kidney pie, more modern ones like duck breast with mango and always game in season. I think there is supposed to be some statement here about English food being good when good ingredients are not mucked about, but too often the high bill seems out of kilter with the concept. The surroundings are well designed as you might expect and there are good pictures supplied by the art dealer Kasmin. Neal Street is a restaurant for the rich who won't mind paying more for what others expect for less. This applies also to the wine list which has some interesting bottles if it's an expense account talking. After the theatre and opera the Neal Restaurant is lively with stylish clientele.

CUISINE: International	*Also vegetarian dishes*
OPEN: Mon to Fri	
MEALS: 12.30 to 2.30; 7.30 to 11	
AVERAGE PRICE: £27	
CREDIT CARDS: Access, Amex, Visa, Diners	
SEATS: 65	

Neal's Yard

In a small complex with entrances off Monmouth Street and Short's Gardens, there is a bakery, dairy, grocery shop, fruit shop and coffee shop. The bakery produces, to my mind, the best wholemeal bread in London as well as various other loaves including a delicious cheese and herb bread – sensational when sliced and toasted. You can buy rolls, sandwiches, quiches, pizzas and sweet baked goods to take away or to eat in the small tea shop upstairs. This connects with the coffee shop (entrance in Monmouth Street). The dairy sells British farmhouse cheeses as well as yoghurts and crème fraîche. The grocery is champion for when you want to stock up on grains, pulses, honey, peanut butter, nuts, oils, dried fruits, herbs and spices, teas and various other commodities. It is, in a sense, bulk buying but the quantities packaged are not swamping. The crowd who mill about in the yard are usually a refreshing antidote to the chi-chi of Covent Garden.

NEW RASA SAYANG

3 Leicester Place, WC2
01-437 4556

Terry Tan who comes from Singapore oversees this group of Malaysian restaurants (see below for other branches) and he has been quoted in interviews as being passionate about the authenticity of food, the need for the correct ingredients and spicing, rather than banking on the quite likely fact that the British will not know the difference between the real thing and a muddle of disparate influences. The Rasa Sayang restaurants are efficiently run and each has its own charm – this one off Leicester Square providing a welcome surreal sort of decor that puts the milling crowds and sleazy-movie cinemas outside your ken. The distinguishing flavours of the food are coconut, peanut, lemon grass, chilli, tamarind and turmeric. At the weekends, which is when it is available, I would advise trying the Hainanese chicken rice which is a more interesting and subtle dish than the name implies. Other times likeable assembles are the lumpia (a form of spring roll), the satay of course, the char kway teow based on broad, floppy rice noodles, ayam perchik, grilled chicken in a spicy coconut sauce, one of the fish curries and the laksa, a coconut soup with rice noodles. If the long choice is daunting, the set menus are imaginatively composed. There are tones of Lee Kuan Yew's Singapore in the didacticism of the menu: 'Patrons kindly take note, all bookings which are a quarter of an hour before last orders will have to have a starter and a main course together', but on the whole these are worthy restaurants and good value. The Rasa Sayang, 10 Frith Street, W1 (01-734 8720) has relatively chic decor and disco. The Rasa Sayang West, 168 Sussex Gardens, Lancaster Gate, W2 (01-402 9142), the newest branch, usually has Mr Tan on hand which bodes well for the food.

CUISINE: Malaysian   *Also vegetarian dishes*

OPEN: Mon to Sun

MEALS: 12 to 3; 6 10.45 (Sat 12 to 11.45, Sun 12 to 10.15)

CLOSED:	Bank Holidays and Christmas
AVERAGE PRICE:	£11. Set Menus: £4.95 (lunch); £24.90 (dinner for two inc. wine)
CREDIT CARDS:	Amex, Visa, Diners
SEATS:	80
PRIVATE ROOM:	(30)
MUSIC:	Piped

NIKITA'S

65 Ifield Road, SW10
01-352 6326

I include Nikita's in part out of sentimentality. It was opened by the late Nick Clarke who helped to change the face of restaurant eating when he opened Nick's Diner (now Martin's *q.v.*) in the early Sixties. Nikita's was first called The Place Opposite but it never took off in the same way as the Diner and the involvement of Shura Shiwarg and the chef from Chez Luba being on the loose led on to the Russian theme and the name Nikita's. Denis Ryan, one of the current owners, was around during the heyday of the Diner (I used to moonlight there as a cashier at the age of about 19) and now Nikita's is, I think, the only Russian-style restaurant in London. What the restaurant is good for, and good at, is celebrations – when the bottles of vodka plain or flavoured sunk into a block of ice come into their own and the blinis with marinated salmon, or smoked sturgeon or caviar and the garnishes of soured cream, melted butter, onion and chopped egg seem festive. The cooking of the main courses is variable and the dishes are only quasi-Russian, e.g. chicken Kiev, boeuf Stroganoff, steak tartare. The safest bet is probably the shashlik dramatically served on a sword and it is worth having the kasha (roasted buckwheat) for £1 extra rather than the vegetables for £2. The Bakst-inspired (very vaguely) decor has seen better days but then, thinking back to myself perched behind the desk at Nick's flirting with the manager, so have I. Since such services are not always easy to find, it is noteworthy that Nikita's offers a comprehensive outside catering service for events large and small, domestic or sporting. Ring 01-846 9637 (daytime) or 01-352 4018 (evening).

CUISINE: Russian	
OPEN: D only: Mon to Sat	
MEALS: 7.30 to 11.30	
CLOSED: Christmas and 1 week in August	
AVERAGE PRICE: £22	
CREDIT CARDS: Access, Amex, Visa, Diners	
SEATS: 50	
PRIVATE ROOM: (12)	
MUSIC: Taped Russian	

♥ # NOSHERIE

12 Greville Street, EC1
01-242 1591

I used to meet a diamond merchant for lunch at the Nosherie sometimes. He worked in nearby Hatton Garden. I loved watching him and his colleagues huddled in doorways showing each other their gems which they produced wrapped in pieces of paper, as if they were Beecham's Powders. I also liked the comforting non-Kosher Jewish food here served by, if not Yiddisher Mommas, at least Aunties. The salt beef was always my choice as a main course and it is particularly well done here. If you are in need of building up, the chicken soup with kreplach (filled dumplings) will do the trick and for the correct range of flavours have the latkes (potato pancakes) and tzimmes (sweetened carrots) as accompaniments to the main course and the lockshen pudding afterwards. The menu has many other choices: fried fish, gefilte fish, various wursts. The value is tremendous. It makes a refreshing change from other kinds of cuisine and the clientele will show you a slice of London business life quite different to other city gents eating – as opposed to noshing.

CUISINE: *Jewish*	*Also vegetarian dishes*
OPEN: *Mon to Fri*	
MEALS: *8 to 5*	
CLOSED: *Bank Holidays*	
AVERAGE PRICE: *£10*	
CREDIT CARDS: *None*	
SEATS: *80*	

ODETTE'S

130 Regent's Park Road, NW1
01-586 5486

Odette's has a woman chef and a woman owner which seems hardly worth mentioning except that it is odd that the restaurant should get such scant recognition in other food guides when the menu is appealing, the place stylish, the service extremely efficient, and the cooking, on the whole, careful and successful. It is in a pretty street which happens to be not far from where I live but it is not only proximity that makes me pro-Odette's. The menu is perhaps too static, though it changes in part seasonally, but there is enough choice and enough variety in influences that it would not pall unless you visited several times a week. The cost of a meal would make that unlikely, for although it has a neighbourhood feeling – and many regulars – these are serious prices. The soups are usually good (and a less expensive option). In winter I have enjoyed the ham, pea and parsley soup and in summer the cold cream of fennel. Gravad lax is popular both as a first course and a main course and they do well a dish I associate with jumped-up wine bars, deep-fried Camembert with a gooseberry preserve. Roast brill on the bone with oyster mushrooms I can recommend unreservedly. Stir-fried chicken with sake and spring onions is swamped by the flavour of soya sauce. Sweetbreads in leaf pastry and braised tongue with caper sauce are favourite dishes. The menu does not tail off lamely with the puddings. There are robust and scrumptious choices like the wet chocolate cake and the

166

brown bread ice-cream. The main dining room is decorated, disconcertingly, with mirrors in ornate gilded frames. The back room, which being a conservatory comes into its own in summer, has a peculiarly inept mural and some cheeky photographs. Downstairs there is a wine bar with much better than average food. Wines are good but no bargain. It was Jonathan Miller, an NW1 resident, who said that he thought of South of the Park as France and perhaps I slightly share his point of view in my espousal of Odette's but I think it compares favourably with a lot of the trendiness down Chelsea way.

CUISINE: Eclectic	Also vegetarian dishes

OPEN: L: Mon to Fri; D: Mon to Sat

MEALS: 12.30 to 2.30; 7.30 to 10.45

CLOSED: Bank Holidays

AVERAGE PRICE: £22

CREDIT CARDS: Access, Amex, Visa, Diners

SEATS: 50

♥ ODIN'S

27 Devonshire Street, W1
01-935 7296

To my mind this is one of the most romantic restaurants in London. As each year passes you appreciate more the glint of Peter Langan's eye where buying paintings is concerned. The warm browns of the walls and the soft, flattering lighting create a perfect environment in which to appreciate the pictures and, I trust, the human being opposite you. The menu cooked by English chef Chris German changes with every meal and although I find it can sometimes lack immediate appeal, i.e. few dishes that call out to be tried, what you choose invariably tastes rather more profoundly good than you expected. The first courses which may seem top heavy due to the fact that many of them are warm or encased in pastry, can be balanced by restrained main courses where the meat or fish is not swamped by sauce. I remember perfect lamb cutlets accompanied by a leek purée, cooked *à point* and served in exactly the right quantity. Though the cooking style is French it is tempered by a wholesome English influence; there is no froggy chi-chi. If I have lost you there something like the hot apple tart or Mrs Langan's chocolate pudding for dessert will clarify the thought. The wines are well chosen. To try Odin's, not exactly on a shoestring but economically, go for the set-price lunch and stay with the decent house wine. The fly in the ointment, despite a manageress built to turn on a sixpence, can be the service. Try to go on romance rather than on business and then the longueurs can be turned to your advantage.

CUISINE: *French*	*Vegetarian dishes on request*
OPEN: *L: Mon to Fri; D: Mon to Sat*	
MEALS: *12.30 to 2.30; 7 to 11.30*	
AVERAGE PRICE: *£33. Set Menu: £12.50 (lunch)*	
CREDIT CARDS: *Amex*	
SEATS: *60*	
PRIVATE ROOM: *(14)*	
Wheelchair Access	

OH BOY

843 Garratt Lane, SW17
01-947 9760

This curiously named restaurant is altogether something of an oddity – Thai cuisine with a French or anyway Western influence, lending the menu dishes like steak Diane which you don't have to go to a Thai restaurant or to Tooting to find. When I visited, which I have to admit was some years ago (but a chef friend of mine living in Wimbledon brings me good reports still), I liked the sudsakhon soup which was a mixture of fish and shellfish in a broth spiked with chilli and made fragrant with lemon grass. The selection of hot hors d'oeuvre included some delicate dumplings and also Wimbledon ball, the fish variety having enough bounce to outface Becker. The King and I is a mixture of steak, seafood and vegetables grilled on a special dish and served with various sauces. A dish I haven't tried but have read about is 'volcano poussin', the bird charcoal-grilled with garlic, chilli and tomato sauce and flamed with brandy at the table, evidently less showy than it sounds. A nice dessert is the coconut sorbet. The outside of the premises twinkles and inside the surroundings have charm with flowers and buds made from jewel-coloured silks and Thai figures stalking the walls. The service, too, is gracious. According to my research both the owner and the chef are women. The Mai-Thai room can be booked for parties in traditional style, i.e. sitting on cushions at low tables. A little more of the French influence would be welcome in the wine list.

CUISINE: *Thai*	*Also vegetarian dishes*
OPEN: *Mon to Sat*	
MEALS: *D only: 7 to 11*	
CLOSED: *Last two weeks in August*	
AVERAGE PRICE: *£13. Set Menu (in Mai-Thai room only): £12.50*	
CREDIT CARDS: *Access, Amex, Visa, Diners*	
SEATS: *28*	
PRIVATE ROOM: *(15)*	
MUSIC: *Piped Thai*	

OLD BUDAPEST

6 Greek Street, W1
01-437 2006

If you cannot get into the nearby Gay Hussar (*q.v.*) or you want a more discreet meeting place at lunchtime but still with a set-price Hungarian menu, this is the place. A former member of staff of Gay Hussar has opened it and apparently the chef he started with has now moved on to Molnars in the Finchley Road; rather *Hungarian* behaviour. Because I love things like smoked sausage in paprika with egg barley, red cabbage, lentils, jellied carp, pressed boar's head and smoked baked beans, I would recommend the Old Budapest for the lunch menu. Of course, if you go in the evening you get the cimbalom player. That is for when you are feeling racked with suppressed tears.

CUISINE: Hungarian	*Also vegetarian dishes*
OPEN: Mon to Sat	
MEALS: 12 to 2.30; 6 to 11.30	
AVERAGE PRICE: £22. Set Menu: £8 (lunch)	
CREDIT CARDS: Access, Amex, Visa	
SEATS: 50	
MUSIC: Cimbalom player in the evenings	

THE OLD RANGOON

201 Castelnau, Barnes, SW13
01-741 9656

'**D**uring the late 19th century, the British Empire spread throughout the world. Amidst the refreshing breeze of the palmetto fans and the romantic aroma of magnolia blossoms, the early colonialist would celebrate sunset with long cool planter's punches and delicious fresh meats cooked over an open charcoal fire. It is to the spirit of this way of life that we dedicate The Old Rangoon.' Thus begins the menu at this pub with a garden, the former Boileau converted by the aptly named Theme Restaurants Limited. That the sun does not always shine, even if it now sets, over this corner of the Empire tends to create a hiccup in the scheme and the fact that the preparation of Eastern-influenced snacks and dishes is less than sublime also could be said to detract, but it is just so heart-warming that someone is trying to do more than provide the minimum and also encouraging families to go out together, that I feel it deserves inclusion in any guide. In good weather they will give you a picnic hamper and a rug to sit on out in the large garden where rabbits hop and ducks paddle. Planning permission is being sought at present for a barbecue. On the terrace or inside where the decor is that current favourite of theme pubs, wickerwork chairs and potted palms and beige paint-work, you can order starters like satay, pakoras, deep-fried potato skins, samosas and mulligatawny soup. There are elaborate salads or grilled kebabs, steaks, chicken tikka and burgers. As well as ice-creams and sorbets there is a Bombay trifle containing sponge fingers, mango, ice cream and plum sauce. As I said, it is not done with great finesse. Because it is licensed for a pub, you may also just drink at The Old Rangoon and types hang out there who would cause apoplexy in colonial colonels. When you have children to divert, think about the afternoon tea served from 3.30 pm (4 pm on Sundays).

CUISINE:	*International/Colonial*
OPEN:	*Mon to Sun*
MEALS:	*12 to 11.30*
AVERAGE PRICE:	*£12*
CREDIT CARDS:	*Access, Amex, Visa, Diners*
SEATS:	*90*
TABLES OUTSIDE:	*(50)*
PRIVATE ROOM:	*Outdoor marquee (150)*
MUSIC:	*Piped*

♥ # L'OLIVIER

116 Finborough Road, SW10
01-370 4199

A room awash with Provence sunshine is not what you expect to find in a basement in Fin-borough Road but Pierre Martin, also the owner of La Croisette, Le Suquet and Le Quai St Pierre (see entries), has worked his magic again, this time centering the main courses on grilled meat and provid-ing the sort of spread you might be offered in res-taurants in the hills behind the Côte d'Azur. If you take the set menu, you are in for a feast. After a glass of kir, a little slice of tarte, some tiny fried fish, a large mixed plate of various hors d'oeuvre, salads and excellent

charcuterie are presented. This is followed by stuffed
vegetables (the thing to miss if you are treading carefully where your appetite is concerned) and either ravioli
or cannelloni. Finally, among the first courses, there is a
splendid soup au pistou. There is then a choice of roast
or grilled meats or fish or one of the plats du jour which
tend to be casseroles. Salad, cheese, dessert and coffee
follow. It is astonishing value and the sensation of the
food keeping rolling is a very festive one. Eating à la
carte I would start with scrambled eggs with truffles (a
rather dingy colour but a sublime flavour) and then
share a Barbary duck, côtes de boeuf, carré d'agneau or
poulet fermier. If you do not feel like ingesting chunks of
meat there are feuilletés with asparagus or sweetbreads, fresh noodles with truffles or langoustines or the
various salads garnished with marinated fish and foie
gras. However, it is easy eating à la carte to equal the
menu price with just a choice of two dishes. Provence
wines are the appropriate choice and I like the Estan-
don in white, red or rosé but there are more classy
bottles if you want to lash out. On the whole there is an
atmosphere of a good time being had by all in this room
decorated in sky blue and Brother Sun prints but there
have been complaints of high-handed service. It is
possible that if a waiter does not understand the customers because he speaks only two words of English, his
attitude will come across as unhelpful: speak loudly to
the chap and beat him when he sneezes.

CUISINE: French (Southern)

OPEN: *Mon to Sun*

MEALS: *12.30 to 2.30; 7.30 to 11.30*

AVERAGE PRICE: *£27. Set Menu: £20 (7 courses, inc. 5 starters, plus kir)*

CREDIT CARDS: *Amex, Visa*

SEATS: *60*

♥

192

192 Kensington Park Road, W11
01-229 0482

Opened by the team that gave you the Zanzibar Club (now tarred with the dull brush of Kennedy Brookes) and, more recently, the fashionable Groucho Club in Soho, this wine bar with a restaurant in the basement is consistently popular with an agreeably raffish clientele. The menu style was set by Alastair Little (*q.v.*) but now the daily changing list is handled by Angela Dwyer. The light touch remains, with tempting small dishes that strike you as exactly what you feel like eating, e.g. a warm tart of wild mushrooms, bresaola with virgin olive oil, a grilled goat's cheese with interesting salad leaves, seafood soup with shiitake mushrooms, lamb pinkly cooked, salt beef; modern food but not gussied-about food. At lunchtimes the menu invites minimalist eating – there is no division into courses as such. In the evenings rather more elaborate ordering would seem to be expected from you. Sunday lunch with its roasts is a nice occasion. The cheeseboard is magnificent and the puddings are proper homely ones. The wine list is enterprising and Ben Wordsworth, a partner and manager, cares. I am not a fan of the cramped downstairs room and would always try to get a table on the ground floor. 192, though it sometimes can be egregiously clubby in feel, is one of those places where they seem to respect the customer's needs.

CUISINE: *Eclectic*

OPEN: *L: Mon to Sun; D: Mon to Sat*

MEALS: 12.30 to 2.30 (Sun 1 to 3); 7.45 to 11.30	
AVERAGE PRICE: £14	
CREDIT CARDS: Access, Amex, Visa	
SEATS: 30 in restaurant; 25 in wine bar	
MUSIC: Piped	

ORSO

27 Wellington Street, WC2
01-240 5269

O rso is an offshoot of Joe Allen (*q.v.*) and is in fact part of the same basement premises but you would not realize this either upon entering the discreet doorway in Wellington Street nor once you are downstairs. Pastel tablecloths, white walls, framed photographs of former movie stars and lampshades apparently made from tin jelly moulds all add up to a deliberately non-style style but the waiters striking poses rather than taking your coat remind you that this opened in 1985. I have long been of the opinion that it would take a non-Italian to open an interesting Italian restaurant in London, so convinced are Mario and Pasquale and Dante and Piero *et al.* of our gullibility when it comes to their cuisine and their particular way of flaunting it. Orso does not quite bear me out but it does have some refreshing new menu departures like fried courgette flowers, a warm salad of spinach and new potatoes that is dressed with balsamic vinegar, proper use of offal like breaded calf's brains or sautéed sweetbreads, vegetables served at room temperature and dressed with oil and lemon juice, soft fruit accompanied by marscapone (a soft pungent cheese) and a wonderful garlic bread that is thin as a skin and dusted with parmesan. They also serve pizzas should you want to trim your bill, and you might well want to. Joe Allen shares a talent with Mark Birley (see entry) in knowing how to please. Touches like the pretty pottery plates – they must have a gem of a washer-up – do not go unappreciated. With the exception of Veuve Clicquot champagne, the wines are exclusively Italian and though sometimes interesting, always overpriced. Like

Joe Allen, Orso attracts a theatrical crowd, performers and spectators, but a more expensive bill sorts the stars from the chorus line.

CUISINE: Italian	*Also vegetarian dishes*
OPEN: Mon to Sun	
MEALS: 12 to 12	
CLOSED: Christmas Day and Boxing Day	
AVERAGE PRICE: £18	
CREDIT CARDS: None	
SEATS: 110	

PALMS PASTA ON THE PIAZZA

39 King Street, WC2
01-240 2939

PALMS PASTA ON THE HILL

3–5 Campden Hill Road, W8
01-938 1830

Both of these are useful lively places for a reasonably priced meal of pasta or one or two other dishes which have been assembled with thoughtfulness and care. The first courses include chicken teriyaki and bagna cauda, raw vegetables served with a warm dip flavoured with anchovies and walnuts. Salads, which can be served as a main course, include a prawn and avocado combination, salade niçoise, that cliché (now) of spinach leaves, mushrooms, bacon and avocado and a version of coronation chicken which they call chicken Indiana. There is spaghetti, fettucine and linguine done this way and that and with an uncooked sauce of tomatoes, celery, basil and garlic that I like, and various stuffed pastas. A dessert that follows on refreshingly is the fresh orange slices with lychees. Andrew Leeman who is the guiding light behind these restaurants is an energetic, canny soul with an eye for the details that count. (I must declare an involvement: if you visit Palms in Covent Garden during the school holidays you might find my eldest daughter Hannah working there.)

On the Piazza

CUISINE: American Italian	Also vegetarian dishes
OPEN: Mon to Sun	
MEALS: 12 to 11.30	
CLOSED: Christmas Day	
AVERAGE PRICE: £12	
CREDIT CARDS: Luncheon Vouchers only	
SEATS: 130	
MUSIC: Piped pop and jazz	

On the Hill

CUISINE: American Italian	Also vegetarian dishes
OPEN: Mon to Sun	
MEALS: 12 to 11.30	
HOLIDAY CLOSING: Christmas Day	
AVERAGE PRICE: £11	
CREDIT CARDS: None	
SEATS: 80	
TABLES OUTSIDE: (12)	
MUSIC: Sunday night jazz. Otherwise piped pop classics	

PAPPAGALLI'S PIZZA INC

7–9 Swallow Street, W1
01-734 5182

I am not a great fan of pizzas. I find dough covered with melted cheese sort of floors me, but I like the effort they make here, giving you the option of a wholemeal bread base if you wish and going in for less obvious portion control with the other ingredients than at some places. Apparently at the Pizza Express chain the manual stipulates one anchovy fillet only with the Pizza Napolitana. As a change from Chicago pizza, here they claim to be Sicilian in style in 'the true tradition of Mulberry Street, N.Y.', whatever that means. Gourmet pepperoni is my choice. They also serve pasta dishes with six sauces that include a clam sauce innocent of tomatoes, which is how clam sauce ought to be. The salad bar is imaginatively composed and a bowlful would precede a pizza more healthily than the garlic bread, chicken wings or baked mushrooms. Children are welcome. They provide booster seats and also colouring sets though I am for encouraging *conversation* as a meal time activity. Pappagalli's is well placed if you are shopping in the West End and has a merciful happy hour and a half from 5.30 pm.

CUISINE: Pizza	*Also vegetarian dishes*
OPEN: Mon to Sat	
MEALS: 12 to 3; 5.15 to 11.30 (Sat 12 to 11.30)	
AVERAGE PRICE: £11	
CREDIT CARDS: Access, Visa	
SEATS: 100	
MUSIC: Piped	

PAULO'S

30 Greyhound Road, W6
01-385 9264

The ground floor of the Torres' house provides the premises for this sympathetic, family-run Brazilian restaurant open only in the evenings, offering a self-service buffet featuring some typical dishes such as vatapa (a mixture of shrimps, fish, coconut milk, peanuts and palm oil), angu (a thick 'porridge' made from rice flour and coconut milk that is served with meat), feijoada, the dish of Rio which is somewhere between a soup and stew made with black beans and pork served with rice, cassava meal, a pepper sauce and sliced oranges, and caruru, a Bahian casserole of shrimps with okra, onions and peppers. The plainer dishes can be more tempting to the uninitiated – it has to be admitted that there is a 'done-up' quality to some of the specialities. Corn-on-the-cob, crab and roast chicken are all readily recognizable. Sometimes there is live music which is fun. For a long time Paulo's was unlicensed. Now they have a licence but are easy about you bringing your own wine and will not charge corkage. An evening here is unlike any other provided by London's restaurants.

CUISINE: Brazilian	*Also vegetarian dishes*
OPEN: D only: Mon to Sat	
MEALS: 6.30 to 11	
AVERAGE PRICE: £11. Set Menu: £6.20	
CREDIT CARDS: None	
SEATS: 52	
PRIVATE ROOM: (16)	

Bob Payton

Bob Payton is a large American from Chicago. He worked for a while in London at the advertising agency J. Walter Thompson and, presumably unhappy with that as well as the available pizzas in this town, he opened the first Chicago Pizza Pie Factory in Crown Passage, St James's in 1977. Success there – customers accustomed to a smear of tomato and cheese on a thin pastry base were astounded by the Chicago-style deep-dish pizza with its cushiony base and mass of filling and altogether overwhelming impact – led to a move to larger premises in Hanover Square. Thanks to Uncle Bob the words Chicago, deep-dish, deep-pan and titles for fast-food outlets with variations on the theme of factory, passed into catering vocabulary. His secret of success, as he tells it, is his attention to detail and tireless energy when seeking out sources, for example the perfect rib recipe (see entry for Chicago Rib Shack for the result). It does not always work, as his attempt to show the English a thing or two about fish at Payton Plaice in Charing Cross Road demonstrates. My theory is that he thought of that name and couldn't resist using it. There are branches of the pizzeria in Paris and Barcelona. Bob Payton likes to live the life of one of the landed gentry – he's come a long way from the windy city – and at the moment of writing is trying to raise finance for a country house hotel.

PEACHEY'S

205 Haverstock Hill, NW3
01-435 6744

I have an American friend who lives in SW3 who drives across London to eat here. This is a man who asked me if it was possible to fly to Reading when I mentioned a good restaurant near there (Chez Nico in Shinfield), so you see the fact has significance. I've always thought of Peachey's as a nice place to have up the road, but it is true that they do cook here with unusual care, and the willingness to be accommodating – even after a *very* long movie at the next door Screen on the Hill cinema – underlines the general approach. Dishes of the day enhance a printed menu from which I have had particularly good fish dishes including monkfish grilled on charcoal and served with a trio of sauces, and a good tart of mussels. I would avoid the dishes where they inject a zizzy oriental influence and stay with the French bistro cooking which they do well and which chimes with atmosphere of antiques and old lace. Originally Peachey's was a wine bar and concern with wine remains although I suspect the conditions for storage are not ideal. There are usually wine 'specials' which can be a bargain. Were you to go for a bracing walk on a Sunday morning on Hampstead Heath, you could reward yourself with a brunch at Peachey's with your cheeks rosy.

CUISINE: French	*Also vegetarian dishes on request*
OPEN: L: Mon to Fri, Sun; D: Mon to Sat	
MEALS: 12 to 2.30; 7 to 11.30	
CLOSED: Bank Holidays	
AVERAGE PRICE: £24. Set Menus (lunch only): £7.50 (2 courses) and £8.50 (3 courses)	
CREDIT CARDS: Amex, Visa, Diners	
SEATS: 38	
TABLES OUTSIDE: (20)	
MUSIC: Piped	
Wheelchair access	

THE PENANG

41 Hereford Road, W2
01-229 2982

A correspondent who works for the BBC World Service told me that the Penang is an absolutely authentic Malaysian restaurant. I took his word for it, but the only authoritative thing I can say is that I had a good meal – the beef satay was well prepared and I liked the 'Lip Stick' chicken, the fried pork liver with scallions and the noodle assembly – and thought the simplicity of the basement premises fitting for the prices. At the take-away counter on the ground floor I tasted a pickle they call achar which was delicious and spoke of loving hands at home. I meant to go back to try the babi manis dan asam in my ceaseless quest to discover whether sweet and sour pork can be a creditable dish. I never did, so perhaps you would like to try.

CUISINE: Malaysian	*Also vegetarian dishes*
OPEN: D only: Mon to Sun	

MEALS: 6 to 11
AVERAGE PRICE: £11
CREDIT CARDS: Access, Amex, Visa, Diners
SEATS: 35

PERFUMED CONSERVATORY

182 Wandsworth Bridge Road, SW6
01-731 0732

On the form I have used to elicit practical details from restaurateurs there is a question about whether children are welcome. The proprietors of this awkwardly named restaurant, Barbara Dean and Jonathan Hayes, have replied that they like them to be 8 years and older and to be quiet. The whole place makes me want to throw a tantrum and drum my heels loudly on the floor, but I am including it because Hayes and Dean don't skate round the subject of English food but attack it head on, even plundering the hedgerows and marshes for ingredients like nettles, samphire and young dandelion leaves. Elderflowers might be plunged into batter to become fritters to accompany duck breasts. Rhubarb, which the Roux brothers think should go with scrambled egg, they feel, quite rightly, better partners pigeon. They title their style English Nouvelle which can be read as referring to tricksy combinations as above but they do cook vegetables simply and well. There is a conservatory with two tables and perhaps the plants do give out a scent; there is also a small garden for use in summer. Other guides have described this restaurant as romantic and candle-lit but I think the mood to go in is when you are feeling combative about the whole subject of whether there is such a thing as British cuisine and how, if you don't feed your two-year-old pear, nettle and pea soup, is he or she going to be able to recognize it?

CUISINE: English Nouvelle	Also vegetarian dishes
OPEN: L: Tues to Fri; D: Tues to Sat	

MEALS:	12.30 to 2.30; 7 to 11.30
CLOSED:	Christmas and Bank Holidays
AVERAGE MEAL:	£22. Set Menu: £14.50
CREDIT CARDS:	Access, Amex, Visa
SEATS:	38
TABLES OUTSIDE:	(4–6)
PRIVATE ROOM:	(20)
MUSIC:	Piped

PHOENICIA

11–13 Abingdon Road, W8
01-937 0120

Open every day, except Christmas Day and Boxing Day, from noon to midnight, the Phoenicia is the place to go to graze among the *meze*, cold and hot. There is a choice of up to 35 dishes (depending on availability) and whilst there are set-price menus that give you a selection, a more diverting meal can be composed by choosing yourself. As well as the items that are now familiar to Westerners such as hoummus, tabbouleh, aubergine purée, there is the more reckless kibbeh nayeh, raw minced lamb mixed with crushed wheat and spices; a salad made with poached lamb's brains; basturma, which is like a more emphatic version of pastrami; and shankleesh, goat's cheese marinated in olive oil, flavoured with thyme and tomato, among the cold hors d'oeuvre. The hot small dishes feature various stuffed breads and pastries, grilled spicy sausages, chicken wings, sautéed lamb or chicken livers and deep-fried aubergines and courgettes. An array of dishes is an agreeable way to eat when you are in a group and at the Phoenicia they are friendly towards Europeans, altogether less militantly Middle-Eastern than at some other Lebanese places. The main courses are various charcoal grills, some in the form of kebab and I find they tend to monotony after the tapestry of a meze. An accompaniment worth ordering is fattouch, a salad made of chopped tomatoes, cucumbers, onions and mint with toasted bread crushed into the dressing; an idea worth reproducing at home. The high cover charge (£1.20) produces fresh salad vegetables and pickles as crudités. Vegetarians fare well at Phoenicia with two meatless set menus.

CUISINE: Lebanese	Also vegetarian dishes
OPEN: Mon to Sun	
MEALS: 12 to 12	
CLOSED: Christmas Day and Boxing Day	
AVERAGE PRICE: £16. Set Menus: £7.95 and £12.95	
CREDIT CARDS: Access, Amex, Visa, Diners	
SEATS: 80	
MUSIC: Piped Lebanese	

PIER 31

31 Cheyne Walk, SW3
01-352 4989/5006

The team that gave you Tai-Pan, Edward Lim and Lord Lichfield (poor dear) moved in on a restaurant belonging in part to Henry Smith called Smith's and turned it into Pier 31. If you can bring yourself to discount a wide road thundering with traffic, this fashion-conscious place can be included among restaurants on the river. There is a view of the rather tacky statue 'The Boy and the Dolphin' and the splendid Victorian ironwork Albert Bridge. Inside all is sleek, grey and marbled with black slatted blinds on the large windows; the post-modern period in restaurant decor. The chef, Mikito, is Japanese and the oriental slant on the menu is, on the whole, to its benefit especially for post-modern minimalist eaters. First courses are called light courses with the implication that you could compose your meal of a few of them, perhaps the sashimi (marinated seafood in a lime dressing), the smoked salmon crêpes and the Pier 31 version of eggs Benedict, which has the egg nestling in an artichoke heart, garnished with ham and hollandaise sauce. 'Balls Brothers' (the name of the wine bar previously at this address), a pair of veal croquettes, is also served as a snack in the bar. They do spaghettini my favourite way – with chili, olive oil and garlic. Main courses are either French or oriental, e.g. tempura, beef teriyaki, with some simple grills and a fish dish of the day. It is food for the jaded palate, requiring little evaluation or involvement and keyed with appetite enhancers like ginger and soya sauce; a menu not without guile. The bar of Pier 31 is a popular place to hang out, and Sunday brunch a popular time to see and be seen.

CUISINE: Eclectic	*Also vegetarian dishes*
OPEN: Mon to Sun	
MEALS: 12 to 3; 7 to 11.30	
AVERAGE PRICE: £22. Set Menu: £9.50 (Sun brunch)	
CREDIT CARDS: Access, Amex, Visa, Diners	
SEATS: 70	

Pierre Martin

Pierre Martin comes from Cannes and arrived in London having worked in the south of France and at Fouquet in Paris. He opened his first restaurant, La Croisette, in 1975. This restaurant with a set-price menu of un-English generosity challenged the old order of fish restaurants – places like Wheeler's, Overton's and Bentley's – by providing varieties of fish like sea bass and bream and red mullet almost unknown on fish restaurant menus and difficult to buy at Billingsgate, a stunning array of crustaceans and molluscs, and a sunny atmosphere with service from young French waiters. The fish was allowed to rejoice in its freshness rather than being muffled in heavy sauces. La Croisette was a success and led to Le Suquet and Le Quai St Pierre, these three restaurants opened in conjunction with Alberto Bracci. In 1986 Pierre Martin bought out his partner and the group, which also includes L'Olivier and Lou Pescadou, is now his, with shares going to his managers. Pierre Martin has said that anyone with energy can succeed in Britain – but that it is a rare commodity among the British.

PIGEON

606 Fulham Road, SW6
01-736 4618

This is a Peter Ilic restaurant with slightly more intimate surroundings than at La Cloche or The Lantern. For the style of food see the entry under La Cloche.

CUISINE: Eclectic	*Also vegetarian dishes*
OPEN: Mon to Sun	
MEALS: 12 to 3; 7 to 12	
AVERAGE PRICE: £12	
CREDIT CARDS: Visa	
SEATS: 75	
PRIVATE ROOM: (30)	
Wheelchair access	

POISSONNERIE DE L'AVENUE

82 Sloane Avenue, SW3
01-589 2457

This crossroads of the Brompton Road by Sloane Avenue and Draycott Avenue is dividing up very clearly between the old guard and the new trendies. It applies to all manner of shops, not just restaurants. To get away from, say, the wearisome high-style of Joe's Café it might be consoling to relax in the Poissonnerie, run now for many years – since 1962 in fact – by Peter Rosignoli. I have always praised the restaurant for offering more than just the luxury fishes; I have had good skate au beurre noir and a homely preparation of smoked haddock. Mr Rosignoli claims that the English like large pieces of fish that they can tackle easily rather than fiddling about dissecting, for example, langoustines. So there you have it: on my left is Le Suquet (*q.v.*) where in clattery surroundings you can nit-pick your way through the stunning plateau de

185

fruits de mer, on my right you have the Poissonnerie with its velvet banquettes where you can enjoy a plate of turbot with hollandaise sauce. Both have their virtues. In season, make use of the long oyster bar.

CUISINE: Fish	*Also vegetarian dishes*
OPEN: Mon to Sat	
MEALS: 12.15 to 3; 7 to 11.30	
AVERAGE PRICE: £24	
CREDIT CARDS: Access, Amex, Visa, Diners	
SEATS: 90	
TABLES OUTSIDE: (15)	
PRIVATE ROOM: (24)	

POLLYANNA'S

2 Battersea Rise, SW11
01-228 0316

In a stretch of Battersea littered with bistros, the name and the folksy appearance of Pollyanna's belie its seriousness and its scope. The chef, Eamonn Connelly, has put together an imaginative menu which changes regularly. From a summery list you could choose among the first courses a terrine of foie gras with truffles and a raspberry vinegar jelly, goat's cheese in aspic with a spinach and watercress sauce, a warm salad of lamb's brains with rosemary vinaigrette or red mullet and sole terrine with a light tomato coulis. As you can see from main courses such as sea bass cooked in butter with candied onions and a cider vinegar sauce, sliced breast of corn-fed chicken marinated in olive oil and basil served on noodles with a Riesling and cream sauce, haunch of venison roasted served on spinach with two crème de cassis sauces, nothing is left well alone but all the 'with this' and 'with that' is usually to good effect and makes a highly defined change from eating at home. There is a note on the menu saying that dishes can be cooked plainly if preferred but it would seem a squashing request. The laudable efforts at making interesting vegetarian dishes are not always successful as perhaps curried tofu and vegetables served on wild rice with banana raita might imply. However, bully for them for trying. The wine list is helpfully and frankly annotated and very fairly priced. It kicks off with ten vintages of Château Gruard Larose with the '71, for example, at £22.50. Champagne starts at £9.25 for NV Canard Duchêne and there are some interesting choices among the second, third, fourth and fifth growth clarets, and an impressive list of burgundies, red and white. It would be a great shame here to opt for the house wine. That the team at Pollyanna's are enthusiastic about food is palpable but should you doubt it, they organize special regional menus and also tributes to various classical chefs, some of the contemporary ones occasionally being persuaded to join in. Sunday lunch is a traditional roast or a steak and kidney pie followed by proper English puddings.

CUISINE: French	Also vegetarian dishes

OPEN: L: Sun; D: Mon to Sun
MEALS: 1 to 3; 7 to 12
CLOSED: 4 days at Christmas
AVERAGE PRICE: £18. Set Menu: £7.95 (Sun lunch)
CREDIT CARDS: Access, Amex, Visa, Diners
SEATS: 80
TABLES OUTSIDE: (20)
PRIVATE ROOM: (36)
MUSIC: Piped jazz and pop

PONTE NUOVO

126 Fulham Road, SW3
01-370 6656

I find Italian restaurants in London so indifferent and so repetitious that recommending one over another often comes down to whether there is a likeable manager or, if the Fulham Road *flâneurs* have decided that it is the 'in' place, the clientele is fun to observe. Walter Mariti who used to be involved with

Enzo Apicella at the Meridiana and Pasquale Lunghi from the Pontevecchio in Old Brompton Road, have opened Ponte Nuovo and from the start it was popular. The interior is smooth and shiny with a strip of mirror running round the walls at eye level so you can do a quick check of the tenacity of your styling mousse. The small size of the premises means that nearly every table is the worst in the room which can take the sting out of wondering if you have been seated sycophantically. The food has some strengths, namely the fresh pasta and the fish dishes. There has been sloppy garnishing with the meat dishes and you have to watch that you avoid tomato sauces cropping up too often during a meal. The dolci del trolley are fairly uninspired. Service can be erratic. All in all, you might infer that I am not recommending Ponte Nuovo wholeheartedly, but within the spectrum of Italian places it is frolicsome and has the advantage of pavement tables surrounded by bushes and covered with an umbrella, worth noting for fine days. The wines are carefully chosen and the long list is exclusively Italian.

CUISINE: Italian	*Also vegetarian dishes*
OPEN: Mon to Sun	
MEALS: 12 to 3; 7 to 12	
CLOSED: Bank Holidays	
AVERAGE PRICE: £16	
CREDIT CARDS: Access, Amex, Visa, Diners	
SEATS: 50	
TABLES OUTSIDE: (20)	
Wheelchair access	

POON'S & CO

4 Leicester Street, WC2
01-437 1528

Sitting at the back of the ground floor of Poon's peering up a fire escape, my companion referred to 'that little patch of blue we prisoners call the sky'. Incarcerated in Poon's you could pass the time happily choosing among the 200 mainly Cantonese dishes including the specialities made with wind-dried meat and sausage, but the attitude of the staff can sometimes veer on prison warden. However, as at most Chinatown restaurants, experiences are not consistent and once I was served by a waiter whose only concern in life seemed to be for us to like the dishes and he urged us towards ones with which they were experimenting which went to prove yet again that emulating Western creamy sauces is a duff idea. Fish dishes are particularly good and I think it is a shame if steamed scallops are left out of the first course. The hot-pot dishes make a change of pace, as far as cooking methods go, and I like very much the one of eel, crispy belly of pork and garlic. The Poon family in its various ramifications have long been associated with Chinese food in London. They have an expensive and disappointing up-market restaurant in King Street, Covent Garden and a cheap unlicensed café in Lisle Street where wind-dried foods hang in the window. This branch seems to me to strike the happy medium.

CUISINE: Cantonese	*Also vegetarian dishes*
OPEN: Mon to Sat	
MEALS: 12 to 11.30	
AVERAGE PRICE: £9. Set Menu: £8.50 for two	
CREDIT CARDS: None	
SEATS: 90	

PORTE DE LA CITE

65 Theobalds Road, WC1
01-242 1154

Open only at weekday lunchtimes, this is a restaurant clearly aimed at the business community but the food is more carefully cooked and the dishes more inventive than expense account eating is generally considered to require. It is most emphatically French. First courses can be substantial as in the fish soup sètoise and the duck terrine or in a more modern vein as with the hot aubergine and courgette mousse served with a tomato sauce and the salade gourmande which contains thinly sliced vegetables, walnuts, prawns and shallots. The fish dishes, reassuringly, change according to marketing. That men like to order steak is a belief borne out by the various ways they present it here including a grilled côte de boeuf served rare wtih a béarnaise sauce, for two to share. A speciality of the house is the slice of hot, melting goat's cheese flamed with marc de Bourgogne – a dish to seal a deal if ever there was one. Enthusiasm and energy in the kitchen is proved by the list of plats du jour that enhance an already quite comprehensive menu. The price structuring – a set price for either two or three courses – makes ordering a pleasure and entertaining more graceful. The house wines are probably the ones to choose. It is worth noting that the restaurant can be booked in the evenings for private parties. Porte de la Cité is under the same ownership as Au Bois de St Jean, in St John's Wood (of course), but I prefer this enterprise.

CUISINE: French	*Also vegetarian dishes*
OPEN: L only: Mon to Fri	
MEALS: 12 to 2.30 (can be booked for private parties in the evening)	
CLOSED: Bank Holidays and Christmas	
SET MENUS: £12.50 (2 courses) and £14.50 (3 courses)	
CREDIT CARDS: Access, Amex, Visa, Diners	
SEATS: 65	
PRIVATE ROOM: (20–25)	

PORTS

11 Beauchamp Place, SW3
01-581 3837

For some impenetrable reason there is a concentration of Portuguese restaurants in the ultra-fashionable shopping street of Beauchamp Place. I think the rising damp of some of the basement premises lends a certain necessary melancholy but Ports is jolly and stylish and also has the best food. The premises are tiled prettily and the chef from Angola brings a bit of cut and thrust to what Quentin Crewe has described as an essentially dismal cuisine. It is true that Portugal has suffered from poverty but sometimes constraints on the ingredients can bring forth benefits – like all their ways with salt cod, apparently one for every day of the year. Here they serve bacalhau na braza which is salt cod bathed in olive oil spiked with garlic, something like an English tourist in Albufeira, but rather more appetizing. Interesting first courses are espadarte fumado – smoked marlin marinated in lemon and rosewater and dressed with chopped tomatoes and shallots – the grilled prawns with a spicy sauce, the grilled squid with a butter-lime sauce and the morcela, Portuguese sausage, served on braised red cabbage. Main courses are strong on fish, including an arroz de marisco, a sort of seafood paella, prepared for two. Meat is served pink in a rather non-Portuguese way. I like the sound of Iscas a Don Theodosio, a dish of liver and sweetbreads served in a sauce of wine, mustard and shallots. Desserts are not an issue but there is sometimes a Portuguese pastry, a puff pastry custard-filled confection which the manager says has Proustian overtones of nostalgia for him. Portuguese wines are a territory worth exploring and if you are eating meat the vintage red Garrafeiras are a good choice. The manager recommends the white Bucelas '79. Ports and madeiras are served by the glass.

CUISINE: Portuguese

OPEN: L: Mon to Fri; D: Mon to Sat

MEALS: 12 to 2.30; 7 to 11.30	

MEALS: 12 to 2.30; 7 to 11.30
CLOSED: Bank Holidays and Christmas
AVERAGE PRICE: £19. Set Menu: £6.50 (lunch)
CREDIT CARDS: Access, Amex, Visa, Diners
SEATS: 45

♥ LA POULE AU POT

231 Ebury Street, SW1
01-730 7763

S entiment pushes me to include La Poule au Pot. It is the stage-set notion of a French restaurant complete with a menu that in these days of food fads is becoming relatively rare. Snails, pâtés, soupe Crécy, coq au vin, lapin à la moutarde, veal chop with a creamy sauce are all likely dishes, all competently cooked. Their approach to cheese is to serve a wheel of Brie in optimum condition. An equally beady ploy is their approach to house wine, which is to serve it in magnums and charge you for what you drink, which, with the candlelight, the open fire in winter, the lace cloths, the French-speaking staff, tables in secluded corners and reminders (in my case anyway) of past assignations, is usually all of it. The set-price three course lunch is good value and a thought when you have designs on someone rather than a yen for designer food.

CUISINE: French	Also vegetarian dishes
OPEN: L: Mon to Fri; D: Mon to Sat	
MEALS: 12.30 to 2.30; 7 to 11.15	
CLOSED: Bank Holidays	
AVERAGE PRICE: £22. Set Menu: £8.45 (lunch)	
CREDIT CARDS: Access, Amex, Visa, Diners	
SEATS: 53	
Wheelchair access	

PRINCESS GARDEN

8–10 North Audley Street, W1
01-493 3223

Related to the Princess Garden in Hong Kong, this has the characteristic of that city of conspicuous consumption. As you approach the restaurant through the circuitous passage you are passed from hand to hand among the members of staff until you feel you have been waited upon before you are even sitting down. Given all that and the well-heeled decor, the prices for food are reasonable, not too dissimilar from some of the Chinatown dives with laminated tables and strip lighting. Starters, including the soups, are about £3, meat and poultry main courses are from £4 and as long as you avoid items like lobster and shark's fin you will not pay over the odds for a luxurious experience. What you might not be getting is the most beguiling Chinese food in London but opulence has its place. And that place is certainly where visiting businessmen from the East feel they ought to be. If for some extraordinary reason you should want to do so, you can ask the management to lay on a special demonstration of noodle-making in one of the private rooms. I suppose it could, as it were, break the ice.

CUISINE: Peking	*Also vegetarian dishes*
OPEN: Mon to Sun	
MEALS: 12 to 2.30; 6.30 to 11.30	
AVERAGE PRICE: £22	
CREDIT CARDS: Access, Amex, Visa, Diners	
SEATS: 120	

LE QUAI ST PIERRE

7 Stratford Road, W8
01-937 6388

This is the smallest of Pierre Martin's fish restaurants (see La Croisette and Le Suquet) and its intimate size gives it a special charm. At the downstairs bar there is no compulsion to eat more than a plate of oysters, a platter of various shellfish or a crêpe or feuilleté with a seafood filling. The tables are upstairs. There you might choose a more copious meal including a luxury fish such as turbot, bass or bream with a beurre blanc. There is a meat dish or two if you have an ornery person in your party who won't eat what is good for them. The waiters can be as *farouche* here as at the other branches but for advice on handling them consult the entry for L'Olivier.

CUISINE: French/Fish

OPEN: L: Tues to Sat; D: Mon to Sat

MEALS: 12.30 to 2.30; 7.30 to 11.30

CLOSED: Christmas

AVERAGE PRICE: £20

CREDIT CARDS: None

SEATS: 60

MUSIC: Taped classical

RED FORT

77 Dean Street, W1
01-437 2525

Differing reports coming out of Red Fort make me hesitant about reiterating the idea that here you might find some of the best Indian (Moghul) food in London. Perhaps the energetic Amin

Ali has bitten off more chapati than he can thoroughly chew, what with this, Lal Qila and The Moghul Brasserie, Wembley, amongst his involvements. The service is styled, the publicity said, to make you feel like a Maharajah but I didn't even feel like a Maharanee when during my first meal there we were continually interrupted by waiters asking if everything was all right, behaviour that seems somehow unlikely in an Indian court. From the first courses I liked the masha which is a pillow of lentils and vegetables wrapped in a layer of onion. The fish dishes based on pomfret work better than those utilizing trout. Quails in a rich sauce are good and meats sizzled on an iron plate (karahi) are a better bet than those doused in spicy gravies. The surroundings are posh, the ground floor preferable to the basement. Set-price buffet lunches are good and, as at most Indian restaurants, vegetarians and non-vegetarians can eat together equally satisfactorily.

CUISINE: Indian   *Also vegetarian dishes*

OPEN: Mon to Sun

MEALS: 12 to 3; 6 to 11.30

AVERAGE PRICE: £19. Set Menu: £6.95 (buffet lunch)

CREDIT CARDS: Access, Amex, Visa, Diners

SEATS: 150

PRIVATE ROOM: (80)

Wheelchair access

THE RED PEPPER

7 Park Walk, SW10
01-352 3546

Courageous magazines have in the past attempted features on London restaurants showing family trees. Mostly they resemble balls of tangled wool. If you were to do one for the Szechuan restaurants of south-west London you would have branches, or twigs anyway, representing The Golden Duck, Paper Tiger, Tai-Pan and The Red Pepper. It is not a direct line of descent, more the outcome of odd couplings. There has been a change of management since the restaurant opened but it remains somewhere to go if you are hankering after the spicy specialities of Szechuan province. A chilli pepper symbol picks out the hot dishes and you might start with frogs' legs or chicken wings or spare ribs all gingered up with fegara pepper. There are milder alternatives including bang-bang chicken, a dish of cold chicken and cucumber in a peanutty sauce that has achieved a sort of fashionability. Camphor wood tea-smoked duck (see Dragon Gate) is available and makes a good centrepiece to the meal. Prawns stand up well to vigorous spicing, and now your taste buds are ready for the challenge it is the moment for crispy beef shreds with chillis and carrots. There are set meals including a 'gourmet's feast' that tempts with the notion that dishes not on the menu might be served. The wine list has a section on Alsace wines with good suppliers, though no vintages mentioned. These wines can stand up to prickly food. Norman Wong, who set up Red Pepper originally, has gone on to open the notably fashionable and successful (book early to avoid disappointment) Mao Tai, 58 New King's Road, SW6 (01-731 2520) which has similar specialities to the above.

CUISINE: Szechuan	*Also vegetarian dishes*
OPEN: Mon to Sun	
MEALS: 12 to 2.30 (Sat and Sun till 3); 7 to 12	
AVERAGE PRICE: £20. Set Menus: £13.50–16.50	

CREDIT CARDS: *Access, Amex, Visa, Diners*

SEATS: *65*

MUSIC: *Piped*

Wheelchair access

THE RITZ

Piccadilly, W1
01-493 8181

A bout the Ritz it has been said that it has the most beautiful dining room in Europe. I would agree with this and were I invited to lunch or dinner there I would never demur. The voluptuous murals and formal *trompe-l'oeil*, the chandeliers and gilded garlanding, the view over St James's Park are inimitable. There was a flurry for a while with the idea that English chef Michael Quinn (now at Ettington Park in Alderminster, Warwickshire) was going to bring great cuisine to The Ritz but you cannot turn a battleship round quickly particularly if all hands are not helpfully on deck. The way to treat the Ritz is as a treat: have a good bottle of wine from the excellent list and some straightforward food; a roast, grilled fish or game. Recently there has been enterprising cabaret on Wednesday, Thursday and Friday evenings with such great jazz singers as Adelaide Hall and cocktail pianists like Steve Ross. On Saturday evenings you may dance.

CUISINE: *International*   *Also vegetarian dishes*

OPEN: *Mon to Sun*

MEALS: *12.30 to 2.30 (Sun till 2); 6.30 to 11 (Sun 7.30 to 10.30)*

AVERAGE PRICE: *£42. Set Menus: £18.75 (lunch); £24.50 (dinner). Available Mon, Tues and Sat*

CREDIT CARDS: *Access, Amex, Visa, Diners, Carte Blanche*

SEATS: *136*

TABLES OUTSIDE: *(20)*

RODOS

59 St Giles High Street, WC2
01-836 3177

Many actors, actresses, chefs and restaurateurs had cause to feel warmly about Rodos when late hours meant that there was a place to unwind after the performance whether in front of the footlights or the stove. Now conventional hours are kept and there is a possibility that the dread hand of 'redecoration' will spoil that endearingly tatty eating-in-the-kitchen quality of the decor. They have promised expansion on to the first floor. With seating for an additional 40–50 people, will the meze stay so plentiful and so good? Let us hope so for the value of the set-price spread is tremendous and the Rodos ideally sited for after theatre or cinema.

CUISINE: Greek	*Also vegetarian dishes*
OPEN: L: Mon to Fri; D: Mon to Sat	
MEALS: 12 to 2.30; 5.30 to 11.30	
AVERAGE PRICE: £16. Set Menu: £9.45 (Meze)	
CREDIT CARDS: Access, Amex, Visa, Diners	
SEATS: 35	
PRIVATE ROOM: (40–50)	
MUSIC: Piped Greek	
Wheelchair access	

LE ROUTIER

Camden Lock, Chalk Farm Road, NW1
01-485 0360

It is the setting of Le Routier that is its unique selling point. In the cobbled courtyard of Camden Lock, the long wooden building gives on to a terrace by Regent's Canal and on summery days it is somewhere to head when you have come to the sad conclusion that little use is made of the Thames. The food is bistro style with the odd thrust of invention and though the staff may look a bit stern you can get away with ordering two first courses, which is something you might prefer to do at lunchtime on a warm day. Inside, the fact that the premises used to be stables is only pleasantly apparent. Decor is the gingham tablecloth school. Sunday lunch, which has two well defined sittings (at 12.30 and 2.30), can be fun. Book ahead for that and for tables outside when you can anticipate sun.

CUISINE: English/French	Also vegetarian dishes
OPEN: Mon to Sun	
MEALS: 12.30 to 2.30; 7 to 10.45	
AVERAGE PRICE: £16	
CREDIT CARDS: Access, Amex, Visa, Diners	
SEATS: 70	
TABLES OUTSIDE: (40)	

The Roux Brothers

The Roux brothers would be the first to admit it: they changed if not the face, then an aspect of the face of British catering when, in 1967, with the backing of some of the families for whom they had worked in private service or embassies, they opened Le Gavroche in Lower Sloane Street. Before Le Gavroche, ambitious, professionally cooked food in England was found mostly in hotels or ocean-liner style restaurants like the Coq d'Or or A l'Ecu de France with menus as long as your arm, cooking methods set in aspic and the chef a nameless figure well sealed in the kitchen. Formally trained chefs as restaurant owners were not the common occurrence in London they are now becoming, thanks, in part, to the brothers who helped set up Pierre Koffmann at La Tante Claire, Jean-Louis Taillebaud (at the moment of writing looking for new premises), Peter Chandler at Paris House (see Worth a Drive) and René Bajard at Le Mazarin. They have installed Christian Germain at the Château de Montreuil in northern France and opened a Waterside Inn in Santa Barbara, California. They have both been awarded three

Michelin stars, Albert at Le Gavroche now in Brook Street and Michel at The Waterside Inn in Bray (see Worth a Drive). Their early training in France was as pâtissiers. They promote the role of the pastry chef as part of the activity of being key figures on the catering scene, a role Michel relishes more greatly than Albert. Albert has twinkly eyes and a business brain as sharp as a chef's knife. It was Michel, the younger, taller, fairer one who did most of the work on their book *New Classic Cuisine* and on their new pastry book, but they refer to one another as Brother – Brother says this, Brother does that – and share credit equally. The former premises of Le Gavroche are now run as Gavvers. There are two Roux restaurants in the City, Le Poulbot and Le Gamin, and soon there will be a chain called Le Gamin serving pre-prepared food (see Sous-vide). They have a butcher's shop, Boucherie Lamartine in Ebury Street, a bakery in Wandsworth, and run a truck from Rungis market outside Paris. It is a little empire, now employing more British chefs than French.

RSJ

13a Coin Street, SE1
01-928 4554

According to the 1986 edition of *The Good Food Guide* this restaurant is one of the most popular among its readers of all the restaurants in London. The location can explain some of the clientele; the National Theatre, National Film Theatre and Festival Hall turn out customers in the evenings, the employees of IPC, London Weekend Television and Shell, and perhaps even County Hall, do so at lunchtimes. Chef Ian McKenzie is apparently now producing a nouvelle cuisine menu and dishes in that style well spoken of are marinated salmon, duck breast, and the vegetables which retain their bite. Entrecôte steak with morels and hare with prunes sound rather more gutsy. When last I visited, which was a few years ago, I liked a haddock mousse, a veal escalope with lemon and rosemary and salmon trout in a champagne sauce. Dessert had been a bread and butter pudding. The wine list is wisely composed and has a notable section of Loire wines, well annotated. The premises, a converted cycle warehouse, make designer use of the eponymous component. Set-price menus, which were once a feature, are no longer offered. The owners, obviously sympathetic to the needs of theatregoers, have also opened Mabileau near the Old Vic at 61 The Cut, SE1 (01-928 8645).

CUISINE: French	
OPEN: L: Mon to Fri; D: Mon to Sat	
MEALS: 12 to 2; 6 to 11	
AVERAGE PRICE: £21	
CREDIT CARDS: Amex, Visa	
SEATS: 50	

RUDLAND AND STUBBS

35–37 Greenhill Rents, EC1
01-253 0148

The fittingly Victorian names happen to be those of the original owners. The Victorian concept of 'a fish ordinary', i.e. a place where you might have some cockles and mussels and a pint of stout or a lobster and a bottle of champagne has worked out in practice reasonably well. It is agreeably unpretentious, almost like an extended pub in feel, with a cheeky menu given the proximity to Smithfield market. There is a meat dish or two but the point of the place is fish, on the whole simply cooked, more ornately in the form of pies or pâtés. I have found the standards of cooking variable. It is safer to stay with items like smoked eel and grilled plaice where, since the buying seems sound, there is little scope for disappointment. The staff are jolly and accommodating. Perhaps because of its location, handy for Fleet Street as well as the market, Bart's hospital and the City, the long bar does get firmly propped up and customers eating there can choose a plateful of oysters, some prawns with mayonnaise, a bowl of mussels or other small meal. You would be wise to book for lunch if you want a table. Sunday lunch is a nice occasion here and on a clement day the area rewarding to stroll in, finding Cloth Fair where Sir John Betjeman lived and other corners of architectural interest.

CUISINE: Fish	
OPEN: L: Mon to Fri and Sun; D: Mon to Sat	
MEALS: 12 to 3; 6 to 11.30 (Sat from 7)	
CLOSED: Bank Holidays and Christmas	
AVERAGE PRICE: £15	
CREDIT CARDS: None	
SEATS: 75	
TABLES OUTSIDE: (12)	
MUSIC: Piped	

RUE ST JACQUES

5 Charlotte Street, W1
01-637 0222

I n conversation with a friend who works in restaurant PR we discussed how it is that a restaurant like this can attract such a flurry of customers and attention upon opening, eliciting tributes such as two stars in the *Egon Ronay Guide* upon its first appearance in the book and the title of Newcomer of the Year in *The Good Food Guide* for 1985 and being named Restaurant of the Year by *Decanter* magazine. This friend is not so helplessly immured in PR that he did not think good food was somehow involved and indeed chef Gunther Schlender came with the credentials of having worked seventeen years at Carrier's restaurant in Islington and the manager, Vincent Calcerano, previously worked at Boulestin. Even so, Calcerano errs on the side of unctuousness and Carrier's had become pretty dismal towards the end. My enthusiasm for Rue St Jacques (I wondered if the *name* was particularly clever) is not unbridled. The food seems to me more expensive than the premises, and more importantly the cooking, can justify. I suppose I have to admit to be increasingly less diverted by dishes like escalope of salmon with a raspberry vinegar sauce and fillet of veal stuffed with pistachio nuts and pimento served with a Calvados sauce or terrine of peach and kiwi Chantilly but, accepting the modern style, I have been disappointed by first course salads, by plonking sauces and less than sublimely fresh-tasting scallops. The time to go to Rue St Jacques, I think, is for lunch upon signing a good deal with a publisher when he will appreciate that you have chosen the set-price (£15) meal. Natty interior design utilizing stretches of mirror makes the premises look larger than they are and the banquettes with their scatter cushions nudge you into relaxation. There is an upstairs room decorated strikingly in raspberry and green, which can be hired for private functions. The wine list is good in parts but energetically marked up.

CUISINE: French	
OPEN: Mon to Fri	
MEALS: 12.30 to 2.30; 7.30 to 11.15	
AVERAGE PRICE: £29 (lunch); £40 (dinner). Set Menu: £15 (lunch)	
CREDIT CARDS: Access, Amex, Visa, Diners	
SEATS: 40	
PRIVATE ROOM: (20)	

RULES

35 Maiden Lane, WC2
01-836 5314

In the November 1985 edition of the newsletter *European Wine and Food*, there is a rave review of Rules, the burden of it being that now, at last, under the new ownership, there is somewhere to take friends and visitors and say with pride, here is British food. In my experience of a meal in November 1985, also to test out the new regime, Rules remains here to reinforce all the negative prejudices visitors to this country might have about our food. Indifferent potted shrimps were served with toast made from spongy white sliced bread. Ham and melon (that famous English duo) was listed as featuring 'matured Cumberland ham' but a bendy piece of Parma ham appeared. Boiled silverside was unpleasantly salty. The dumplings would have been more usefully employed as draught excluders. The only redeeming feature of that meal was the Welsh rarebit (hard to do badly) and the steamed pudding, spotted dick, with the custard charged as an extra. A system agreeable for the customer of service charge as well as VAT being included in the prices seems to result in the staff being disaffected and unco-ordinated in their service. What is wonderful about Rules and what has not been marred, is its appearance. The interconnecting rooms of what were two eighteenth century houses hung with historic prints and pictures are some of the most delightful in London and repay well a visit to see 'London's oldest restaurant' and trace links with what was a distinguished and artistic clientele. What a shame the food cannot be modernized, i.e. cease to be a token gesture towards what is basically now a tourist clientele, become a reflection of all that British chefs have recently learned and a place of pilgrimage for the English. To go back to the *European Wine and Food* review, the inference must be that you can choose luckier than I did but somehow I find it hard to believe the writer's contention that 'When I had my first spoonful of Cockie Leekie soup (£1.50), I immediately imagined that a Scotswoman had rung the neck of her cock and dug up some leeks that very morning.' Mmmm. Was it a dew-kissed morning and did the cock leave behind him happy hens? The wine list is long but will inflate what can be – if you stay with, say, the house claret – a fairly reasonable bill.

CUISINE: Traditional English	*Also vegetarian dishes*
OPEN: Mon to Sat	
MEALS: 12.15 to 2.30; 6 to 11.15	
CLOSED: Christmas and Bank Holidays	
AVERAGE PRICE: £22. Pre-theatre Menu: (to 7.30 pm): £9.50	
CREDIT CARDS: Access, Amex, Visa, Diners	
SEATS: 120	

SABRAS

263 High Road, NW10
01-459 0340

This Indian vegetarian restaurant featuring the food of Gujerat would take the prize, were I to offer one, for the establishment serving the most interesting and delicious food for the least money. However, it is functional rather than fancy and therefore of interest when food and money are the prime concerns, which has to be admitted is not always the case in the complicated social exchange that constitutes eating out. The star turn of this style of food is the rice and lentil flour pancake called dosa, large as a dinner plate, golden and crisp, often wrapped round spiced potatoes when it becomes masala dosa. Vada is a fried patty made with chick pea or lentil flour mixed with shredded vegetables and served with yoghurt or various chutneys. Moong dal vada is one variety served. Bhajias are another kind of fried snack, more like a fritter based on vegetables. Sambar provides a spicy liquid curry to accompany the crisp or the softly steamed as in the flavoured and spiced rice cakes and semolina. If you have ever considered vegetarian food limited or monotonous it is a revelation to pick and choose among the menu here, contrasting textures, temperatures and tastes, in a manner that can be highly sophisticated. The owners, the Desai family, are friendly and helpful and the menu is adequately explained, so do not feel intimidated because you could not describe what is ragada patish. It is a spicy potato cake grilled on a hot plate and covered with yellow peas in sauce, tamarind chutney, chopped onions and coconut: exquisite. Corkage on your own wine, should you wish to stray from lassi (diluted yoghurt) is 40p. It is the sort of place to take someone who thinks they know it all where food is concerned, a French person perhaps.

CUISINE: Vegetarian Indian

OPEN: *Tues to Sun*

MEALS: *12.30 to 8.30 (summer to October till 9.15)*

HOLIDAY CLOSING: *2 weeks July/August and 2 weeks mid December*

AVERAGE PRICE: *£8. Set Menus: £3.75 and £5.75*

CREDIT CARDS: *Access, Amex, Visa, Diners. Luncheon Vouchers*

SEATS: *24*

MUSIC: *Piped*

ST QUENTIN

243 Brompton Road, SW3
01-589 8005

The blessed person we are invoking here is one of the partners, Quentin Crewe, the man who can be credited with turning restaurant criticism into a lively branch of journalism and who was my predecessor on *The Evening Standard* (as it was then called). The premises which were previously The Brompton Grill, a lovely stately restaurant, were first called Brasserie St Quentin but in the interests of accuracy the brasserie appellation has been dropped. Now generous restaurant hours are kept with last orders at midnight and weekend lunches lasting until 4 pm, and the menu under chef Marc Legros has assumed a pleasantly straightforward shape with a preponderance of grills, both fish and meat in the main course. A typical meal might start with beignets de foie de volaille en salade or pithiviers au Roquefort followed by rôti de lotte à l'orange or rognons de veau dijonnaise. Sorbets, cakes and fruit tarts made by an excellent pâtisserie are the appropriate desserts. St Quentin is fashionable and the etched mirrors give additional scope for people watching. Tables are close together and you must be fond of your fellow man or opt to eat in Siberia downstairs. One of the interesting things about this operation is their shop, Les Specialités St Quentin, 256 Brompton Road, SW3 (01-225 1664) where there is a room specially fabricated to bring on the unpasteurized French country cheeses imported from Philippe Olivier and also the team of pastry chefs referred to above who handle the baking which includes croissants claimed by some to be the best in London. Terrines, quiches, sandwiches, etc., are also sold. At the moment of writing St Quentin are about to open a café serving the output of the shop plus dishes prepared *sous-vide* (vacuum-packed) and grills. It will be at 7 Cheval Place, SW7 adjacent to a new Thai restaurant called Khun Akorn.

CUISINE: French	
OPEN: Mon to Sun	
MEALS: 12 to 3 (Sat and Sun till 4); 7 to 12 (Sun till 11.30)	
CLOSED: 2 weeks at Christmas	
AVERAGE PRICE: £22. Set Menu: £9.50 and £12.90	
CREDIT CARDS: Access, Amex, Visa, Diners	
SEATS: 80	
PRIVATE ROOM: (30)	

SALLOOS

51 Kinnerton Street, SW1
01-235 4444

Indians visiting London are invariably scathing about Indian restaurants here, deriding us Westerners particularly for favouring places like The Bombay Brasserie. Salloos, which is a Pakistani restaurant, usually gets grudging praise and I can understand why. It has always struck me as a serious and authentic place and what impresses me is that dishes featuring offal are usually available. Often you think how nice to have spicy kidneys or brain masala only to be told it is 'finished', i.e. no one since the menu was printed has ever requested it. A clientele that includes Arabs perhaps accounts for this feature as well as dishes like haleem akbari, shredded lamb cooked with whole wheat, lentils and spices. The surroundings beg the question of your spending money and the service can be overbearing but it is a sound place, particularly at lunchtime when you see lone diners, obviously *minding* tremendously about their food, having a good tuck in.

CUISINE: *Pakistani*	*Also vegetarian dishes*
OPEN: *Mon to Sat*	
MEALS: *12 to 2.30; 7 to 11.30*	
CLOSED: *Bank Holidays*	
AVERAGE PRICE: *£22*	
CREDIT CARDS: *Access, Amex, Visa, Diners, Carte Blanche*	
SEATS: *70*	

SAN FREDIANO

62 Fulham Road, SW3
01-584 8375

Since the late sixties this trattoria has been buzzing, in part because prices have always undercut others, in part because of the staff who really understand the art of serving and in part because of the food which, in the daily dishes particularly, added in pencil on the printed half of the menu, show the results of shrewd marketing and imaginative cooking. If none of those offerings appeals, look to the right hand side of the menu which is the section that changes regularly and features items like home-made ravioli with mushroom sauce, marinated herrings with beans, frogs' legs in butter and garlic, knuckle of veal (osso buco) and a fresh crab salad. What I like about San Fred's is that for once it does seem conceivable that a restaurant like this would exist in Italy. They are nice to you even if you are not a regular which is another plus. The wine list is, rightly, all Italian and is not marked up with the exuberance of the general atmosphere. It is noisy; you have been warned.

CUISINE: *Italian*	*Also vegetarian dishes*
OPEN: *Mon to Sat*	
MEALS: *12.30 to 2.30; 7.15 to 11.15*	
AVERAGE PRICE: *£18*	

CREDIT CARDS: *Access, Amex, Visa, Diners, Carte Blanche*

SEATS: *85*

SAN LORENZO

22 Beauchamp Place, SW3
01-584 1074

S an Lorenzo has long been one of the places where the chic meet to eat and it shows no sign of fading. Without doubt one of the reasons is the constant presence of Mara and Lorenzo Berni reassuring regulars that they are still loved. Another reason is the almost tropical decor which is like another world, or anyway another part of the world, somewhere you might well prefer to be, like Bali. Masses of plants, trees almost, split bamboo blinds and a sliding roof in good weather contribute to that feeling, but pictures of Marilyn Monroe and Victorian busts convey other considerations. The menu, which is presented stapled to a wicker tray, is more interesting than at the average London Italian restaurant and should be appreciated for its strengths – diet dishes such as carpaccio, bresaola and crudités with bagna cauda, pasta dishes and the rice with squid in its ink, game and rustic items like zampone and pigeon – but ignored when it leans towards clichés like salad Creola or veal pizzaiola. From observing the clientele I can't believe the creamy calorific desserts are frequently ordered. They will only add considerably to what will already be a bill to reckon with. House wine is Sardinian and perfectly good. Joan Collins tends to be treated better than you and me but the impassivity of the waiters would seem to convey that we are all equal in their eyes. Bookings tend to fall into definite sittings and you may well find yourself kept waiting when you arrive to claim your table. But it will be fun looking round.

CUISINE: *Italian*   *Also vegetarian dishes*

OPEN: *Mon to Sat*

MEALS: *12.30 to 3; 7.30 to 11.30*

AVERAGE PRICE: £28

CREDIT CARDS: None

SEATS: 120

SANTINI

29 Ebury Street, SW1
01-730 4094

I've always liked Gino Santini's establishments. I like his wine bar and pasta shop in Ealing (70 The Mall, W5, 01-567 5237) and I recollect a good lunch at his restaurant, now closed, near the river in Richmond. Having skirted the centre of London, with this enterprise he is making a distinct bid to go upmarket. The interior is cool and calm in white and grey trimmed with the colours used to shade sugar almonds. Pictures of Venice, presumably Signor Santini's home town, are echoed by Venetian specialities in the menu. As well as the printed card there is a daily menu and should you encounter the owner and should you convey a lively interest in the food, you can be rewarded by dishes like a risotto with wild mushrooms or, in season, white truffles shaved on to pasta. Out of season, or not wishing to shell out for white truffles, I recommend the tagliatelle with a sauce of aubergines and black olives or a simpler pasta dish with just tomatoes and basil. Main courses that might make you think of the Ocean's nursling are the quails with polenta; the artichokes served with garlic, parsley, white wine and Parmesan; the coda di rospo (monkfish) cooked in the oven and, indeed, carpaccio. Sauces on the meat and fish can be heavy-handed and vegetables over-buttered. The wines are not well described. A bottle of Prosecco, which was a recommended wine of the day, brought back memories of a wonderfully simple meal of fish in the Arsenale quarter of Venice, but unless it has associations for you I would look to other choices. I feel that Italian restaurateurs need encouragement to resist sinking into doling out the clichés both in food and style of service. Santini seems to be keeping his head above water.

CUISINE: Italian	Also vegetarian dishes

OPEN: L: Mon to Fri; D: Mon to Sun

MEALS: 12.30 to 2.30; 7 to 11.30

AVERAGE PRICE: £25. Set Menu: £9.50 (lunch, 2 courses and coffee)

CREDIT CARDS: Access, Amex, Visa, Diners

SEATS: 65

SEA SHELL FISH BAR AND RESTAURANT

49–51 Lisson Grove, NW1
01-723 8703

Recently the Sea Shell moved a little way along the road so that now nearly twice as many customers can enjoy the sparklingly fresh fish delivered daily from Billingsgate. The chips are cooked in groundnut oil which is healthier than beef dripping even if not so moreish. In the restaurant you could start with a prawn cocktail or soup or cod's roe or a fish cake and move on to halibut, sole, salmon, plaice, haddock, skate, cod, scampi and rock salmon depending on availability. Prices which start at £3.20 for rock salmon include chips. It is an interesting reflection on the times that the only main course item cheaper is quarter of a chicken. Peas, coleslaw, pickled onions, cucumbers and salad can be had on the side, ice cream or apple pie afterwards. By now they should be licensed and perhaps have put into practice their idea of a salad bar and the option of grilled fish and poached salmon. Seems to me that if you do fish and chips well, which they do, there is an argument for sticking with that.

CUISINE: Fish

OPEN: Tues to Sat

MEALS: 12 to 2; 5 to 10.30

CLOSED: Christmas

AVERAGE PRICE: £5 (without wine)

SHAMPERS

4 Kingly Street, W1
01-437 1692

Wine bars, which were all the rage in the seventies – 'What shall we do? Let's open a wine bar' – are rarely interesting for food and, more unforgivably, often have dull wine lists, that is unless they are attached to wine companies like Balls Brothers or Davy's, both with several branches in the city. Don Hewitson runs a group of commendably ambitious wine bars with long and enterprising lists, usually featuring a promotion keyed to a wine producing area and much better than average food. This Kingly Street branch has, as the name implies, a wide selection of champagnes. The food, both cold and hot, is carefully prepared. Dishes change daily and play variations on the themes of composed salads, casseroles and pies. I met Australian Hewitson on a press trip to Loch Fyne whence come farmed salmon, smoked salmon, oysters, crayfish and various pickled and marinated fishes including some excellent herrings, some of which Hewitson serves at his bars. The first, and some say the best, wine bar is Cork and Bottle, 44–46 Cranbourn Street, WC2 (01-734 7807), handy for pre-theatre meals. The food especially comes in for praise at Bubbles Wine Bar, 41 North Audley Street, W1 (01-499 0600), notable in an area not famed for reasonably priced places to eat.

CUISINE: Wine bar	Also vegetarian dishes

OPEN: L: Mon to Sat; D: Mon to Fri

MEALS: 11 to 3; 5.30 to 11

CLOSED: Bank Holidays

AVERAGE PRICE: £11

CREDIT CARDS: *Access, Amex, Visa, Diners. Luncheon Vouchers*

SEATS: *100*	
PRIVATE ROOM: *(60)*	
MUSIC: *Piped*	

SHEEKEY'S

28–32 St Martin's Court, WC2
01-240 2565

S heekey's used to be a wonderfully plain and functional wood-panelled fish restaurant with some sort of strange licence or permission that meant they could only boil or steam, not fry or grill. Since Scott's Restaurant bought Sheekey's all that has changed and also the interior has been titivated but not so as to spoil it. It is still very much a theatre restaurant with photographs of stars to attest to that, and also the odd recognizable customer. There is an attractive oyster bar and leading from it a series of interconnecting rooms with tables covered in gingham cloths. The menu is extensive and ranges from the sublime, in price terms anyway, to the gorblimey, e.g. those fashionable items fish cakes. The cooking is adequate rather than superlative and the same applies to the wine list. However if you can afford a meal out as well as theatre tickets, Sheekey's is a fitting venue for before or after the performance.

CUISINE: *Fish*	
OPEN: *Mon to Sat*	
MEALS: *12.30 to 3; 6 to 11.15*	
CLOSED: *Bank Holidays*	
AVERAGE PRICE: *£20*	
CREDIT CARDS: *Access, Amex, Visa, Diners*	
SEATS: *120*	
PRIVATE ROOM: *(15)*	
MUSIC: *Piped classical*	

SIDI BOU SAID

9 Seymour Place, W1
01-402 9930

If you refer to the entry for Laurent, you will observe that I am keen on couscous. It is served in this Tunisian restaurant, as is that beguiling first course brik à l'oeuf, which is here embellished with parsley and capers or with tuna fish in brik au thon. They make a good tagine – a dish cooked in an earthenware casserole – of lamb. A first course to have alongside the brik (an egg sealed in an envelope of filo pastry and deep-fried) is the salad mechouia of chopped grilled peppers, tomatoes, onions and garlic, laced with tuna fish. The blue and white decor is tricked out with white wire birdcages but music is from the tape recorder and is Arabic. Sidi Bou Said would seem to be on the list for students or other impecunious folk. On a cold day customers have been known to wish they were in Tunis rather than Marble Arch, so inadequate is the heating. Some toing and froing with the licensing authorities means that even though they are now licensed perhaps they will look kindly on your own bottle – and it would be a kindness to yourself to take it.

CUISINE: Tunisian	*Also vegetarian dishes*
OPEN: Mon to Sat	
MEALS: 12 to 3; 6 to 12	
AVERAGE PRICE: £12	
CREDIT CARDS: Access, Amex, Visa	
SEATS: 35	
MUSIC: Taped Arabic	

Soho

The image of Soho has changed. Gone, due to a crack-down by the Westminster Council, are most of the visible trappings of sex and seediness, or sauciness, depending on how you view it, and much in evidence is a restaurant revival. *L'Escargot, Alastair Little, Frith's, La Bastide* and the *Soho Brasserie* (see entries) are new and interesting arrivals, the Soho Brasserie attracting a fashion conscious crowd who spill over into *Pollo, 20 Old Compton Street.* Two new clubs have opened, *Groucho (45 Dean Street)* and *Moscow (52 Frith Street)* used by what is called a media crowd, who if not eating in the clubs will be patronizing L'Escargot, Alastair Little etc. There are two Vietnamese restaurants, neither quite up to an entry, though were the service not so abysmal I would have included *Saigon, 45 Frith Street* as the food can be diverting. *Maison Bertaux, 28 Greek Street,* and *Pâtisserie Valerie, 44 Old Compton Street,* are somewhere to drink tea or coffee and have good pâtisserie. The best espresso coffee in London is still at *Bar Italia (22 Frith Street).* Although some grocery shops have closed, Soho remains a prime food shopping area with fruit and vegetable markets on Berwick Street and Rupert Street. Brewer Street can supply you with great fish at Richard's, fine meat at Slater, Cooke, Bisney & Jones and Italian delicatessen and pasta at Lina's. Buy your coffee at The Algerian Coffee Stores and more Italian provisions at Camisa, both in Old Compton Street.

SOHO BRASSERIE

23–25 Old Compton Street, W1
01-439 3758

At the moment of writing it seems conceivable that the licensing laws in England will soon be relaxed. When that happens expect more conversions such as this one; a centrally located pub that serves breakfast until 11.30, coffee, tea and snacks in the bar area all day and meals in the restaurant at the back at lunchtime and in the evening. Some 'theme' pubs have been disastrous and rightly so but Ind Coope have done a good job here with initially the inspiration for the food coming from Sue Miles who has worked at L'Escargot Brasserie among many other places. The full-on licence means that during licensing hours you may just have a drink and many customers do just that while showing off the latest styles and striking poses. The restaurant menu has a list of light dishes that sometimes sound better than they taste. Brioche with oyster mushrooms proved to have a brown roll standing in, the sweet pepper tart had not gyrated quite long enough in the microwave but smoked chicken salad and the nice offering of bourride (garlicky fish stew) were good. This sums up the last meal I had at Soho Brasserie. I loved watching the fashion parade of customers; definitely somewhere to go to see and, if you are in the running, be seen. Book ahead or take a chance late in the evening.

CUISINE: Eclectic	*Also vegetarian dishes*
OPEN: Mon to Sat	
MEALS: 10 am to 11 pm (L: 12 to 3)	
CLOSED: Bank Holidays	
AVERAGE PRICE: £15	
CREDIT CARDS: Access, Amex, Visa, Diners. Luncheon Vouchers	
SEATS: 72	
TABLES OUTSIDE: (6)	
MUSIC: Piped jazz and classical	

Sous-vide

This method of storing and cooking food, much vaunted at the moment as a breakthrough for catering, has been around for a long time, sometimes known under the rather less felicitous term boil-in-the-bag. Foodstuffs in a raw or cooked state are packaged in a plastic pouch from which air – the agent for spoliation – is removed. Some items, salmon is an example, apparently benefit from being so wrapped and cooked. Shrinkage is lessened and moistness is retained. However, the interesting application to the restaurant business is the removal of chefs from a restaurant kitchen. Dishes can be prepared during a normal working day by chefs employed in a central kitchen in some area where rents are low. Food thus prepared can be kept, chilled but not frozen, for up to eight days and it just needs to be micro-waved or cooked in a wet convection steamer near the moment of service. Costs are obviously quite dramatically lessened. What strikes me as depressing is the uniformity of the product and the absence of any human *tension* which traditionally, and often usefully, belongs to the heat of the kitchen. Job satisfaction must be altered too. Although *sous-vide* dishes are used in a small way in many restaurants, the first establishments openly to depend on them will be the Le Gamin chain owned by the Roux brothers, serviced by their kitchens in Park Royal, North London. The first Le Gamin of this style is opening at Finsbury Circus in the City. At a chefs' conference I watched a slide show presented by a Hilton International executive chef demonstrating how the same 'nouvelle cuisine' dishes can be served all over the world. Whether you are in Delhi, Dubai or Rio de Janeiro you can get the same fanned-out fillet of lamb surrounded by the same little sauce. My heart plummeted.

LE SOUFFLE

Inter-Continental Hotel, 1 Hamilton Place, W1
01-409 3131

My criterion for including a restaurant in this guide has been an imaginary conversation where I hear myself recommending a visit to a friend. Friend has been loosely defined in some cases. With Le Soufflé, which is the rather awkwardly designed ground floor restaurant of a large impersonal hotel, I see myself addressing a friend of a friend, a visitor with a resilient expense account. The food, coming from the kitchens of Peter Kromberg, is very good. The menu changes and an understanding of the potential of ingredients is palpable. The service is assiduous and also caring. Prices hit the roof and I mean the one 30 floors up or whatever it is and nowhere more obviously than on the wine list. However, my last meal which totalled about £68 before service and with a modest bottle of wine, included praiseworthy dishes of ravioli of pigeon in a morel mushroom soup, calf's kidney baked in a salt crust with a garnish of vegetables pared so thinly they became a sort of tagliatelle and, not for me but for my companion, poularde stuffed with morels (yes, more morels) and served with a creamed truffled sauce. She was not so happy with her first course of a soufflé of salmon and spinach with anchovy sauce, one of many soufflés for which the restaurant is famous. We both were attracted to the peeled and cut fresh fruit displayed on the dessert trolley which the waiter combines on the plate. The rest of the display, though not bad, makes me take sides with the aggressors in the Great Trolley War which aims to put pâtissiers back into the kitchen working until the end of service. Le Soufflé is a good example of the way hotel restaurants have become serious but the surroundings, I have to say, despite the romance of the singer who can be heard from the bar, would not make me recommend it for anyone's special night out. It is for the rich who don't want to move too many steps from Park Lane.

CUISINE: Modern French

OPEN: L: *Mon to Fri and Sun; D: Mon to Sun*

MEALS: *12.30 to 3; 7 to 11.30*

AVERAGE PRICE: *£34. Set Menus: £16 (lunch); £28 (8-course dinner)*

CREDIT CARDS: *Access, Amex, Visa, Diners*

SEATS: *74*

MUSIC: *Sunday brunch pianist*

Wheelchair access

♥ # LE SUQUET

104 Draycott Avenue, SW3
01-581 1785

This was the second of Pierre Martin's (*q.v.*) fish restaurants in London. Unlike La Croisette the menu is à la carte but otherwise the successful formula of lively Provençal decor, the freshest of fish and shellfish brought by an in-house transport system, and the *je m'en fiche* staff is adhered to. Being at Le Suquet always raises my spirits and although that ought to be a commonplace function of a restaurant, in practice it isn't. Swiftly to transport yourself to the Mediterranean or, less ambitiously, to the northern coast of France, order the plateau de fruits de mer, a heap of all manner of shellfish and crustaceans served on a cork board with mayonnaise as sauce and various pins and other winkling-out implements to keep you busy and out of mischief for at least half an hour. Although the look of the plateau is festive I prefer the ease of eating salade Le Suquet which has various marinated fish, artichoke hearts, edible seaweed, langoustines and other appropriate garnishes. To follow choose a dignified fish such as sea bass or *daurade* (gilt-head bream) simply cooked or perhaps grilled over fennel (in the case of bass) and served with an appropriate sauce. As at the other restaurants in the chain there are less grandiose alternatives like feuilletés of seafood or asparagus. There are even meat dishes, but that would be foolish given the whiff of the briny implicit in the surroundings. Also after some fillets of

John Dory in a sorrel sauce it is easier to imagine a yacht parked outside rather than a car clamped in Walton Street. Cheese and salad and a fruit tart follow on happily. The consistent business of Le Suquet attests to its quality but also makes their occasional shortcomings in helpfulness easy for them to brush aside as unimportant: Si vous parlez français, it helps.

CUISINE: Fish/French	
OPEN: Mon to Sun	
MEALS: 12.30 to 2.30; 7.30 to 12	
CLOSED: 2 weeks at Christmas	
AVERAGE PRICE: £28	
CREDIT CARDS: Amex	
SEATS: 55	

♥
SWEETINGS

39 Queen Victoria Street, EC4
01-248 3062

Sweetings is my favourite restaurant in the City. It dates from 1906 at these premises. No bookings are taken and you have to be quick off the mark to nip in ahead of City gents who remember nice straightforward food like this being recommended by their nannies. You wait until a place becomes vacant either at a counter or at a table in the small restaurant part and there order perhaps half a dozen oysters, some dressed crab, smoked cod's roe served simply sliced – taramasalata, what's that guv? – or jellied eels followed by a slab of poached turbot with a sauce that never heard of that fashion of leaving out the flour, salmon fish cakes, smoked haddock with an egg on top, fish pie. Steamed puddings complete the nursery meal but it was at Sweetings that a young stockbroker taught me how to eat Welsh Rabbit which is a good accompaniment to a glass of port. You get a knife and crosshatch the melted cheese. You then shake on the Worcestershire sauce which dribbles away into the runnels, cut up and enjoy. The staff are used to handling a noisy crowd and in the end everyone gets served even if only with a crab sandwich and a glass of blanc de blanc.

CUISINE: *Fish/English*	
OPEN: *L only: Mon to Fri*	
MEALS: *11.30 to 3*	
AVERAGE PRICE: *£18*	
CREDIT CARDS: *None*	
SEATS: *65*	

TAI-PAN

8 Egerton Garden Mews, SW3
01-589 8287

Tai-pan, which apparently means European big boss, is also the name of a venomous snake, but no doubt the two things are considered synonymous. The tai-pan here is Patrick Lichfield who in partnership with Chinese Edward Lim and Shura Shiwarg (a Russian educated in China) opened this colonial style basement restaurant featuring Szechuan and Hunanese dishes in an otherwise Peking menu. The showy clientele the place attracts does nothing to encourage the kitchen in enterprise but that is all the more reason not to opt for the set meals nor items like the basket of hot appetizers which takes the cooking mode of deep-frying to quite unnecessary lengths. In fact the menu has some interesting dishes, for example the shower-fried Yu Ling chicken, Ganshow prawns in gingery sauce, twice-cooked Szechuan pork with Chinese cabbage and peppers, chef's boned and sauced poussin with mushroom and bamboo shoot stuffing and Hunan fish in hot bean sauce. Duck is prepared in four ways including a camphor wood- and tea-smoked duck. Take off time from drinking to thy companion only with thine eyes and prod the chefs into action with challenging ordering. Only this way can restaurants stay big boss in the culinary world. Cocktails suit the Raffles atmosphere but Shura's involvement – another finger he has in another pie is the Ebury Wine Co. – means that there are decent bottles from which to choose.

CUISINE: *Chinese*	
OPEN: *Mon to Sun*	
MEALS: *12 to 2.30; 7 to 11.30*	
CLOSED: *Bank Holiday lunchtimes and Christmas Eve*	
AVERAGE PRICE: *£22. Set Menus: £14 and £16*	
CREDIT CARDS: *Access, Amex, Visa, Diners*	
SEATS: *80*	
MUSIC: *Piped*	

♥ LA TANTE CLAIRE

68 Royal Hospital Road, SW3
01-352 6045/351 0227

A couple of years ago I moved house and I have noticed that a change of kitchens has altered my cooking. The food I cook is not necessarily better or worse but it is different. This tedious anecdote is here to indicate that I think M. Pierre Koffmann's new kitchen in his expanded and revamped premises seems to have had an influence. He also of course started up in the autumn of 1985 with a new brigade and, although I wouldn't know from personal experience, that probably affects things. I have had two meals here since the pretty stylized dining room picked out in lemon and blue came into being and neither has had the magic of meals remembered. However, it is incontestable that M. Koffmann is one of the most gifted chefs working in Britain and it must be the case that after a tactful pause – to take in evidence of the amount of money spent on the new decor and the formality of the service – Michelin will award him a third star. Koffmann, who trained at Le Gavroche (*q.v.*) has a slightly more racy style than his mentor Albert Roux: for example he will stuff a pig's trotter with morel mushrooms and serve that with mashed potatoes, and sauce a fillet of hare with raspberry vinegar and bitter chocolate. There is an effective bush telegraph where fashions in food are concerned and the pig's trotter of Koffmann might be compared with the Paris chef Joel Robuchon's dish of pig's ears also served with mashed potatoes. This might be thought to be cocking a snook at nouvelle cuisine, but the important lessons are adhered to and it would be unbalancing the menu not to mention also dishes like the rougets rôtis au cumin et aux tomates, gâteau de foies and the filet d'agneau chartreuse de persil et son jus à l'ail. Desserts are almost faultless and for chocolate lovers heaven awaits in the assiette du chocolatier. I prefer the millefeuilles au caramel et au pamplemousse and the version of tarte Tatin made with quinces. First courses can cost more than £12, main courses more than £15 so the sage way to approach Tante Claire is via the set-price lunch where two well-balanced three course menus with coffee are offered for £18. To experience skills such as Koffmann has at his disposal, it is a bargain. The wine list has some treasures but expect to pay for them.

CUISINE: French	*Also vegetarian dishes*

OPEN: Mon to Fri

MEALS: 12.30 to 2; 7 to 11

CLOSED: Christmas–New Year, 1 week at Easter and 3 weeks in August/September

AVERAGE PRICE: £27 (lunch); £44 (dinner). Set Menu: £18 (lunch)

CREDIT CARDS: Amex, Diners

SEATS: 45

Wheelchair access

TASTE OF INDIA

25 Catherine Street, WC2
01-836 2538

This is one of the Indian restaurants that followed on from the success of Last Days of the Raj started by a Bengali Workers' Action Group funded by Camden Council, proving that Bengalis in action are a force to be reckoned with. What now marks out Taste of India as special is the opening of a wine bar called Jewel in the Ground in what was the downstairs private room. Pre-theatre, or any time, it is pleasant to nibble on spicy snacks. Whilst some wine lovers might recoil at the thought of wine with chilli or other strong flavourings, others might find the prospect diverting. Fizz, e.g. champagne, I think holds its own. The restaurant proper is sound but the wine bar has the advantage of bargain basement prices.

CUISINE: North Indian/Bengali	*Also vegetarian dishes*

OPEN: Mon to Sun

MEALS: 12 to 2.30; 5.30 to 12

AVERAGE PRICE: £15. Set Menu: £6.95 (pre-theatre)

CREDIT CARDS: Access, Amex, Visa, Diners

SEATS: 90

PRIVATE ROOM: (20)

♥ TATE GALLERY

Millbank, SW1
01-834 6754

There was a rumour going round that Egon Ronay used to have the Tate Gallery left out of his guide so that not too many people would find out about the marvellous and reasonably priced list of wines. If true, it has proved futile, for you must always book here for lunch in the Whistler room. The food is self-consciously British with those terrible historical recipes such as Joan Cromwell's Grand Sallet, which you wish could be left peacefully buried. However, if you stay with the simpler options like potted crab and roasts and pies, including a good steak and kidney pie, you can let rip with the wines. The restaurant has been recently revamped, the mural cleaned, a new ventilation system installed, but the result from this customer's point of view just seems to be more customers packed in. The service does its best in the circumstances and would that all public institutions were as adventurous and industrious with their catering as the Tate. Lunch here with a great bottle or several halves – some probably unobtainable at the price from wine merchants – after an exhibition or just a wander in the gallery is one of London's treats.

CUISINE: English		Also vegetarian dishes
OPEN: L only: Mon to Sat		
MEALS: 12 to 3		
CLOSED: Christmas and Bank Holidays		
AVERAGE PRICE: £17		
CREDIT CARDS: None		
SEATS: 140		
Wheelchair access		

TEXAS LONE STAR SALOON

154 Gloucester Road, SW7
01-370 5625

Andrew Leeman (see Palms) with the backing of Ernie Corret opened this Tex-Mex restaurant which has an authentic inauthenticity. Research in the Southern states and California done by Leeman has resulted in suitable artefacts decorating the walls and some better than usual recipes for chilli con carne, tacos, guacamole, ribs, steak sandwiches and Margaritas. Videos of Westerns run silently and ceaselessly and Tex-Mex music is played in the late evening. The first time I went to Lone Star there was someone playing a banjo, an instrument I find extraordinarily *galvanizing*. Children love eating here and do not mind the noise or the occasional need to queue.

CUISINE: Tex-Mex	Also vegetarian dishes
OPEN: Mon to Sun	
MEALS: 12 to 11.30	
AVERAGE PRICE: £11	
CREDIT CARDS: None	
SEATS: 155	
MUSIC: Live Tex-Mex from 9.30 pm	
ENTERTAINMENT: Video Westerns	

THIERRY'S

342 King's Road, SW3
01-352 3365

T hierry's, owned by Thierry Cabbane for many years now, fulfils most people's expectations of a romantic French restaurant and it is an interesting reflection on the development of the London restaurant scene that there are now relatively few places presenting the flickering candle on the table, cosy, intimate experience you find here. All too often these days you find that an architect has been let loose on a restaurant and, without wishing to ally myself with Prince Charles' views, it has occurred to me that most architects are mystified by human functions like talking, eating, sitting at a desk or sleeping. They are quite good at people going up in lifts. Anyway, the food in haute-bistro style is good. I could describe a meal of several years ago but it is probably more to the point to quote other current guides who praise the soufflés, the quenelles of pike and the carré d'agneau. My last report on Thierry's was from a friend who went on New Year's Eve – a great test – and was delighted. The set lunch has always been good value here. It still is. The waitresses can usually be counted on for charm and a pleasing profile.

CUISINE: French	*Also vegetarian dishes on request*
OPEN: Mon to Sat	
MEALS: 12.30 to 2.30; 7.30 to 11.30	
CLOSED: Public Holidays and last two weeks in August	
AVERAGE PRICE: £21. Set Menu: £5.75 (lunch)	
CREDIT CARDS: Amex, Visa, Diners	
SEATS: 60	
PRIVATE ROOM: (20–30)	
MUSIC: Piped	

TIGER LEE

251 Old Brompton Road, SW5
01-370 2323

For six years the Michelin Guide has awarded Tiger Lee one star (the one London Chinese restaurant now decorated). It bears out my theory that only by imitating the French will you get into the good graces of Michelin. Prices at Tiger Lee certainly banish the, perhaps erroneous, assumption that ethnic food should cost less and they might narrow down your ordering to the structure of a Western meal. Fish is the speciality and some of it swims live in tanks which can be upsetting for the soft-hearted. Twice I have ordered the steamed fish (bass) with shredded meat sauce and found it indistinguishable from the way other restaurants prepare steamed fish with ginger and spring onion but the waiter assured me that it was correctly done. Deep-fried prawns with yam make an interesting use of the sweetness of the vegetable. Other dishes I have admired are the braised eel with garlic, quick fried squid with black beans and chilli, and both rice and a mixture of chicken and mushrooms steamed in a lotus leaf, an assembly you seldom find outside the restaurants of Chinatown that serve dim sum. The best way to approach Tiger Lee is in a group, for six or eight, preferably rich, people will be able to extract the best from the relatively brief menu and feel justified in ordering the more spectacular dishes like the deep-fried crispy chicken, the Cantonese equivalent of Peking duck, served chopped into pieces on a heap of prawn crackers. The price of wine, starting at nearly £8 for house wine, suggests the wisdom of an abstemious evening supping jasmine tea. The restaurant is decorated with restrained good taste. Service is assiduous and culminates in that dubious ritual of handing the female customers a rose as they leave.

CUISINE: Cantonese   *Also vegetarian dishes*

OPEN: D only: Mon to Sun

MEALS: 6 to 11

CLOSED: 1 week at Christmas

AVERAGE PRICE: £25

CREDIT CARDS: Access, Amex, Visa, Diners

SEATS: 50

PRIVATE ROOM: (20)

TOPKAPI

25 Marylebone High Street, W1
01-486 1872

In 1984 Capital Radio, in conjunction with the Ad Lib column of *The London Standard*, voted Topkapi Restaurant of the Year. It was the overall winner as well as the winner in the mid-price category. Such recognition showered upon them seems to have improved the service, in particular the welcome to women eating out together, a concept that Turks have to tussle with. The long list of mezeler (hors d'oeuvre) would seem to be prepared freshly daily. Apart from soup they are all one price which makes picking and choosing between such items as stuffed vine leaves, stuffed aubergine (imam bayildi), tabbouleh, cheese and egg stuffed pastries, meat balls, hoummus and the notably good taramasalata a pleasure. The grilled meats include a doner kebab upon which you feel you can safely graze, various styles of kofta (minced spiced lamb), kidneys and marinated breasts of chicken which are excellent. The special dishes bring you closer to the Greek experience of long stewed food. What deeply impressed the judges of the above-mentioned award was the value implicit in the set-price meal and indeed it is a good way of handling the menu. Tables are cramped. In winter there is a gas-fired fire which introduces a flicker of romance into a pragmatically costed meal.

CUISINE: Turkish	Also vegetarian dishes

OPEN: Mon to Sun

MEALS: 12 to 12

AVERAGE PRICE: £12. Set Menu: £8

CREDIT CARDS: Access, Amex, Visa, Diners

SEATS: 60

TOP WOK

30 England'sLane, NW3
01-586 8619

Ricky Cheung who was formerly at Paper Tiger in South Kensington and then Crystal Palace in Earls Court has opened Top Wok (good name) describing the cooking as Imperial Chinese. It features dishes from Canton, Peking, Hunan and Szechuan, the last two often being fiery hot from the inclusion of chillis. Venturing north of the park seems to have put new zip into the chef Mr Lau. Most dishes have an edge that sets them apart from and above the offering of typical neighbourhood Chinese restaurants and it is not just the sting of pepper. Dumplings are good. The steamed scallops with black bean sauce are a model of that dish and the frogs' legs with a pungent sauce are worth trying. Drunken fish – sole in a wine sauce – I enjoyed and I have never had better sea-spice auber-gine. When you peer into Top Wok it usually looks empty because most of the tables are downstairs but in clement weather I prefer the ground floor. The staff are militantly attentive but they succumb to that wretched habit of leaving the total on the credit card slip empty even after the levy of a 15% service charge. The Pinot d'Alsace is a reasonably priced wine well matched to the food. There are symbols on the menu pointing to the vegetarian dishes.

CUISINE: Imperial Chinese	*Also vegetarian dishes*
OPEN: Mon to Sun	
MEALS: 12 to 3; 6 to 12	
AVERAGE PRICE: £18. Set Menu: £12.50	
CREDIT CARDS: Access, Amex, Visa, Diners	
SEATS: 80	
PRIVATE ROOM: (20)	

TOTO'S

Walton House, Walton Street, SW3
01-589 0075

Opened by Antonio Trapani from Montepeliano, a restaurant which emulated the style and success of San Lorenzo (*q.v.*), Toto's is another venue for a meal when meeting and greeting is more important to you than thinking long and hard about the consistency of the sauce on your escalope of veal. Built in what was originally the squash court of Lord Walton's residence, the look of the restaurant with its creamy marble floors and ornately carved fifteenth-century (so they say) fireplace is more stunning than the experience of eating there, for the menu is predictable, even slightly stolid with the one flash of culinary daring being the addition of curry powder to various dishes. Tagliatelle Toto has a good pinch thrown in with not very satisfactory results. However, I have had well made cannelloni, stuffed with spinach and ricotta which works a great deal better than minced meat, and the waiter did seem genuinely concerned to discover that the sea bass was overcooked. Good gnocchi and tagliolini gratinati free from the curse of the curry powder would seem to indicate that pasta is a wise choice but then the problem comes when you can't do up the zip on your Gianfranco Ferre skirt. Such are the dilemmas of fashionable life. In summer at lunchtime there are tables set in the courtyard.

CUISINE: Italian	*Also vegetarian dishes*
OPEN: Mon to Sun	
MEALS: 12.30 to 3; 7.30 to 11.30	
CLOSED: Bank Holidays	
AVERAGE PRICE: £22	
CREDIT CARDS: Access, Amex, Visa	
SEATS: 80	
TABLES OUTSIDE: (40, lunch only)	

LE TROU NORMAND

27 Motcomb Street, SW1
01-235 1668

When I reviewed this restaurant in *The London Standard* I pointed out how bizarre it might seem if someone were to open a restaurant specializing in the food of Kent and yet when we consider visiting a Normandy place we might well anticipate dishes such as poulet Vallée d'Auge, duck rouennaise, sole dieppoise, tripes à la mode de Caen and generally a liberal use of butter from Isigny, cream and Calvados. There is no reason that in Kent and thereabouts they should not have come up with comparable dishes and ingredients but they haven't and that is the difference between us and the French where food is concerned. This establishment decorated with posters of Honfleur and other appropriate scenes is managed by the son of Alberto Bracci who was previously the partner of Pierre Martin (*q.v.*). The dishes you correctly suppose will be there are, e.g. mussels, seafood salads, tripe, poulet fermier, turbot, côte de veau au cidre. Perhaps because of the former association with Le Suquet and La Croisette, live lobsters do a quadrille in a tank near the door and can be served grilled at a not unreasonable price. A dessert I chose of tarte Tatin was Normandized with Calvados and thick cream and very delicious too. A champagne and oyster bar has recently been opened in the basement of these attractively weathered looking premises where Stephen Pulman (now chef at the Mirabelle) ran his own restaurant. If you can't make it to Portsmouth and the ferry to Le Havre, try here. Le trou normand, the shot of Calvados mid-meal, will encourage you to face the breaded calves' feet if, indeed, demand has maintained the supply.

CUISINE: French

OPEN: Mon to Sun

MEALS: 12 to 2.30; 7 to 11.45

CLOSED: Christmas and New Year

AVERAGE PRICE: *£22. Set Menu: £8 (lunch: 1 course and coffee)*

CREDIT CARDS: *Amex, Visa*

SEATS: *45*

TABLES OUTSIDE: *(12)*

PRIVATE ROOM: *(25)*

TUI

19 Exhibition Road, SW7
01-584 8359

T his is a particularly stylish Thai restaurant with the sort of minimalist decor that is fashionable in designer clothes shops. The black and white effect throws into relief the staff, particularly the women in silk cheongsams (if that is the right word for Thai dress) and the pictures which, sensibly, take food as their subject. The menu is long but not so long as to floor you. If you decide, as I often do, that you know about satay and want to move on, then try the kanom jeeb, steamed dumplings containing pork, and the gai yang, charcoal grilled chicken served with a sweet hot sauce, apparently a popular 'road-side' dish. Their version of spring rolls is good too. Tom yum is a dish that Thais consider essential to a meal. From what I am told, they would not countenance even sitting at the table unless they could be sure it would be served. It is a soup flavoured with lemon grass and chillis and can taste like diluted Night Nurse but is good here and comes in three versions depending on the garnish. Prawns are the most satisfactory. Yum by itself refers to a cold spicy salad and the one incorporating squid, yum plameuk, is excellent. Stir-fried meats and fried fish compose most of the main courses. Mee grob, crispy rice noodles served with prawns and pork, has an interesting sauce flavoured with tamarind and some sweet ingredient almost like jaggery. Accompany a stir-fried dish with a curry, for example the green curry with beef, gang keowan. Desserts include iced rambutan (a lovely fruit) and pineapple in syrup. Sancerre rosé seemed to me an appropriate accompaniment to what is necessarily a mix of ingredients. The menu states that vegetarians should just mention their predilections and they will be catered for. I hope the quick popularity of Tui will not erode the cooking standards.

CUISINE: Thai	*Also vegetarian dishes*
OPEN: Mon to Sun	
MEALS: 12 to 2.30; 6.30 to 11	
AVERAGE PRICE: £15	
CREDIT CARDS: Access, Amex, Visa, Diners	
SEATS: 50	
PRIVATE ROOM: (35)	

TWENTY TRINITY GARDENS

20 Trinity Gardens, SW9
01-733 8838

'Chef Joanna van Rooyan says she is longing to show the marvellous things to be done with the wide variety of fresh produce available in Brixton market.' So said the press handout of the summer of 1984 when Twenty Trinity Gardens opened. The joys of Brixton market can presumably pall just like anything else including being gracious to customers. There have been reports of debby-snotty service in this attractively decorated neighbourhood restaurant owned by David Spence and Jane Mann who previously ran The Rose Tree Restaurant in the Cotswolds. There have been ups and downs with the food too and the original shining optimism of being open seven days a week lunch and dinner has, understandably, dimmed and retreated given the sheer slog that implies. However, there are not masses of restaurants to recommend in the Brixton area and this one remains very good value and shows enterprise with the food which is English in the sense that it acquiesces easily to foreign incursions, e.g. stir-fried pork in satay sauce, spiced rack of lamb with Kashmiri rice. However, there are stauncher dishes and true blue puddings like spotted dick or gooseberry fool. Lunch is a great bargain when it is possible to have one light dish. The wines are well chosen. 'Savings' on food can be well spent on drink.

CUISINE: Eclectic	Also vegetarian dishes

OPEN: L: Mon to Fri; D: Mon to Sat

MEALS: 12.30 to 2; 7 to 10.30

AVERAGE PRICE: £16 (1-course lunch £3.50). Set Menus: £7.25 and £10.25 (2 courses); £8.75 and £11.75 (3 courses)

CREDIT CARDS: Visa

SEATS: 56

TABLES OUTSIDE: (8)

MUSIC: Piped classical

VARNOM'S

2 Greenman Street, N1
01-359 6707

Nico Ladenis owner/chef of Chez Nico in Shinfield near Reading (see Worth a Drive) put the cat among the pigeons when he said on a TV programme that chefs needed no formal training. The sort of French chefs who belong to Academies of this and that and who wear discreet little badges on their lapels were outraged. John Varnom is of the Ladenis school – self-taught – and certainly you could not accuse his cooking of being hidebound by classicism or tradition. Influences crowd in from the Orient and elsewhere, e.g. grilled maize-fed chicken breast with papaya and coriander chutney, ragoût of scallops Bangalore. Lately he seems to have become mercifully a little less peripatetic in his cooking pots, although a holiday in Italy had provided the nice inspiration of a creamy soup flavoured with parsley and sage and garnished with chopped raw radicchio and, no doubt, the idea for boned roast rabbit 'Capanna kind' with wild mushrooms. There are dishes of interest particularly to vegetarians such as the spinach and aubergine pancake steamed in cider and the warm salad of oyster mushrooms. They will also make main courses for vegetarians and this is the moment to note that every main course is served with at least five fresh vegetables, rather too many I think. Varnom is keen on game. Grilled mallard with game glaze, raspberry vinegar and green peppercorns is a representative dish where you will note that the accoutrements of nouvelle cuisine have not been ignored. Bottled fruit and home-made sorbets make a nice dessert. The dining room is in the basement of the premises and is clerically decorated in grey, a modish colour for restaurants at present. Varnom's girl friend Binna Walde is the attractive manageress. It is a praiseworthy enterprise at an unlikely address. The set-price meals are a good deal and at Sunday lunchtime the chef will often cook bouillabaisse, cassoulet, couscous or similar dishes, difficult to find in most London restaurants.

CUISINE: Eclectic	Also vegetarian dishes

OPEN: L: Tues to Fri, Sun; D: Tues to Sat
MEALS: 12.30 to 3; 7 to 11
CLOSED: 2 weeks in January and August
AVERAGE PRICE: £22. Set Menus: from £11.95
CREDIT CARDS: Access, Amex, Visa, Diners
SEATS: 46

Vegetarian Eating

Restaurateurs, ever on the lookout for which side to butter their bread, have cottoned on to the fact that a significant number of would be customers now espouse vegetarianism and it has become increasingly unlikely, though not unknown, that someone asking for a meatless meal will be fobbed off with a plateful of over-buttered vegetables or a cheese omelette. Many restaurants, particularly the more fashionable ones, list a vegetarian main course. In Italian and Indian restaurants it is easy to avoid meat but you have to watch out for chicken or pork based stocks in Malaysian and Chinese cooking. Apart from the vegetarian restaurants with individual entries (see index), here are a few suggestions of places that do better than the leaden quiches and bitty brown rice salads once associated with the genre, but for reasons of opening hours (ring to check) or remedial surroundings do not attract a full description: *Food for Thought, 31 Neal Street, WC2 (01-836 0239)* known for their stir-fried vegetables and tempting puddings. Enquire about the Saturday night gourmet meals. *Govinda's, 9–10 Soho Street, W1 (no phone)* run by the Hare Krishna Temple but pleasant even if that doesn't ring a bell with you. *Wilkins Natural Foods, 61 Marsham Street, SW1 (01-222 4038)* useful in a barren area. *Windmill Wholefoods, 486 Fulham Road, SW6 (01-385 1570)* is more comfortable and welcoming than most. *Cherry Orchard, 241–245 Globe Road, E2 (01-980 6678)* has quite inventive food and sometimes live music. Run by friends of the London Buddhist Centre. *East/West, 188 Old Street, EC1 (01-608 0300)*. Remember macrobiotics? The Eastern influence is all to the good, and the Western influence supplies wine. *Mandeer, 21 Hanway Place, W1 (01-323 0660)* Gujerati food, highly spiced, in rather endearingly romantic surroundings in the main dining room. *Shanti, 185 Battersea Park Road, SW11 (01-720 9928)* friendly family-run establishment serving Southern Indian food. *Diwana Bhel-Poori House, 121 Drummond Street, NW1 (no phone)* astonishingly cheap Southern Indian food.

♥ # VIJAY

49 Willesden Lane, NW6
01-328 1087

The Vijay was a restaurant name that cropped up when I was in India talking with Indians about eating out in London. It is a favourite of mine and, it would seem, of many others, for the rather youth hostel style rooms are always buzzing. Southern Indian vegetarian dishes make up one menu and more conventional Indian food complete with meat curries constitute the other. All of it is remarkably cheap but considering the preparation involved, the dosa, sambar, avial, uppama and other vegetarian dishes are a steal. Even if you are a meat eater don't forgo some of these dishes made of lentils, vegetables and steamed grains. The masala dosa – a crisp, lacy rice and lentil flour pancake wrapped around spicy potatoes and served with coconut chutney – will convert you immediately to the cause.

CUISINE: Southern Indian	*Also vegetarian dishes*
OPEN: Mon to Sun	
MEALS: 12 to 2.45; 6 to 10.45 (Fri and Sat till 11.45)	
CLOSED: Christmas and Boxing Day	
AVERAGE PRICE: £9	
CREDIT CARDS: Access, Amex, Visa, Diners. Luncheon Vouchers	
SEATS: 74	
MUSIC: Piped	

VILLAGE RESTAURANT

8 High Street, Wimbledon, SW19
01-947 6477

This is south-west London's answer to Odin's (*q.v.*) for good reasons like the chef Nick Rochford and one of the owners, Annegret Wood, both hailing from there. The look of the place is a diluted version in that the selection of pictures covering the walls does not cover so densely nor so interestingly, but the menu stands comparison. The cooking has sparkle and dishes that you thought done to death like salad of pigeon breasts or a hot fish pâté have life breathed into them. A main course of loin of lamb sautéed with mint, spring onions and wild mushrooms had the immediacy of Eastern food but the lasting satisfaction of a French dish. Also good on the same occasion was a grilled saddle of lamb with a piquant mustard sauce. The desserts I have tried which are a chocolate marquise and a selection of sorbets were well made. The attention to detail, as in the *amuse-gueules*, is what you might expect in the West End but be pleasantly surprised by in Womble country. There is a short but interesting wine list. Prices are high; the chances to economize are with the set lunch and in the downstairs bistro.

CUISINE: French

OPEN: L: Mon to Fri; D: Mon to Sat

MEALS: 12 to 2.30; 7 to 11

AVERAGE PRICE: £28. Set Menu: £9.50 (lunch)

CREDIT CARDS: Access, Amex, Visa

SEATS: 50

Wheelchair access

WALTON'S

121 Walton Street, SW3
01-584 0204

The Michelin gives this restaurant a star and rightly so. Why *le tout Londres* does not talk much about Walton's is perhaps to do with its expense account air and the curiously oppressive boudoir decor in shades of lemon and grey enlivened only by the gunmetal glint of stainless steel service plates. The last time I went to Walton's was after a trip to Reims with some English chefs who were all talking about it, at least about the capabilities of chef David Nicholls. I tried the very good value set-price lunch where there were four choices in each of the courses and an opportunity to put together an enterprising vegetarian meal. The chicken timbale enclosing a mousse of Roquefort garnished with apples and celery was a combination where the notes of mildness, sharpness and sweetness harmonized. Duck's legs which seemed to have been slightly smoked served with a cider-based sauce was also liked and the dessert of lemon meringue pie had the appropriate zestiness. This meal which includes the price of coffee is a steal when you consider that main courses alone from the à la carte menu are considerably more expensive. A modern approach is evident in most of the dishes but self-consciousness rears up with the harking back to the historical. Eighteenth-century saffron chicken is described as 'An old English recipe lifted into today's repertory served with a "ragoo" of grapes and "cowcumbers"'. I really don't think we need that sort of thing. Many of the dishes justify their cost with luxury ingredients such as fresh foie gras, lobster, morels, and fresh crayfish but they do not stand in for invention, viz. the Old English country soup served with boned chicken wings, fillet of wild salmon with a compôte of spring onions, tomatoes and fresh horseradish served with a mint and lime sauce, and the noisettes of Southdown lamb with fennel and a creamy sauce of foie gras and bay. There is a savoury, a mini Welsh rarebit, made according to 'an enigmatic recipe' as well as desserts. The wine list is sumptuous and though you could run amok financially in the high reaches there are some interesting modest bottles. There is a notable collection of champagnes. Supper after 10 pm at a set price of £17.50 is another moment to think of Walton's.

CUISINE: *English*

OPEN: *Mon to Sun*

MEALS: *12.30 to 2.30 (Sun till 2); 7.30 to 11 (Sun till 10.30)*

AVERAGE PRICE: *£44. Set Menus: £11 (lunch); £17.50 (after 10)*

CREDIT CARDS: *Access, Amex, Visa, Diners*

SEATS: *64*

PRIVATE ROOM: *(12)*

♥ THE WHITE TOWER

1 Percy Street, W1
01-636 8141

This family-run (since 1938) sedate Greek Cypriot restaurant is beginning to find favour anew with other restaurant guides. If you wait long enough even food fashions will come full circle – but 48 years? My heart has always gone out to The White Tower. Despite the sad death of John Stais, his wife and niece maintain the restaurant's comfortable immutability and the menu, originally written by literary critic Daniel George who also worked as an editor at the publishing house of Jonathan Cape, continues to enchant. Its nine pages of lyrical prose are aided and abetted by little slips attached with paper clips giving dishes of the day or new ideas. The rooms are soberly decorated with plush seating and suitably Byronic portraits on the walls. Both the ground floor and the upstairs rooms have their attractions. The waiters are stately and skilled and it is one of those restaurants where you would like to be a regular and treated as such. The food is Greek Cypriot with a French influence; the old-fashioned style as opposed to the taverna. The claim of the best taramasalata in London has been made for the cod's roe pâté served here and many people choose it as part of a first course meze that also includes a creamy chicken dip and a duck's liver pâté. I like the fish salad made with turbot trimmings and when hungry and longing for a sunny holiday, the imam bayildi, an aubergine stuffed with onions, garlic and tomatoes. The first question I invariably ask at The White Tower is if there is the roast duck stuffed with bougourie (cracked wheat mixed with almonds, dried fruit and seasonings) available. So good is this, it is worth ordering in advance. If you have neither foresight nor luck, the poussin is the next best in that vein. I have also enjoyed a dish of veal with sweetbreads and the calm, subtle poularde, good for a fragile day. Fruit salad or baked apple or a pancake stuffed with rose petal jam make apposite desserts. Some people have remarked that, in common with many Greek restaurants, lunch will be better for being closer to the time when the dishes are cooked. If that is your theory, stay clear of moussaka and the like. There are many more interesting dishes to choose from that cannot be left to sweat it out. I am always delighted when friends discover the virtues of The White Tower. Even those diverted by places like The Caprice and Joe's Café know that they have hit upon the real thing. Note the weekend closing.

CUISINE: Greek/Cypriot	
OPEN: Mon to Fri	
MEALS: 12.30 to 2.30; 6.30 to 10.15	
CLOSED: 3 weeks in August and 1 week at Christmas	
AVERAGE PRICE: £27	
CREDIT CARDS: Access, Amex, Visa, Diners, Carte Blanche	
SEATS: 70	
PRIVATE ROOM: (16)	

WILTON'S

55 Jermyn Street, SW1
01-629 9955

Since the Savoy Group and banking firms took over this long-established St James's restaurant its style and exclusivity seem to have become a bit threadbare but it remains one of the haunts of the rich and influential in business and politics. The straightforward English food, relying heavily on oysters, shellfish, fish and game is expensive and of good quality but details such as game chips or the allure of the bread sauce can be less than studiously attended to. It is an intimate restaurant with the air of a private club, enhanced by the delightful Edwardian decor, parts of which have survived two moves from the original address of Wilton's when it was established at the turn of the century. Photographs of loyal customers which would seem to include the Royal Family help put you in your place if the service neglects to. I still view Wilton's as a treat if invited there by one of the regulars but both nepotism and good sense make me prefer the nearby Green's Champagne and Oyster Bar and Restaurant (*q.v.*) where my sister cooks and where oysterman Peter Manzi, previously at Wilton's, now wields his stubby little knife.

CUISINE: English Fish and Game Also vegetarian dishes on request

OPEN: L: Mon to Fri; D: Mon to Sat

MEALS: 12.30 to 2.30; 6.30 to 10.30

AVERAGE PRICE: £33

CREDIT CARDS: Access, Amex, Visa, Diners

SEATS: 85

PRIVATE ROOM: (16)

THE WINE GALLERY

49 Hollywood Road, SW10
01-352 7572

That this is an eminently sensible set-up for reasonably priced eating is borne out by its expansion to two other addresses: 232 Brompton Road, SW3 (01-584 3493) and 294 Westbourne Grove, W11 (01-229 1877). Owned by John Brinkley who also runs the eponymous restaurant next door, the kitchen offers a list of interesting small dishes starting with various soups including fish soup, gazpacho and home-made leek and potato served either hot or cold, continuing with various salads such as spinach and bacon or avocado and mozzarella and moving through various ways with seafood, such as hot buttered shrimps, a mousse of Arbroath smokies and a timbale of scallops with a crab sauce. Those are among the first courses. Filo pastry is wrapped round cheese and deep-fried and baked potato is served with soured cream, smoked salmon and chives. Fairy appetites can be appeased with Bayonne ham with lemon and orange and heartier ones with kedgeree or sausage, beans and mash or cottage pie. It is a well-constructed menu with prices ranging from 90p to £3.90. Wines are also fairly costed and the house wine pleasant. The staff are friendly. Noise can be a problem. At lunchtime in summer there are tables in the garden. What I like about The Wine Gallery – puzzlingly it is something often ignored by restaurateurs – is that the benefits accrue to the customers who are only making the seemingly reasonable demand of a thoughtfully prepared and reasonably priced meal out.

CUISINE: English/French	
OPEN: Mon to Sun	
MEALS: 12 to 3; 7 to 12 (Sun till 11.30)	
AVERAGE PRICE: £11	
CREDIT CARDS: None	
SEATS: 80	
TABLES OUTSIDE: (30)	
PRIVATE ROOM: (18–24)	

WOODLANDS

37 Panton Street, SW1
01-839 7258

Woodlands have a chain of South Indian vegetarian restaurants with branches in India and the USA. There are three in London. The Panton Street restaurant is the newest and has special charm inherent in offering such virtuously delicious dishes in a street off tacky Leicester Square. Spurn the grease and the grabbiness of the fast food joints round about, or indeed forgo the expensive experience of the faux-Maxim's almost next door, and embrace a kancheepuram idli (spiced steamed rice cakes) or rasa vada (a lentil patty mixed with shredded vegetables served with a spicy sauce). Those are first courses you could choose. The most dramatic of the main courses is the masala dosa, a lentil and rice flour crisp golden pancake wrapped around spicy potatoes, or the paper masala dosa which is thinner and lacier. It is unnecessary to describe uthappam as a kind of pizza in order to make it seem desirable, but they do. Try the mixed uthappam which is topped with tomato, onions and coconut. To understand South Indian food you have to give pickles, chutneys and raitas their due as means of enlivening interesting ways with carbohydrates, which includes various delicious breads. Once you get into the swing of it I have no doubt you will say to your companion something along the lines of 'I could easily be a vegetarian if someone would prepare food like this for me all the time.' If the menu seems impenetrable at first, opt for a thali, a tray containing a range of dishes. At weekends they serve bisi bele hulianna which is a combination of rice and lentils subtly spiced. The decor here is, how shall we say, uneventful, but I can vouch for the diverting properties of the food. Other branches of Woodlands in London are at 77 Marylebone Lane, W1 (01-486 3862) and 402a High Road, Wembley, Middlesex (01-902 9869).

CUISINE: Vegetarian Indian	
OPEN: Mon to Sun	
MEALS: 12 to 3; 6 to 11	
CLOSED: Christmas and Boxing Day	
AVERAGE PRICE: £14. Set Menu: £7.25 (thali)	
CREDIT CARDS: Access, Amex, Visa, Diners	
SEATS: 120	
PRIVATE ROOM: (65)	

Worth a Drive

Included among the restaurants listed below that are outside London are some that the French Michelin guide night describe as 'Une des meilleures tables, vaut le voyage' but that we more prosaically say are worth a drive. They are restaurants for special occasions, not necessarily anniversaries of one kind or another, which seem to be the galvanizing factor in eating out for many Britons, but for when you decide that the treat you want to give yourself and others will take the form of superb food and wines. For three

Michelin stars, the goal, it has to be said, of all serious chefs, lavish amenities and gracious surroundings are required. These are somewhat cheaper to rustle up in the country, rather than in town, and that explains the location of Chez Nico anyway and probably played a part in that of Le Manoir restaurant. On a clear day these restaurants are within an hour's drive – or so – from central London. Book well ahead at:

The Waterside Inn, Ferry Road, Bray-on-Thames, Berkshire (0628 20691). Chef, Michel Roux. The setting by the river is intensely romantic.

Le Manoir aux Quat' Saisons, Church Road, Great Milton, Oxfordshire (08446 8881). Chef, Raymond Blanc.

Chez Nico, Church Lane, Shinfield, near Reading, Berkshire (0734 883763). Chef, Nico Ladenis.

Paris House, Woburn Park, Woburn, Bedfordshire (052525 692). Chef, Peter Chandler.

Less ambitious, perhaps 'vaut le detour' (sometimes rather a long one) are:

Chez Max, 85 Maple Road, Surbiton, Surrey (01-399 2365).

The Bell Inn, Aston Clinton, Buckinghamshire (0296 630252).

The Feathers Hotel, Woodstock, Oxfordshire (0993 812291).

The Old Lodge, High Street, Limpsfield, Surrey (08833 2996).

Flitwick Manor, Church Road, Flitwick, Bedfordshire (0525 712242).

Gravetye Manor, West Hoathly, East Grinstead, West Sussex (0342 810567).

ZEN

Chelsea Cloisters, Sloane Avenue, SW3
01-589 1781

Zen, under the same ownership as I Ching (*q.v.*) but not quite Pun (ownership of Chinese restaurants is a nebulous affair) it is generally agreed, is the most ambitious Chinese restaurant in terms of its menu, its appeal to Westerners and its wild decor which incorporates features like a rock face down which water skims, horoscopes on the walls and tinted mirrors on the ceiling. It is a remarkable achievement given the history of the premises, a ground floor restaurant in a block of service flats, which since the Minotaur closed about eight years ago has seen one venture after another bite the dust. No longer must you go through the entrance to the flats, Zen has its own door and once through that you can forget, for a while, the mundane world. The menu has over 100 dishes to choose from, too many really as, unless you are out on your own or with a totally undiverting companion, you probably will not wish to devote the time for study and contemplation it needs. There are nearly thirty hot appetizers, some of these dim sum (dumplings) and some without meat – a vegetarian meal is a delight to compose at Zen. I have liked the crispy veal sticks, the minced quail wrapped with lettuce, the egg rolls stuffed with chicken livers, steamed scallops in black bean sauce and from the cold appetizers the spicy duck's tongues (the Chinese let nothing go to waste) and the bean thread skin cold-tossed with Szechuan peppercorn salt. There are various duck dishes but when you branch out and choose, for example, the crispy thousand flowers sesame duck fillets wrapped with lettuce, it tends to be less satisfactory than the Peking duck with plum sauce, spring onions and cucumber and pancakes. Nam King duck gives you the skin served that way with the meat sautéed with vegetables. The seafood menu shows some enterprising ideas. In particular I appreciate the either/or approach of dishes like prawn balls sautéed in two different styles or poached squid served with two different sauces. Lobs-

ter is a speciality and the ideal highlight of a feast if you are set to spend money the way the Chinese do. The meat and poultry section tends to be less interesting than other parts of the menu and the Chinese way with vegetables, usually involving a cornflour-thickened sauce, never appeals to me. Chi-chi dishes like the rice with chicken and diced pineapple served in a pineapple shell seem to me to traduce the basic integrity and interest of the menu. If you like the sort of desserts based on sweetened bean pastes you will do well here. The wine list is quite enterprising but you might wish to keep the price of your meal in check by ordering a modest bottle. Lawrence Leung and his partners, including the head chef Michael Leung (no relation), strike me as the most 'integrated' group of Chinese restaurateurs, quick to spot gastronomic trends. By the time this book appears their new venture, ZeNW3 in Hampstead High Street should be under way and worth a look.

CUISINE: Chinese	*Also vegetarian dishes*
OPEN: Mon to Sun	
MEALS: 12 to 3; 6 to 11.15 (Sat: noon to 11.15, Sun: Noon to 11)	
CLOSED: Christmas Day and Boxing Day	
AVERAGE PRICE: £27	
CREDIT CARDS: Access, Amex, Visa, Diners	
SEATS: 40	
PRIVATE ROOM: (24)	
MUSIC: Piped	

ZIANI

45 Radnor Walk, SW3
01-352 2698

Managers maketh well-manned Italian restaurants and Roberto from La Nassa is the welcoming presence at this small, crowded, noisy and successful trattoria. Residents of Radnor Walk wish that customers didn't like to party so long and loud, particularly in summertime when ebullience seeps on to the pavement. Rather better than average food is, I am glad to say, also a draw. I have had excellent fresh fettucine with a seafood sauce, almost equally good cheese-filled pasta with a basil and tomato sauce and an admirable dish of what Americans would priggishly call variety meats, i.e. brains, liver, sweetbreads and kidneys, all crisply, quickly fried. Vitello tonnato lacked the same style. As I said in my original review, every table in the L-shaped space is the worst in the room unless coveting your neighbour's wife is your particular weakness.

CUISINE: Italian	*Also vegetarian dishes*
OPEN: Mon to Sun	
MEALS: 12 to 2.30; 7 to 11.30	
AVERAGE PRICE: £17	
CREDIT CARDS: Access, Amex, Visa, Diners	
SEATS: 60	
TABLES OUTSIDE: (20)	

Indexes

CHELSEA AND FULHAM

Astrix
Bagatelle
La Croisette
Drakes
Eleven Park Walk
Foxtrot Oscar
The Garden
Gastronome One
Henry J Bean's
Martin's
Nayab
Nikita's
L'Olivier
Perfumed Conservatory
Pier 31
Pigeon
Ponte Nuovo
Red Pepper
San Frediano
La Tante Claire
Thierry's
Zen
Ziani

EARL'S COURT AND KENSINGTON

The Ark
Bangkok
Blakes Hotel
The Bombay Brasserie
Clarke's
Daquise
Hilaire
I Ching
Launceston Place Restaurant
Ma Cuisine
Lou Pescadou
Palms Pasta on the Hill
Phoenicia
Poissonnerie de L'Avenue
Le Quai St Pierre
Le Suquet
Texas Lone Star Saloon
Tiger Lee
Toto's
Tui
Walton's
The Wine Gallery

BAYSWATER, HOLLAND PARK, NOTTING HILL GATE

The Ark
Belvedere
Geale's
Julie's Wine Bar
Kalamaras
Khan's
Leith's
Malabar
Monsieur Thompson's
192
The Penang

WEST LONDON

La Dordogne
Maxim
Minar
Paulo's

BLOOMSBURY

Chez Gérard
Heal's Restaurant
Ikkyu
Mr Kai of Russell Square
Rue St Jacques
The White Tower

MARYLEBONE

Cinecitta Roma
Don Pepe
Langan's Bistro
Mumtaz
Le Muscadet
Odins
Sidi Bou Said
Topkapi

NEWSPAPERLAND AND THE CITY

Brasserie du Coin
Bubbs
Corney & Barrow
Gonbei
Nosherie
Porte de la Cité
Rudland & Stubbs
Sweetings

HAMPSTEAD AND FINCHLEY
Cosmo
Fontana Amorosa
The Gallery Boat
Green Cottages
Koto
Laurent
Lemonia
Peachey's
Le Routier
Top Wok

NORTH LONDON
Anna's Place
Beau Rivage
Le Bistroquet
La Cloche
Eleganza
Great Nepalese Tandoori
  Restaurant
Jacques
Lal Bhag
The Lantern
Odette's
Sabras
Sea Shell
Varnom's
Vijay

SOUTH OF THE RIVER
Archduke Wine Bar
L'Arlequin
La Barca
Blades
Bretts
Mandalay
Oh Boy!
The Old Rangoon
Pollyanna's
RSJ
Twenty Trinity Gardens
Village Restaurant

By Nationality
AFGHAN
Caravan Serai

AFRICAN
Calabash
Laurent
Sidi Bou Said

BRAZILIAN
Paulo's

BURMESE
The Mandalay

CARIBBEAN
The Caribbean Sunkissed Rest.

CHINESE
Chuen Cheng Ku   C
Dragon Gate   Sz
Eleganza
Fung Shing   C
The Gallery Boat   P
Green Cottages   C
I Ching
Joy King Lau   C
Ken Lo's Memories of China
Maxim   P
Mr Kai of Russell Square   P
Mr Kong   C
Poon's & Co   C
Princess Garden   P
Red Pepper   Sz
Tai-Pan
Tiger Lee   C
Top Wok   Sz
Zen
C = Cantonese; P = Peking;
Sz = Szechuan

EASTERN EUROPEAN
Daquise (Polish)
Gay Hussar (Hungarian)
Nikita's (Russian)
Old Budapest (Hungarian)

ENGLISH
British Harvest
The Connaught Restaurant/Grill
The Dorchester Grill
Drakes
Duke's Hotel Restaurant
The English House
The Greenhouse
Green's
Launceston Place
Perfumed Conservatory
Rudland and Stubbs

English – *cont.*
Rules
Sweetings
Tate Gallery
Walton's
Wilton's

FRENCH
The Ark
L'Arlequin
Auberge de Provence
La Bastide
Brasserie du Coin
Bubbs
Le Café des Amis du Vin
Café Pélican
Café Rouge
Capital Hotel Restaurant
Le Chef
The Chelsea Room
Chez Gérard
Chez Nico
Ciboure
The Connaught Restaurant/
  Grill
La Croisette
La Dordogne
Gastronome One
Le Gavroche
Gavvers
Inigo Jones
Jacques
Lou Pescadou
Ma Cuisine
Langan's Brasserie
Le Mazarin
Mon Plaisir
Monsieur Thompson's
Le Muscadet
Odin's
L'Olivier
Porte de la Cité
La Poule au Pot
Le Quai St Pierre
Rue St Jacques
St Quentin
Le Soufflé
Le Suquet
La Tante Claire
Thierry's
Le Trou Normand

GERMAN
Cosmo

*GREEK AND
GREEK/CYPRIOT*
Beoty's
Kalamaras Mega & Micro
Lemonia
Rodos
The White Tower

IBERIAN
Don Pepe
Ports

*INDIAN/PAKISTANI/
  NEPALESE*
The Bombay Brasserie
Great Nepalese Tandoori
Khan's
Lal Bhag
Last Days of the Raj
Malabar
Minar
Mumtaz
Nayab
Red Fort
Sabras
Salloos (Pakistani)
Taste of India
Vijay
Woodlands

ITALIAN
La Barca
Beccofino
La Capannina
Cinecitta Roma
Eleven Park Walk
La Finezza
La Fontana
Fontana Amorosa
Orso
Ponte Nuovo
San Frediano
San Lorenzo
Santini
Toto's
Ziani

JAPANESE
Ajimura
Gonbei
Ikeda
Ikkyu
Koto

JEWISH
Nosherie

KOREAN
Arirang

LEBANESE
Phoenicia

MALAY/SINGAPOREAN
Equatorial
New Rasa Sayang
The Penang

SCANDINAVIAN
Anna's Place

TEX-MEX
Café Pacifico
Texas Lone Star Saloon

THAI
Bangkok
Chiang Mai
Oh Boy
Tui

TURKISH
Topkapi

USA
Henry J Bean's
Joe Allen
Kettners
Pappagalli's Pizza Inc

Where to go for . . .
ROMANCE
La Bastide
Belvedere Restaurant
Blake's Hotel Restaurant
Connaught Grill
Duke's Hotel Restaurant
The English House

Green's Champagne Bar
Hilton Hotel Roof Restaurant
Julie's Wine Bar
Kettners
Langan's Brasserie
Mélange
Mon Plaisir
Monsieur Thompson's
Odin's
L'Olivier
Peachey's
La Poule au Pot
The Ritz
Tai-Pan
Tate Gallery
Thierry's
The White Tower

GARDENS/CONSERVATORIES
Anna's Place
Archduke Wine Bar
Bagatelle
Beccofino
Le Bistroquet
The Bombay Brasserie
Le Café des Amis du Vin
Café Rouge
Le Chef
La Croisette
Fontana Amorosa
The Garden
Geale's
Henry J Bean's
Launceston Place
Lemonia
Lou Pescadou
Odette's (conservatory)
The Old Rangoon
Peachey's
Perfumed Conservatory
Pollyanna's
The Ritz
Le Routier
San Lorenzo (sliding roof)
Toto's L
The Wine Gallery
Ziani

INTERESTING WINE LISTS
Auberge de Provence
La Bastide

Interesting Wine Lists – *cont.*
The Capital Hotel
The Connaught Restaurant/
  Grill
Corney and Barrow
Don Pepe
L'Escargot
The Gay Hussar
Le Gavroche
Inigo Jones
Au Jardin des Gourmets
Maxim's de Paris
Ménage à Trois
Neal Street Restaurant
192
Pollyanna's
RSJ
Le Soufflé
La Tante Claire
Tate Gallery
Twenty Trinity Gardens
Walton's

BARGAIN HAUTE CUISINE SET LUNCHES
L'Arlequin
Auberge de Provence
The Bombay Brasserie
The Capital Hotel
The Chelsea Room
Chez Nico
The Dorchester Grill
Le Gavroche
Hilaire
Inigo Jones
Odin's
Rue St Jacques
Le Soufflé
La Tante Claire
Walton's

POWER LUNCHING
Alastair Little
Bubbs
Camden Brasserie
Le Caprice
The Connaught Restaurant
Corney and Barrow
L'Escargot
Le Gavroche
The Gay Hussar

Green's
Inigo Jones
Rue St Jacques
Tate Gallery
The White Tower
Wilton's

CHILDREN'S TREATS
Astrix
Blades Barbecue
Chicago Rib Shack
Chuen Cheng Ku
Cinecitta Roma
The Gallery Boat
Geale's
Henry J Bean's
Joe Allen
The Old Rangoon
Palm's Pasta
Pappagalli's Pizza Inc
Seashell Fish Bar
Texas Lone Star Saloon

SOMEONE ELSE'S EXPENSE ACCOUNT
The Capital Hotel
Chelsea Room
The Connaught Restaurant
The Dorchester Terrace
Le Gavroche
Inigo Jones
Leith's
Maxim's de Paris
Rue St Jacques
Le Soufflé
Walton's
Wilton's

NOTEWORTHY NEWCOMERS
Alastair Little
Auberge de Provence
La Bastide
Brett's
Chez Nico (Phillip Britten)
Clarke's
La Dordogne
Ikkyu
Langan's Bar and Grill
Launceston Place
Lou Pescadou
Orso

Top Wok
Tui

ECLECTIC
Alastair Little
Bagatelle
Blake's
Le Caprice
Clarke's
La Cloche
L'Escargot
Foxtrot Oscar
Frith's
Heal's Restaurant
Hilaire
The Lantern
Mélange
Ménage à Trois
Odette's
192
Pier 31
Pigeon
Soho Brasserie
Twenty Trinity Gardens
Varnom's

PEOPLE WATCHING
The Bombay Brasserie
Le Caprice
Clarke's
Eleven Park Walk
L'Escargot
L'Express
Joe Allen
Langan's Bar and Grill
Langan's Brasserie
Ménage à Trois
192
Orso
Pier 31
San Lorenzo
San Quentin
Soho Brasserie
Wilton's

VEGETARIAN
Brett's
Cranks
The Garden
Green Cottage II
Sabras
Woodlands

FISH
Beau Rivage
Brett's
La Croisette
Frère Jacques
Geale's
Grimes
Manzi's
Poissonerie de l'Avenue
Le Quai St Pierre
Rudland and Stubbs
Sea Shell Fish Bar
Sheekey's
Le Suquet
Sweetings

OPEN SUNDAYS
Plus most hotels, and
Indian and Chinese restuarants
Ajimura   D
The Ark   D
Astrix
L'Auberge   L
Le Bistroquet
Café Pacifico
Café Pélican
Camden Brasserie   L
Le Caprice
Caravan Serai
The Chanterelle
Chicago Rib Shack
La Cloche
Cosmo
La Croisette
Daquise
Don Pepe
Drake's
The English House
Equatorial
L'Express
La Fontana
Fontana Amorosa
Foxtrot Oscar
Henry J Bean's
Jacques
Joe Allen
Julie's Wine Bar
Kettners
Langan's Bar and Grill
The Lantern

Open Sundays – *cont.*
Launceston Place Restaurant
Laurent
Leith's
Lou Pescadou
Manzi's   D
Le Metro   (Breakfast)
L'Olivier
192   L
Orso
Palm's Pasta
Peachey's   L
Phoenicia
Pier 31
Pigeon

Pollyanna's
Ponte Nuovo
Le Routier
Rudland and Stubbs
St Quentin
Santini   D
Texas Lone Star Saloon
Topkapi
Toto's
Le Trou Normand
Tui
Varnom's   L
Walton's
The Wine Gallery
Ziani